Around the World in 80 Gardens
Monty Don

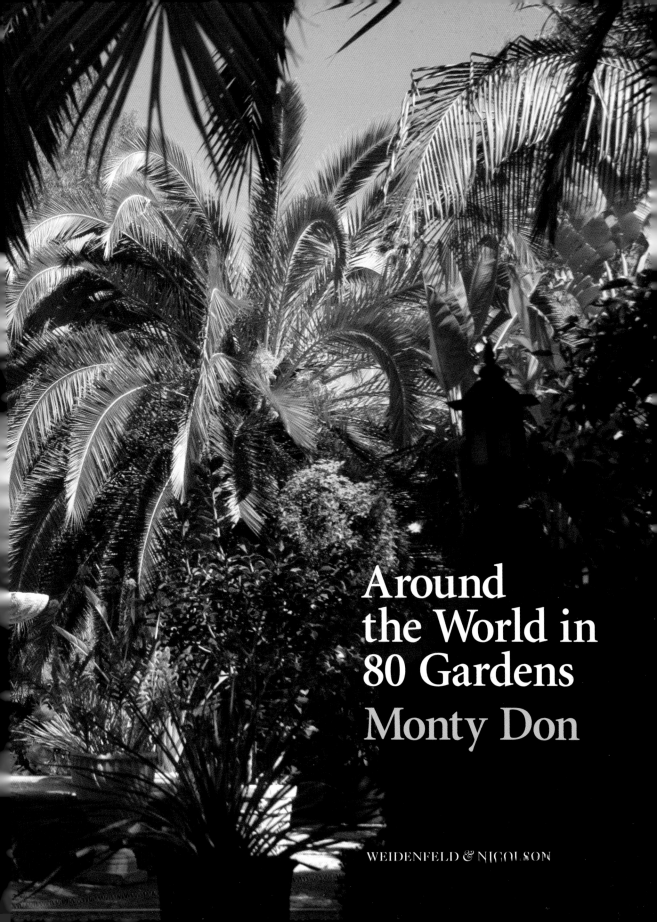

Around the World in 80 Gardens

Monty Don

WEIDENFELD & NICOLSON

Contents

Introduction

The expression 'a trip of a lifetime' gets bandied about easily yet this really was just that. It was actually ten trips in total, returning to base after each one, and spread over eighteen months, but conceptually it was one journey with ten different stages. They were not done in any particular sequence and although we tried to visit each country at the most perfect time of year to appreciate its gardens, inevitably this was rarely exactly the case. In fact, the only time that it was generally agreed that it was the most perfect moment in the year, at Stellenberg in South Africa, we had torrential rain all day long. But that is life. I saw what I saw on the day I was there, for better or worse.

However, for me it was always better. I have travelled relatively little and this adventure took me to places that I would never have been to and probably will not get the chance to return to again. I was aware throughout every single day of it that this was something more than just special. It was unique.

I did not travel alone, save when I set out to join the film crew that had gone ahead of me to pick up 'pretties' of the gardens. The process of filming obviously drove the journeys and meant that I had to write very late at night or early in the morning to keep on top of the relentlessly accumulating notes, but it added to the fun. Good experiences are always better shared. It was television too that gave me the brief that determined the choice of gardens, which was to get under the skin of a culture through their gardens.

I must stress that this is not intended to be the 'best' eighty gardens in the world in any sense. Anybody else would draw up a list that would be different. If I were to do it again I would certainly drop some and add others. That is not the point. It is an exploration of this astonishing planet through the medium of eighty gardens of every kind, in every possible situation. It is also unapologetically about cultures and people as much as about plants. In fact, having made this incredible journey, I remain more convinced than ever that the most interesting thing to be found in any garden is the person that made it. People are always more interesting than plants.

Amongst the dozens of cases of state-of-the-art film equipment that we travelled with, along with carnets, excess baggage and teams of porters to lug it, the two most important pieces of kit that I took round the world with me on each trip were a new Moleskine 3½ x 5½ ruled notebook and a favourite Rotring pen with a broken clip that I have had for twenty years. Both lived in my trouser pocket and I carried them literally every waking hour everywhere I went and jotted notes the whole way. This book is drawn almost entirely from these notes plus interviews that I recorded and then painfully slowly transcribed. Having the extra dimension of knowing that I was writing this as we went along added to the pleasure enormously. This is my personal and unfiltered journey.

I say 'almost' because I am enormously indebted to the research work done by Almudena Garcia in Spain, Mexico, Cuba and South America, Katharine Arthy in South East Asia, India and South Africa and David Henderson, who did a huge amount of research for the gardens in Australia and New Zealand, China and Japan, Northern Europe, Italy and North America. Their invaluable legwork allowed me the luxury of concentrating on my own subjective reactions and observations in every garden.

And now, having finally finished, it seems incredible that I have really been to the Taj Mahal and floating gardens on the Amazon, the mountains of China and the Andes, seen gardens in Hollywood and the Australian outback, in townships in South Africa and the klongs of Bangkok as well as 200 miles inside the Arctic Circle and the rooftops of Manhattan. But it is true. I did it all. And here it is.

MONTY DON, 2007

Gardening as part of artistic popular culture is extraordinarily strong in Northern Europe, and is founded upon a gardening history that goes back over 300 years.

1 Chasing the Light

Northern Europe

Northern Europe

hoosing seven or eight gardens to represent the whole of Northern Europe was always going to be a tricky, if not absurd, proposition. I could easily have done the entire eighty gardens there and still have some to spare. But the guiding principal of this whole venture was that it was personal, biased and only definitive insofar as it seemed a good idea at the time. By definition my mind would be altered if not changed by completing the journey.

I thought of including my own garden on the grounds that this is where all my horticultural journeys begin and end, but decided that it was a wasted opportunity to visit somewhere that I had never seen before. In the end I rationed it severely: two gardens only in England, two in France, my long time hero Jacques Wirtz's garden in Belgium, two gardens in the Netherlands and the northernmost botanic garden in the world, 200 miles inside the Arctic Circle in Norway. It would be a mixture of gardens that I knew and was eager to revisit and those that I had long wished to see.

It seemed to me that there was a pattern to trace. Gardening, as part of artistic popular culture, is extraordinarily strong in Northern Europe and is founded upon a garden history that goes back over 300 years. There are literally hundreds of historic gardens that one can visit and millions of people do just that every year. Personal history or, most intoxicating of all, 'celebrity' inevitably pulls the crowds. Sissinghurst is justifiably renowned for its extraordinary beauty and expertise but I reckon that it would not draw half the visitors that it does without the shade of Vita Sackville West falling over it. How many of the garden visitors have read a word of her work? Would half a million people a year visit Giverny if it had been created by an anonymous bank clerk rather than Claude Monet?

Yet historic gardens that have no such powerful ghosts still attract vast figures. There is clearly a common desire to touch, smell and walk through the past via the medium of a garden. Gardens that have not been altered in anything but minutest detail over hundreds of years bring the past alive in the most vivid way possible because, unlike a building or a painting, the components are alive only in the intense present.

There is an overriding paradox in the maintenance of all such historic gardens. How do you hold them still, locked in the specific time that they commemorate and yet still maintain the vitality and constantly shifting life of plants that is inevitable in any kind of garden and, more than that, an essential part of any garden's attraction?

I waited until midsummer to visit these gardens on the basis that this would probably be the best time to see gardens in Northern Europe, but it happened to be one of the wettest, dullest years in living memory. I have never visited a garden anywhere or at any time without someone telling me that it would look better had my visit been last or next week. But on this trip that was almost certainly true, except when I got up to Tromsø, inside the Arctic Circle.

Rousham

Oxfordshire, England

I SET OFF FOR ROUSHAM on a wet Sunday morning in curiously anticlimactic mood. Rather than starting with a journey to exotic places, Rousham is just a couple of hours' drive from home. I need not have worried about any disappointment. It was that day, and is at any time, one of the greatest garden experiences on this earth.

Rousham is acknowledged to be one of the great masterpieces of garden design and yet is astonishingly unknown. Save for the grassing over of the majority of the walled kitchen garden, it is as though it has been untouched by time. This is clearly not true – most of the trees that dominate the garden are not original, and plants are like skin, constantly growing and renewing themselves. But the essence of the garden is unsullied. Rousham is a garden preserved in amber.

William Kent is the genius responsible for Rousham. In 1738 he was hired by its owner General Dormer (the Dormer-Cottrell family still own and live there) to vamp up the designs of the royal gardener, Charles Bridgeman, who had laid out gardens in the 1720s in the new, landscaped style that was beginning to emerge as a contrast to the severely formal Dutch and French influence of the late seventeenth century. Alexander Pope said of Bridgeman's garden that Rousham was 'the prettiest place for water-falls, jetts, ponds, enclosed with beautiful scenes of green and hanging wood that I ever saw'. Kent's brilliance was to take this established, 'prettiest place' and transform it into greatness with a relatively light hand.

Kent was at the centre of the picturesque movement that, in the second quarter of the eighteenth century, established a revolutionary style of garden design that placed classical scenes within the English landscape. He took the idea of arcadia and set it into the rural countryside as it then was rather than creating the idyll of the garden as a park or an estate, as Capability Brown so successfully did a generation later. Kent clearly loved and admired the countryside as it was and did as little as possible to it, framing it here, closing an aspect there or adding a folly on the skyline to direct your view. It is the very English ideal of a domestic, small landscape: the 'eye-catcher' (a contrived ruin on the horizon) and road are almost cosy.

William Kent was no gardener. We know that he avoided visiting the site as far as he could and was notoriously careless on details of construction. But he was, without question, a genius of the first order. He saw the garden as a medium to create a series of living stage sets and at Rousham every path and ride through the trees culminates in a statue or building, creating a sequence of tableaux. What makes them exceptional is that they need humans to make the pictures exist. Kent included people in the same spirit that he made buildings, paths or planted trees. So, as you drift around Rousham, entranced by the way that it uses the physical here and nowness of the landscape to transport you into a dream, there is this extraordinary sensation of making it happen, of your presence being the vital ingredient that brings the buildings, trees, ground-cover, even the water of the river Cherwell and the sky into being. This is enormously flattering – hardly something that you expect from a garden.

Whereas classical mythology is a code which most twenty-first century people are unable to crack, the meaning of Kent's classical scenes at Rousham would have been

intensely vivid to those contemporaries for whom the gardens were made, creating an intellectual subtext to the gardens. Classical allusion indicated by a statue or style of garden building would inform and enrich the experience of the visitor in the same way that a modern garden thematically dedicated to a soap opera would be able to use visual references to characters and story lines that would have added meaning for dedicated viewers.

But even without understanding, let alone spotting the classical references, what remains is more than the sum of most gardens. The house itself, worked on and added by Kent at the same time that he did the garden, is impressive rather than beautiful, although the honey-yellow stables and car park are entrancingly informal and un-National-Trusty. Although this is one of the nation's most precious horticultural treasures, open to the paying public, Rousham is also a private home. In fact, it only gets a meagre 10,000 visitors a year, a puny figure compared to the Hidcotes or Sissinghursts of this world.

Although it has been calculated that there are over 1,000 circuits that you can take round the garden, which is an extraordinary tribute to the way that so much has been fitted into a relatively small site (only 25 acres), you are likely to take a route which starts by going round the back of the house past a yew hedge cut with lovely wonky exactness and across the bowling green. Most owners would have succumbed at some stage in the past 200 years to clutter this with a Cedar of Lebanon, Wellingtonia or, worse, stolidly pretty herbaceous borders. Mercifully, it has been left as a monumental open space of grass with wide surrounding paths and an enormous flanking hedge. A single statue stands at the end against the skyline. This zen-like emptiness clears the mind before you turn onto a small path down the hillside. Immediately you are aware that the garden is a journey with intervals of contemplation rather than a series of pleasant images.

The first thing that strikes you, and which will be reinforced throughout, is the absence of flowers. The overwhelming impression is of green in every shade, from the lime-yellow of new leaves on box and lime trees to the blue-green of ivy underneath the yew trees. The sophistication and delicate beauty of this is anything but drab – rather than reducing the picture, it intensifies it. Green light spatters through the trees onto ivy, wild garlic, herb Robert, holly and tightly cropped laurel. The yews are dark. The mind is open and clear, garden-ready.

As a startling touch of colour you look down onto vermillion fish in a brown pool. This is fed by a rill that snakes down the centre of a path through the trees. It arrives via an octagonal plunge pool with a small building in the middle of the trees. A thread-like canal no more than a foot wide and a few inches deep, the rill and its plunge pool are still shockingly modern and inspiring. It is a sinuous intruder that

A dark green avenue, sheltered by beech and lime trees, leads towards a lone statue, framed in the light at the end of the tunnel.

snakes through the curves of the landscape right into the heart of the classical
orders and references. It is as minimalist
as the bowling green, but, like all good
minimalism, liberates the essence from
clutter so that it can fill a space, endors-
ing Wittingstein's sentiment that 'the
bad architect succumbs to every detail'.
So many gardens from Repton to the
present day succumb to an accumulation
of pointless detail.

All the trees around the plunge pool
were flattened in the early 1970s in a
great storm. All were replanted except for
two of the yew trees. The laurels were
also crushed, causing total devastation.
But regeneration is always a good thing
in the long run, and at Rousham the run
has so far been very long.

Laurel can be sometimes heavy with
the dreariness of Sunday afternoons in
middle England, but here it works well
as a sculptural plane of green beneath

The eighteenth-century visitor to Rousham would have been instantly able to identify the statues hidden in every nook and cranny of the grounds.

the beeches and limes of the woodland, given a flat top cut so that it creates boxy
planes of green on steep, shaded slopes. Head gardener Jenny Bond told me that the
laurel takes four people doing nothing else for a month to cut using secateurs, usually beginning in late September and nearly always when it is sodden, pushing through
the glossy leaves like wading through water.

The severely Classical buildings, including the seven-arched portico Praeneste,
Townsend's building (a temple with, very charmingly, a distinctly unclassical sash
window in the side), and rusticated arches gushing water in the Vale of Venus, are
constructed entirely from vernacular materials, an important factor in the integration
of the very English countryside with filtered images of ancient Rome. It is fortunate
that the local stone is a beautiful ochre limestone that makes any building look good,
but it is also used on the paths through the grass and woods, unifying the picture.

Turn and walk back down to the Vale of Venus down a green nave. Rain and a dark
sky intensifies the colour and light. The Vale of Venus would have been very different
in 1740 – not least because the structure would have been much more dominant compared to the trees. But we have the maturity of 300 years although inevitably for most
of that time the work has been to contain and cut back growth rather than nurture it.
The gardeners keep cutting huge quantities each year to keep the views open but have
let some beeches grow to hide traffic lights.

Rousham is a theatrical set waiting for its actors for the drama to be played out.
The visitor is needed to make the scene come alive. You are the protagonists making the
show complete. This was my third visit after an interval of ten years and it confirmed
my initial impression that it is the greatest masterpiece of English gardening – a flawless work of genius.

Sissinghurst

Kent, England

Above After a sudden downpour, the brick paths glisten between the pleached lime trees of the famous Lime Walk.
Opposite Vita's famous tower rises above the famous White Garden. Cosmos, Artemisia, Aruncus, Hydrangea and Gaura lindheimeri fill the box-edged beds, while the overarching canopy of Rosa mulliganii was only added in 1969.

SISSINGHURST REPRESENTS AND EXEMPLIFIES all that the English aspire to in a garden, not least because it is the setting for the kind of aristocratic sex romps and jollifications that the British so love. Gardening and sex! Days out don't come much better than that, especially if there is a cup of tea and a piece of cake thrown in too. But the 'best garden' tag is an albatross around Sissinghurst's neck, and if such judgements incline you to be truculent and contrary, you will pay your first visit looking for evidence to bring it down a peg or two. Or maybe that's just me.

But it is hardly Sissinghurst's fault that it has had such lofty judgements foisted upon it. I can tell you that it just is awe-inspiringly magnificent. One of my oldest friends lives there and I have been visiting the garden for twenty-five years now, at all times of year, and have never found it less than lovely. Of all the gardens made in Britain in the twentieth century, this is the paradigm, fulfilling modern expectations of a breathing, tangible past. But that, as with almost everything about Sissinghurst, is just another layer of irony. In a way we all go there to mourn what might have been or even what never was.

As ever, the garden must be placed into context to be understood at all. Geographically this is a Kentish place, growing out of a large Kentish estate and informed by the broader Kentish countryside. In the twenty-first century metropolitan world, the significance of counties in England is often overlooked and underestimated. But nationality is a tenuous thing and cities are a curious amalgam of strangers and the extreme parochialism of a few streets. Anyway, most people don't live in cities but in suburbs or towns that are defined by the county that they are in as much as any other factor. It is the counties of England that provide real identity and inspire loyalty over and above nationalism.

Sissinghurst is a castle. What remains now is splendid but in a particularly unfortified, rural way. It is completely unmartial and domesticated – a castle as a series of follies and cottages in the garden, approached by a long private lane surrounded by beautiful countryside, making it the most desirable of all homes to the English psyche. Of all the possible res's this is the most des.

The human context has to be known too. No ghost inhabits a garden more fully than Vita Sackville West at Sissinghurst. She died in 1962 but it is still her garden. Vita was a complex and contrary figure, an aristocrat with Spanish gypsy blood, a lesbian with a long and enduringly loving marriage, a poet and novelist best known for her *Observer* gardening column (she wrote this from 1946–60 and her presence was still tangible in that role when I took over the job from 1994–2006), an impulsive and exotic figure deeply entrenched in the Kent countryside. She fufils all the textbook fantasies of the freedom that money and birth seem to be able to buy. The truth is, of course, much more three-dimensional than that, but all the books, television programmes, film and endless articles about her have done nothing to reduce her obvious glamour.

FOR ALL ITS ELITISM, MONEY AND GRANDEUR, IT IS A GARDEN ACCESSIBLE TO ANYONE WITH A BEATING HEART.

Her husband Harold Nicolson was an altogether more conventional figure. A politician, diplomat and respected author (although he too was famously homosexual), he effectively designed the garden at Sissinghurst. They were a team and in every sense he provided the framework within which Vita could be free to flourish.

The final element of context that one needs to know about is Knole. Knole is said to be the largest house in Britain, a vast palace with endless courtyards where Vita was bought up, and which she felt was rightfully hers. One of the most important things to understand about Sissinghurst is that it is not Knole. Adam Nicolson, Vita's grandson, who took Sissinghurst over in 2005, told me that Sissinghurst is 'defined by the absence of Knole. It therefore has a faded, broken glamour from the outset. By the 1930s – when Sissinghurst was begun – Vita's world was going – she was already an anachronism. Sissinghurst was her retreat and escape from the "modern" world of the 1930s and 40s. Certainly the annual 185,000 visitors would have been a horror to her.' However, the visitors flock to Sissinghurst, undaunted by Vita's dismay. You park the car and walk to the modest but very beautiful brick gatehouse. The whole castle is built of a beautiful peachy brick and its amalgam into the tower, farm buildings, cottages and garden walls feels completely harmonious. The importance of the structural architecture to the garden cannot be underestimated. The harmony between the two is the great achievement. It is the English dream made flesh – a castle in the garden, fading and ruined and yet grand and habitable. A castle made into an ersatz cottage with cottage garden planting yet with a sophistication and labour force beyond the imagining of any cottager.

The first courtyard is a foyer and not for lingering in, despite the skirting borders. This is because it is dominated by the tower, a magnificent building of a type built in the brief period between about 1470 and 1530 when the last castles were built primarily as status symbols rather than fortifications. Go immediately to the roof of the tower and look down on the garden and its place in the surrounding countryside. This is where Harold Nicolson's great gift is best seen, with the structure ingeniously worked into an awkward series of angles, buildings and irregular spaces. It is one of the unfairnesses of history that it is usually known as Vita's garden. In fact, his claim is as strong as hers and his working of the spaces and sensitivity to sense of place is as enduring as a horticultural monument.

Viewed from the tower the strength of Harold Nicolson's layout can properly be seen, especially the way he solved the problem of irregular angles and awkward corners.

This aerial view also clearly shows how the house is, in fact, a series of buildings, remnants of the castle, that in Harold and Vita's time had specific functions – for eating, sleeping or working in. The garden then acted as corridors and courts through which the family strolled to lunch or the study. Just as Vita might have done at Knole…

From the foot of the tower you proceed into another grassy courtyard – the tower lawn – enclosed by walls on three sides and by a yew hedge that is one half of the famous Yew Walk. In fact, a great chunk of this has had to be dug out and replanted as a result of phytophera caused by poor drainage, opening out the tower lawn and to my mind improving it greatly – although it is right that it should be replanted and restored to the original design. Sissinghurst, like Rousham, is a historical monument and radical change, even

for the better, would be as much a form of vandalism as making a few alterations to a Picasso or Rembrandt painting.

Turn left and you enter the White Garden, the most famous, copied and misunderstood of all Sissinghurst's elements. There are two great secrets of the White Garden at Sissinghurst. The first is the structure provided by the box hedges, especially the height of them. The site is on a slope and the hedges are cut with a level top so that they almost double their height as they cross the site. This creates spaces with real volume so that the white flowers burst out of boxes rather than beds. In winter it has a stark, three-dimensional geometric beauty. As with the rest of the garden, none of the angles are square so all the beds are irregular: Harold coped with this by gradually losing the deviation from 90 degrees as the beds approach the centre of the garden so that the two main paths cross at exactly right angles. Simple but effective.

The much-imitated White Garden is one of the most popular of the garden rooms at Sissinghurst. Seen from underneath the Rosa mulliganii *arbour, it is even more evident that green is the dominant colour.*

The second secret is that it is not really a white garden at all but a green garden. Green of every hue dominates it. The brick paths and walls – which always look best against grass, box or yew – are another vital element; paving would mute this monochromatic intensity. And yes, there are a lot of white flowers, beautiful ones, dashed palely against the green.

The Yew Walk is probably too narrow for its length but has a kind of genius. It is always a visceral pleasure to enter into it, a long, dark corridor made unscary by the sky. There is the rose garden, the yew rondel, the cottage garden with its blaze of sophisticated plants against a corner of the castle, imbued with the simple charm that only money can create, the moat walk with the azalea bank, the herb garden, the nuttery, the pleached Lime Walk, the orchard and even Delos, an area of the garden flanking the White Garden whose charms have always evaded me. You walk from area to area, honing in on individual plants or plant combinations – like reading a menu or browsing the counter in a cake shop, spoilt for choice.

The point is that, Delos aside (and that just adds a touch of mortal fallibility), it is almost perfect. Nothing jars. It is as we should want our own garden to be had we but millions to spend and talents and skills beyond our dreams. It is also above all a performance. 'Sissinghurst,' says Adam Nicolson, 'is Grand Opera.' But unlike at Rousham, the public are the reverential audience, not the actors.

The management of this drama is colossal, with forty permanent staff, eight full time gardeners and 120 volunteers that dead head, primp and weed in shifts. This is where the National Trust excels at brilliantly preserving complex living spaces that would have either disappeared or been perverted by commerce. The performance changes from season to season but the story is always the same. It is a requiem to a dream that was only ever made real here in this garden. It is admired and understood by almost every gardener that visits and yet was conceived by people as atypical and removed from the population at large as is virtually possible. This, finally, is one of the many ironies of Sissinghurst and the one that surely would have most perplexed Vita. For all its elitism, money and grandeur, it is a garden accessible to anyone with a beating heart.

Villandry

Loire Valley, France

Above *The Garden of Love is divided into four different squares, each symbolic of a separate aspect of love. This is Fickle Love, with the box carefully cut into the shapes of fans and horns, standing for flirtation and cuckoldry.* Opposite *The vast potager is made up of nine equally-sized squares, each consisting of a different geometrical pattern. Here purple basil, marigolds, cabbages and peppers are planted in low box-edged beds, with standard roses providing vertical interest.*

CHOOSING JUST TWO GARDENS FROM FRANCE was as hard as selecting just two from Britain. But I never troubled myself with any idea of picking the best or most representative as this would inevitably be subjective – so I decided that I might as well make the choice entirely on personal whim and accept that at another time I might have chosen an entirely different two. I had always wanted to visit the potager at Villandry, and had read and heard so much about Monet's garden at Giverny in Normandy, so I decided to go south first to Villandry and then head up to Normandy before moving on to Belgium.

We stayed in a small hotel just outside the walls of the château which is at the edge of the village of Villandry in the Loire Valley. This is an area full of orchards for dessert fruit as well as vineyards, so the potager is a highly organised, decorative version of what the region is best known for. The weather had been awful for weeks but that morning it was bright and clean-aired with a blue sky above the rich green. As I had breakfast I could hear the hum and whine of what proved to be hedge cutters in the garden.

The existing château was first built by Jean le Breton, a minister of François I (he of Field of Cloth of Gold fame), between 1532 and 1536 on the site of an earlier fortification and was one of the last of the great string of Renaissance castles built along the River Loire. Le Breton had first been ambassador to Italy and the garden that he made at Villandry was ornate, extensive and drew on his Italian horticultural experiences.

Villandry stayed in le Breton's family until 1754 and then passed through a number of hands until the nineteenth century. At the end of the eighteenth century the Renaissance formal gardens in their terraces were all swept away and replaced by an English-style landscape park, following a trend that had begun in England in the late 1730s, around the time that Kent was remodelling Rousham. This effectively obliterated the garden that had been there for the previous 200 years, burying it under sand and soil as the parterred terraces were turned into grassy tree-dotted slopes.

Then in 1906 the château was bought by Dr Joachim Carvallo who, aided by his heiress wife Ann Coleman, set about restoring the castle and Renaissance gardens with the added element of medieval vegetable production. To a degree the archaeology of the original garden was preserved beneath the late eighteenth-century landscape park but Cavallo did not set out to scrupulously restore these gardens. Using archaeology and engravings of sixteenth-century gardens he created the Villandry that we see today – the spirit of the Renaissance garden.

The potager is the most famous part of Villandry and really the only aspect of the garden that I knew about and came specifically to see. In fact, despite its presence right next to the château – try and think of a British castle or mansion with the vegetable garden laid out butting onto the walls of the house – it was the last thing that I saw there. I was met by the current owner, Henri Cavallo, grandson to Joachim, and the first thing he did was take me up to the roof of the tower in the corner of the château. This gives a bird's eye view of the entire garden, which was astounding (my notebook says this in capitals and heavy underlining). For a start I had not realised that it is so big. It covers nearly 15 acres. A substantial proportion of that is clipped box, yew or hornbeam. The whole thing is on a scale that is simply breathtaking.

The garden is divided into four main areas, linked by wide avenues of pleached limes and hornbeam hedges, with a fifth area currently under construction. The château is built against the side of a steep hill and the garden abuts two sides of it with the potager on its longest face and the Garden of Love on the other frontage, which in turn connects to the Music Garden. On a higher level is the Water Garden. Looking down, I was immediately struck by its sculptural physicality. The box hedges that make up the acres of patterned parterres are chunky and massively three dimensional, whereas the smaller box hedges, made of *Buxus sempervirens* 'Suffruticosa', the dwarf box, are more two dimensional and exist as framework for the vegetables. Elsewhere the box is the garden, and is entirely unexpected and powerful.

The Garden of Love with its interwoven box parterres punctuated by yew finials, is essentially a series of chunky sculptures dealing in defined space as much as plants. Nevertheless it is a highly codified symbolism that would have been immediately accessible to the Renaissance viewer. To the modern visitor it makes a series of pleasing shapes with just vague hints at a further meaning. The planting within the hearts, crosses and rigidly symmetrical geometric shapes of the Garden of Love seem to my eye gaudy and wholly unnecessary but are entirely consistent with a true recreation of a medieval and Renaissance garden. Whereas I am deeply satisfied with layer upon layer of green, they wanted colour – as bright as possible and plenty of it.

Going downstairs, Henri walked me around the garden. He takes his role as custodian of the garden seriously, seeing it as his duty to preserve it so that as many people as possible can visit and experience it. He is very hands-on and walks round the garden each morning to make sure that every detail is properly attended to. As I had heard in the morning, there was a team focussing on hedge cutting – a huge job. It is not just the box that needs to be cut – although that alone is an epic endeavour – but the hornbeam and limes that provide the structural backdrop. When I was there this was half-done, giving me a perfect visual explanation of how the garden held together, with the shaggy, untrimmed half threatening to slip into anarchy and the newly shorn part a corrective, restoring order.

This order has to be constantly renewed so that it might look perfectly still. Hedging plants die and are replaced by the hundreds each year – the garden does have its own nursery but they still have to buy in a lot each year from Germany. They also raise some 150,000 bedding and vegetable plants (essentially edible bedding), half the amount that they need, buying in the rest. This is the measure of the place. Everything is on a grand, expansive scale. Yet it is the combination of the vast and the intense detail that is so beguiling. The garden is chunky and visceral, yet as delicate and intricate as fine lace.

To reach the huge Water Garden you walk along a lime-flanked, raised platform. This is open, clean and clear, a kind of purification after the intense physicality of the parterres. It has a perambulation around the outside, flanked with avenue of limes on top of a steep grassy bank or *talûs* – so you can look down on the water. This acts as the reservoir that feeds all the fountains and springs, running into the moat and then back up to the top to circuit again. The grassy slope down from the promenade to the ground level is immaculate, cut with a hedge-trimmer type cutter fixed to a tractor that operates on the lower level.

Going down a terrace you come to the Music Garden. This, I think, is one of the great pieces of garden design. The simplicity and scale is beyond anything I have seen anywhere else in the world. It is a couple of acres large and yet is made from massive slabs of box that is effectively installation art of the highest order. At ground level the pattern is only established by lavender planted in the interstices of the box – otherwise it is one vast block of green. I love the practical detail of how they trimmed this to its perfect crispness. I had imagined that it involved hoists and gardeners dangled over the surface but apparently the solution is much simpler and more prosaic: they merely wade straight through the green, pushing the bushes aside to get into the middle, do their cutting and then allow them to close behind as though they had

From this angle, the coloured flowers in the centre of the box shapes cannot be seen, but the vast scale of the Garden of Love is readily apparent.

never been disturbed. The whole thing is cut to about 30 inches high with a square profile which, for the record, is a very satisfying proportion.

The moat runs down from the Water Garden, the water cascading down stone steps and under bridges where house martins ride the surface like an aerial Cresta Run to snatch insects inches from the water. This is covered by a vine whose fruit is deliberately planted with a variety of dessert grapes so visitors can pluck the fruit as they pass, walking down, finally, to the famous potager.

Now this is where honesty becomes tricky. I was disappointed with it, not because it failed to meet my expectations – in scale and detail it far exceeded it – but because the rest of the garden is so spectacularly wonderful. The potager was in the process of a mid-season change over when I was there, all the spring vegetables having finished and the summer crops still in their earliest stages. This meant that it was thin and rather bony compared to the fullness of the rest of the garden. But by any standards it is superb and should be celebrated for what it is rather than criticised for what it is not. It is made up of nine squares, each subdivided into hugely complex geometric beds marked out and edged in box, arranged around a central fountain. Where four squares meet there is another, larger pool and fountain, so there are thirteen water features in the vegetable garden alone. To fill the kitchen garden requires approximately 30,000 flower plants and 50,000 vegetable plants for the spring planting and 30,000 for the summer planting; that is to say 110,000 plants for the two plantings each year.

Vegetables here are eaten of course – this is France, after all – but the rhythm of colour and form built up by chard, cabbage, chicory and courgette is purely decorative. There is an inevitability about it that depends upon taking vegetables seriously and with respect, in the same way that the French address a good meal in a fine restaurant. The one thing that it lacks – or lacked to my eye on that day – is the charm of the rest of the garden.

Finally, knowing I had to rush away to reach Normandy before our hotel there locked its doors, I visited the antithesis of the famous potager, an empty, slightly overgrown and dark lawn leading off the herb garden which was an entirely green space fringed entirely with three tiers of pleached limes rising behind on the slope to the top terrace, and walled with hornbeam hedges and stone wall on one side. I got the impression that visitors did not do more than poke round the entrance, see that it was 'empty' and move on. In fact it was a retreat, filled with green light and the aura of centuries of gardening – the perfect way to leave Villandry with all its complexity and martialled energy.

Giverny

Normandy, France

GIVERNY IS ONE OF THE most famous gardens in Europe, if not the world. It is an icon of colour and light and the embodiment of the creative relationship between painting and gardening. It is, in marketing terms, a win-win situation. Therein lies the problem. Giverny is big business. Whereas Sissinghurst – physically three or four times the size – feels crowded with 200,000 visitors, half a million people arrive in this little Normandy village to see the garden every year. The draw for most of these people is, I guess, as much about personality as plants. Monet is a big attraction, especially to Americans – Giverny is largely funded by American money. My own interest in the garden began forty years ago on a trip to the National Gallery in London where I saw one of his huge water lily canvases and was entranced. When I learnt of his obsession with his garden and how he painted it constantly for decades, I too fell under the spell of the potent mix of painting, gardening and a flamboyant personality. I have books on the garden and had seen endless pictures but had missed many opportunities to go. Now was clearly the moment to rectify that.

When Monet came to the Maison du Pressoir in Giverny in 1883, it had been a cider farm and in front of the house was an orchard with a central path leading down to what was then the narrow track (now a thundering main road) flanked by spruce, yew and box. Monet had always gardened and he set to in this new home with a will. He wished to remove the trees but his wife Alice resisted: the yews still remain and the spruces were only cut down and replaced by the present metal arches in 1920, after Alice's death. But Monet soon made broad beds flanking the path, raised in a mounded 'carp's back' style to accentuate the height and colour of the flowers. In fact these broad beds are almost like floral hedges or berms with the rounded arches mirroring their curve.

In order to compress as much colour as possible into the given space, height is used everywhere. The layout shows a series of narrow beds laid out in ranks, not unlike the Chelsea Physic Garden, but the effect on the ground is of narrow paths with broad reaches of flowers rising on either side. In fact the borders are like uncut country hedges flanking narrow lanes. They are 5 ft wide with 4 ft paths and the height of the borders is at least 5 ft – often more. This makes tunnels of colour, leading the eye deep into the garden along very restricted lines in which colour can be carefully manipulated. It is all very clever.

Short lateral beds work like one long wide one with access paths. These are thirty-eight 'paint box' beds laid out in pairs planted in imitation of colours on Monet's palette. The appearance of each of these small beds is a bit chaotic, but the small areas are all interplaying, like an orchestra or a canvas painted by a certain Claude Monet perhaps. It has a fuzzy formality that is beguiling, the edges of all the paths spilling over with plants and despite all the straight lines, not a hard edge to anything.

Crocosmia 'Lucifer', lilies, hemerocallis, *Alchemilla mollis*, lysimachia – planted to catch the light of the setting sun and intensify it – all make a superb combination down at the bottom of the

MONET LIKED TO PLANT BRIGHT COLOURS IN THE SUN AND COOL COLOURS IN THE SHADE TO INTENSIFY BOTH.

garden by the gate to the road. Monet liked to plant bright colours in the sun and cool colours in the shade to intensify both.

Beds are joined overhead by metal gantrys to support clematis and roses and the smaller beds appear to amalgamate to form one huge one. Everywhere is the branded 'Monet green' – on the ironwork, chains blocking paths, posts, signs, house, gates. As greens go it is a visual itch – being told that it has to be manufactured exclusively does little to ease the sense that it is used as a brand rather than because it improves things.

The overwhelming problem I faced at Giverny was that there was very little colour. I went on June 28th in what was proving to be the wettest summer for a very long time. I have never visited a single garden without being told that I should have come last week, next week, September, May – any time other than the actual day I was there. But in the end you judge as you find. It is all about colour. Without that it hardly exists – the plants could just as easily be vegetables or herbs if all are colourless. It makes the choice and meaning of plants irrelevant beyond their flowering. The fact that there was relatively little colour when I went exposed this cruelly.

The weather did not make Giverny a bad garden or even not worth the visit but it did expose its weaknesses as a garden as opposed to part of the Monet theme business. These are that it has little structure or form beyond the lines of paths and planting and to sustain the intensity of planting and expectation that the gardeners have to fulfil means that nothing feels grounded. Few of the plants look bedded in or settled – most look awkwardly perched because their roots are not really growing into the soil – the whole thing is a stage set. It is also hugely intensive. Monet had six full-time gardeners for this 2 acres and now there are ten. I am sure that they are needed to keep the show going but I am equally sure that the garden suffers as a result.

Cross the road (or actually go under it via the especially built subway) and you reach the lily pond. The pond and its lilies are beautiful in their own right, and fascinating to me as the source of my childhood meeting with the painting in the National gallery. I would have happily gone to Normandy just to have seen it alone. But the planting around the edges is horrid. Feeling sacrilegious, I asked about this and was told that it was necessary to stop people walking into the pond and that in Monet's day there was much less planting at the water's edge. I checked and the old photographs do look much nicer.

It is a tough one. The bits that I liked best were where the gardeners were working – protected by Monet-green plastic chain to keep the traipsing visitors back – with trays of plants, abandoned jerseys or buckets of weeds. But on the whole Giverny felt to me more like a museum or Madam Tussauds than a living garden. Everything is always an interpretation. The modern keepers of the garden have to pay homage to the memory of Monet and his ghost. What would he have done in this situation? How can we best interpret that? It is always a problem. Nothing is the thing itself. I think that this is at the heart of my problem with the garden and perhaps at the heart of all historic and famous gardens. If ever they become a search for what they were, then they are lost.

Yet you have to visit if you are remotely interested in Monet – and I guess that includes everyone interested in painting. As a garden it is a little confusing because all the things that Monet gave it are now lost, and yet that is precisely what they strive so hard to preserve. You cannot hold onto that quirkiness. It slips away.

I shall try and go back some future early June day to see the irises in their glory and hope that the sun shines and my rather glum response is gloriously challenged and transformed. But it will be a detour rather than a special journey.

Jacques Wirtz's Garden

Schoten, Antwerp, Belgium

I TOOK A TRAIN FROM PARIS TO ANTWERP, where it was a short taxi journey to Schoten, north-east of Antwerp, to see the home garden of Jacques Wirtz. Jacques is a garden designer whose work I have only seen in books but that was enough to make me revere him as a designer creating seemingly truly original and yet instantly pleasing gardens. From photographs of his work it appeared that he, as much as any living garden designer, was creating genuinely sculptural forms from plants and the spaces they create. To be allowed to visit his garden at home was to be allowed into an inner sanctuary.

Jacques Wirtz was born in Antwerp in 1924 and studied landscape architecture and horticulture at Tuinbouwschool, Vilvoorde. This gave him a detailed knowledge of plants and how they grow, something that he considers absolutely essential for any would-be garden or landscape designer. Since 1950 he has worked as a landscape architect in Schoten and established an international reputation. His sons, Martin and Peter, joined the firm in 1990 and together they have designed and built gardens in Belgium, Spain, Portugal, England, Switzerland and the USA.

More than any other living garden designer, Jacques Wirtz has harnessed the magic of sculptured plants and the spaces that exist between them.

In 1970 the family moved to the gardener's house of a great estate with an old walled garden of some 4 acres to garden in. When they arrived this was almost entirely derelict apart from some mature fruit trees and the remnants of box hedging. Finding these, Jacques did not impose a preconceived plan but went with it and used this raw material, transforming the garden into one of the most recognisable and idiosyncratic in the world.

The garden is set back from the road and surrounded by a tall beech wood, giving it a completely green backdrop. You are met with his trademark impeccably clipped hornbeam hedges (I confess that my own garden is measured out in hornbeam entirely influenced by Jacques Wirtz) screening the house. There is a lot of clipping in a Wirtz garden (the box hedges alone take two people six weeks to cut) but, I was firmly told, always with an electric hedge cutter if possible or by hand, never with a petrol-driven machine. These green walls make spaces of monastic quiet and calm.

I was nervous about meeting him. As one always is with heroes. As a rule it is a disappointment but not this time. He is a tall, benign, smiling man and incredibly active and sprightly for someone in their mid-eighties. He still works every day on new projects, and still loves his own garden with the excitement and passion he had when he first arrived nearly forty years ago. The house is modest but beautiful inside and out. Breakfast on the lawn, white tablecloth and perfect manners, clean spaces filled with light inside. All is modest and restrained and yet wholly relaxed.

The garden is an irregular rectangle divided into four by paths flanked with the famous astonishing cloud pruned box hedges. Jacques told me that this was simply a practical way of dealing with old hedges that had become so shaded and overgrown that they consisted of individual, lanky bushes with gaps between them. By clipping them with the existing curves and undulations he encouraged them to grow together to make a sinuous form that is billowingly beautiful. Half of the quarter nearest to the house might be called a conventional garden, with a lawn, borders, pond and greenhouse and there is a hidden garden in another quarter but the rest is entirely given up to nursery stock planted in informal beds. This description does no service to it at all. For a start you are hardly aware of any of this. Other than the quartering paths the garden seems to be a seamless whole. Yet it is quite unlike anything you are likely to have experienced before. It has the clipped formality of Villandry, yet is as unostentatious as possible – rather as though one has stumbled upon an attic full of beautiful, yet slightly forgotten, objects or into a sculptor's studio filled with work in various stages of completion.

There are clipped yews, hollies, some so huge that they can only be trimmed from vast cranes. There is a sense of *Alice through the Looking Glass* here – everything is familiar but strangely so. Things are bigger, more trimmed and clipped and yet more wild than one is used to. Parts of the garden are like a quarry with blocks of green standing waiting to be carved. The bubbling curves of the cloud hedges and the clipped shapes beyond them in every direction shape the spaces between the plants, sculpting the green air.

I SPENT TWO DAYS IN THE GARDEN AND NEVER TOUCHED A MOMENT OF LESS THAN WONDER AND DELIGHT.

Very little is presented. Most of the garden is literally hidden. Almost everything is hinted at or glimpsed, rather than presented with a fanfare and carefully staged backdrop. This saturates it with charm without ever becoming whimsical.

You stumble across a range of cherries bred because none could be satisfactorily bought, or a collection of box that was bought in, kept for clients, yet never used and became part of the garden as it was planted. The Wirtzes use the garden to test the hardiness of plants and simply to observe how they grow before using them for clients. There is something genuinely artless about it – which is one of the ways that it so easily reaches art.

This transcends horticulture. The English obsession with horticulture is at best a display of great skill and craftsmanship but very rarely art. At worst it deludes itself that because it is carefully and skilfully done then it must be good. But horticulture is always a means to an end. The end is where judgements of design should be made. Judging a garden by the quality of its plants is like judging a building on the quality of its bricklaying. That might be entirely admirable in its own right but it is never enough to make a good building. This is not to suggest that Jacques Wirtz's garden lacks horticultural skill. It may have the jumbled air of an attic but everything is perfectly clipped, grown and maintained. But that is a given and the horticultural skill necessary is worn very lightly indeed.

And there are flowers too. Lots of them. But no traditional borders. Everything has a utilitarian shape about it. They grow their flowers in rows and do so even in the gardens of their clients. This might seem brutally functional but, although I would not have guessed it until confronted with the evidence, Jacques is right when he says that a 'good selection of perennials is always beautiful when planted in rows'. He started sowing like this in the garden to store for clients but now likes it in its own right. The flower garden thus takes on the easy confidence of an allotment, avoiding the slight anxiety of performance. The result – of course – is a really good show. The lesson is loud and clear.

So delphiniums, nigella, cornflowers, roses, sweet peas, azaleas, weeping cherries, irises, nursery stock, herbs, annuals, perennials and shrubs are all in merging blocks and rows divided by narrow earth paths. Tulips and peonies each have their blocks in amongst the topiary and then are left to die back gently. It does not look abandoned or negligent. Things have simply moved on from their moment, like coming across a patch of bluebells gone to seed in a wood.

The very light, sandy soil affects what they grow and how they grow it. Jacques says that he would love better soil. It does mean that the excellent drainage enables the paths to be made just of bare soil so that the beds can shift where and how they choose. On my heavy clay soil at home this would be impossible for most of the year. It also makes the transplanting of stock much easier. Thus geology shapes the way the garden has evolved as much as the Wirtz design brilliance.

I spent two days in the garden and never touched a moment of less than wonder and delight. But adoration is never quite enough. The best work inspires you to do, to do again and to do more. I left determined to review the work of the previous sixteen years in my own garden at home and completely revamp it. It convinced me that great gardens are never complete. Of course plants are in a constant state of flux but the human creativity must match this. As well as being profoundly spiritual and healing, gardening can be high art – but only if it is constantly changing and evolving. Try and hold it still and the magic slips away like sand through your fingers.

Het Loo

Apeldoorn, The Netherlands

FROM JACQUES WIRTZ'S paradisical modern garden outside Antwerp we drove down the motorway to Amsterdam, where we caught a train to Apeldoorn and back in time 307 years to a precisely calibrated 1700. This is the year that the garden at Het Loo (pronounced 'Het Low') has been meticulously restored to and maintained at. I first visited the garden in 1994, just as the last of the restoration was complete. I thought that in the years since then it might have matured and mellowed but, in fact, if anything it seems newer and brighter now. That is the point of the place: the intention is to hold it at 1700 when it was complete but absolutely new. The topiary and hedging is kept deliberately compact and replaced constantly to stop it growing too big – which is exactly what would have happened at the beginning of the eighteenth century. Man's complete control and dominance over nature was to be seen and celebrated in every manifestation of the garden.

Though it is a scrupulously accurate historical restoration of the garden in 1700, Het Loo's appearance is shockingly brash and gaudy, more Las Vegas than Hampton Court.

William of Orange and his young wife Mary came here in 1684, but they thought the original castle, tucked in the woods beyond the garden walls, was too small, old and unmodern. William wanted to build something to proclaim his power and, above all, send a message to Louis XIV's court at the recently completed Versailles. So now, 310 odd years after it was made, this is a garden in its youthful prime – given a second life at about twenty-five years old. It is seen as it was intended to be seen, rather than having been restrained, repaired and held static. The curator, Ben Groen, speaks of a garden 'frozen' in 1700. What we see now is the virility of Het Loo – not its noble fading.

The approach to the front of the new palace is via three radiating double avenues of beeches. They are beautiful but the grandeur is stated from the outset. In fact, the palace is pretty much hidden until the last 100 yards or so and is surprisingly modest and modern looking. This is because Louis Napoleon had it covered in stucco which preserved the bricks and stopped them weathering. When the stucco was removed in the 1970s, the bricks emerged looking in mint condition. This sets the tone for the whole of Het Loo. Everything looks brand, spanking new. This is perfectly historically accurate – late seventeenth-century baroque was crass, brash and not necessarily very tasteful.

Go round to the rear of the palace, and the garden is spread out in all its considerable glory. There is absolutely nothing loose, soft or 'natural' about it. Everything is clipped, constrained, trained and ordered, with symmetry evident in every aspect.

This is the natural world bought to heel. In the light of all our modern trends, where we try and work with nature wherever possible, it is hard to assimilate. But it is important to stress the regality and display of power of the garden. The intention was to convey the message that the man that ruled this was in command of unruly nature. This is only fifty years before Rousham, but Het Loo is the mould that Rousham broke.

The Great Garden is a rectangle designed to be viewed from high elevated terraces with hugely wide paths running through it, ideal for perambulation three or four abreast with the parasols, canes and broad skirts of the late seventeenth century. The scores of yew cones are all exactly the same size – rather small by modern standards and expectations (about 5–6 ft) – and would be replaced by others a little smaller as they 'outgrew' their spot. Nothing is meant to grow into being or to evolve.

Above *The golden swans spouting water were the orginals from which the lead swans at Rousham were cast.* Opposite *Queen Mary's private garden, with its elaborate, ornate parterres can only be properly appreciated from above.*

The plants lining the paths in the ribbon beds are all single specimens rather than borders in any modern sense. They were laid out like china (of which there was a large collection at Het Loo) to be admired as a collection – piece by piece. Ben Groen stressed to me that the garden deliberately has no naturalism at all. Plants grow precisely where they are told. All the shapes and forms are man-made and entirely artifical – propaganda for the King to show how he could control nature. The maintenance is extraordinarily intense. I saw over a dozen gardeners all clipping box in one small area – all the miles of dwarf box hedging are cut by hand with shears so as not burn the freshly shorn leaves.

They aim to keep the plants 50 per cent European and 50 per cent exotic (introduced) because, after 1700 there were more exotics than European plants. However, the list of plants available for the garden is extensive and remarkably familiar. I jotted down from one bed *Acanthus spinosus*, clipped junipers, *Lychnis chalcedonica*, *Lysimachia*, salvias, honeysuckle, *Centaurea montana*, oriental poppies, *Digitalis ferruginea*, snap dragons, sweet peas (newly introduced to Europe), *Achillea*, *Lavatera*, *Echinacea purpurea*, nasturtiums (rare in 1690) – all lined out with lots of bare earth around them, in thin rows one plant deep like sentinels flanking the paths.

The garden is full of what we rather lumpenly call 'hard landscaping', with fountains, gilded figures, two orbs, rills and canals and arbours to sit in. They are marvellously hideous. I love it at Het Loo but would not want any of it within a mile of my own garden, but then Baroqueness is fantastically kitsch to the twenty-first century eye: Het Loo is a cross between Las Vegas and Ancient Rome.

Leave the Great Garden and it changes dramatically. The two canals either side of the approach road were discovered by archaeologists when they removed 6.5 ft of sand. Unlike the rest of the garden there was no written evidence of them. They were wholly original until a few years ago (2003) when they were replaced by modern materials. They look shockingly modern in every way. Cool, uncluttered and stylish. But this merely confirms our aesthetic prejudices and preferences. We like this sort of thing and recognise it. The other side of the wall, with the parterres, could be Pompeii for all its artistic and cultural remoteness.

The end section, beyond the crossing road and canals, was a vegetable garden until 1692. Then the garden designer Daniel Morot returned from Hampton Court, very influenced by that and made a new garden in 1692–94. It is even more accessible than the rest with a rather park-like feel, perhaps because there are still a few large trees left from the early nineteenth-century landscaping including an oak, a large tulip tree and some beeches. This was so that some mark of that phase of its garden history would remain – which seems odd when you think how complete the rest of the restoration has been. In fact 99 per cent of the garden has been wholly reconstructed – just some of the original steps remain.

Finally, like some delicacy at the edge of the plate, I left what I think is the best bit to last, the Berceaux. A berceaux is really a glorified pergola with hornbeams planted along a substantial wooden framework and trained to completely clad it, making architecture from plants. The idea was to provide the queen with shelter and privacy whilst she walked. The light flickers through the leaves in an entrancing way and it is not the least gloomy. I think that it is quite brilliant gardening.

Het Loo is the best living history lesson I know. It is a time machine and brings the year 1700 completely alive. But I left rather saturated by the past, and eager to return to a garden of the present.

The Boon Garden

Oostzaan, Amersterdam, The Netherlands

Above Looking down from the end of the garden, the black water of the swimming pool appears to lead right into the house. *Opposite* The front of the house does not house the average front garden. Instead it uses massive sculptured shapes of box, yew and beech.

FROM APELDOORN AND THE TIME WARP of Het Loo I went back to modern Amsterdam and a very modern garden. Holland in 1700 had been realised to the last leaf and petal. I now wanted to see what the twenty-first century Dutch garden was like, so looked to the work of another modern garden designer that I have huge respect for, Piet Oudolf.

The garden of the Boon family is at Oostzaan, just twenty minutes to the north of Amsterdam but surrounded by fields. Piet and Karin Boon are both designers and hired Oudolf to create a garden to accompany the house that they were building there. So the whole thing was made from scratch as a garden integrated with the house and designed especially for the tastes and uses of the Boon family. This specificity humanises and personalises the garden and, with the shining exception of Jacques Wirtz's garden, after visiting historic and grand establishments I wanted to see somewhere that was primarily a home. The garden is really quite small and is domestic in every aspect of scale. Before I came I knew that it was hardly a typical back garden – a slice of everyday Dutch horticultural life. This is self-conscious and confident 'Good Design' and to that end they have hired one of the best people in the business. It seemed to me that this is probably very 'un-British' and would therefore be an insight into an attitude more general to this part of Northern Europe. I had expected – and found – a garden that was not so much a status symbol and tribute to a successful life but an adjunct to a life where good design was evident in all that they did and used and where a garden was for leisure and pleasure rather than horticultural ends in itself.

Although only twenty minutes from the centre of Amsterdam (the city's skyscrapers can be seen from the house), it is in fact completely surrounded by low lying (and when I was there, very wet) fields and canals.

The house is on a small but busy road and almost completely screened off by a high beech hedge. Once inside the front gate you are inside a parterre constructed out of massive blocks of beech hedging 4 ft high and equally wide. The exterior hedges are precisely 8 ft high. I give these measurements because they are carefully chosen and maintained and are the specific heights that Piet likes to use for hedges. Why? How does he arrive at these numbers? 'Because they feel right.' Interestingly, these are the same proportions as used in the Garden of Love at Villandry. The sheer mass of the hedges is completely surprising and unexpected as a front garden. Piet is proud of this but apparently it is unused. 'No one uses the front path – just the milkman. It is viewed only from above. Everyone arrives by car, parks and then walks round the side to the house.' Piet sounds sad but resigned to this. Instead of being the front face of the house and garden it is effectively a hidden area, tucked away from house, road and the rest of the garden.

The private, much-used garden is round the back of the symmetrical, rather brutally utilitarian house, whose interior betrays every sign of the occupants' professions. Nothing is left undesigned. These are successful modern people, easy in their well-toned skin.

The garden is dominated by a long pool, twenty paces by five with raised walls that are 18 inches wide and 18 inches high and a wooden decking walkway around it that is 5 ft wide. The water is like glistening black rubber. A pavilion sits at the end beyond it and it is flanked on either side by more massive, low hedges, this time in yew. On one of the wettest, greyest days of an exceptionally wet, grey summer the greens shine out of the gloom. The immediate first impression is of blocks of vegetation and water tethered to the ground. Everything is simplified down to big spaces. No mess but lots of mass.

The proportions everywhere are solid and massively confident, tethering the garden to the ground against the enormous sky, like great green moorings. I find myself measuring everything: the yew hedge is 3 ft tall and 3 ft wide (I suspect 1 m actually), the surrounding beech hedge 4 ft. The boundary hedge is cloud pruned, softening the edge as it fades into sky – literally against clouds. On the other side the apple trees have same effect. It is as crisp as possibly can be at the centre, radiating from the empty blackness of the pool outwards and then gradually softening as it goes out to the sky. This is very well done. The very low horizontals hold the precision close to the ground.

Like the house, everything here is designed. There is hardly an accident to be stumbled across. I like the confidence of this but it suggests that any gardening is done in the same spirit as housework – largely unseen and certainly not by the owners.

This does seem to be a very un-British thing. We are proud of our gardening skills and the very rich will brandish their earth-scarred hands along with the humblest allotmenteer as a badge of horticultural honour. Here on the flatlands outside Amsterdam, this garden is self-consciously and unashamedly a hands-off object of design.

I like it. I like its confidence and the satisfying confidence of the planting and spaces. Oudolf's training as an architect structures the spaces with great boldness, softened and humanised by his planting. It does not enforce or impose itself onto the landscape but I very much like the way that the garden relates exactly and carefully to the particular terrain around it. That is its great skill. In all this huge open, flat space it would be very easy for a small garden like this to be overwhelmed.

Beds of Deschampsia caespitose *flank the long, dark pool, softening the solid masses of hedging.*

However, whereas Jacques Wirtz's garden was like a breathing studio liable to change in the course of a day, this is a finished, honed piece of design: it is a display. It is like the kitchen or the living room – all tidy and clutter-free and filled with very self-conscious pieces of designed good taste. Remember David Hockney's definition of design and art: 'Good art changes your life – good design improves the quality of your life.'

I don't mean this as criticism. There is a lot of paddling under the surface to keep that appearance of immutability. The hedges all have to be clipped, of course, and the flower beds, dominated by Oudolf's trademark use of grasses but rich with flowers, need care and constant stocking up. The *Deschampsia* in the beds flanking the pool has to be replaced every two or three years to preserve its 'look'.

The main beds flanking the pool are planted extremely simply – and strongly – with *Deschampsia*, *Amsonia orientalis* and the red clover *Trifolium rubrens*. But the big border separating the pool area from the little orchard contains – or so I quickly jotted down – *Rodgersia*, *Anemone*, *Thalictrum*, *Eupatorium*, *Geranium*, *Salix*, *Polygonatum*, *Campanula*, *Filipendula*, *Aconitum*, *Phlox*, *Sedum* and the grasses *Stipa* and *Molinia*. It looks great but the only access is via a very narrow path. To view it you look across the top of the great, low yew hedge. The path is for maintenance, not to bring you closer to engage with the plants. This is not bad but all my instincts were to touch and rummage, both manually and visually.

Talking to Piet was fascinating to see how he reconciled the limitations of working with a client and his own tastes and standards. It appears to have been a pretty pain-free process, leading the Boons into a planting that they would never have considered but that satisfied their desire for an easy, instantly stylish space.

The big idea – for Piet – is the way that the hedges create the low, blocky space. There are fixed volumes, like a hedge or wall, and dynamic ones that grow and change like a border. The relationship between these two creates the energy and tension of a garden. In this case maintenance had to be low. In fact, he reckons that maintenance is 35 per cent of the cost of a garden. So cutting maintenance costs makes a real long-term saving.

Oudolf also believes in planting that looks as natural as possible. Ideally his borders should appear as artless as a meadow. They do mostly, although the context of this garden is as artless as a rather swish modern hotel. But he is tapping into a very modern need to escape the intense depersonalisation of the city. His plants are chosen either as species or varieties that look as though they might be species. No intensely-bred hybrids with huge blooms for him. He likes smaller, much more natural flowers and planting that is sustainable both environmentally and for do-today maintenance. His flowering plants are chosen as much for their form as their flowers. The result is that both in appearance and concept his designs are always confidently, coolly modern.

A rounded statue of a reclining woman balances on the edge of the pool, dipping her toe delicately into the water.

OUDOLF'S TRAINING AS AN ARCHITECT STRUCTURES THE SPACES WITH GREAT BOLDNESS, SOFTENED AND HUMANISED BY HIS PLANTING.

On that note it seemed to be an appropriate time to leave the Netherlands and conclude my trip into Northern Europe. But before I went home I wanted to follow the summer sun and go north. In fact, as far north as I could possibly go and still visit a garden.

The Botanic Garden

Tromsø, Norway

Above *Even though this is the northernmost botanical garden there is an astonishing range of plants growing. Chinese rhubarb,* Rheum palmatum, *grows in tall spikes, and is totally at home in this northern climate.* Opposite *The small, upright yellow-flowered* Campanula thyrsoides *thrives in the European Alps garden, alongside the poppies* Papaver rhaeticum *and P. sendtneri, two species of alpine poppy.*

I GOT ON MY FIRST plane of the trip to fly from Amsterdam to Oslo and from there 200 miles inside the Arctic Circle to Tromsø, right up on the north coast of Norway. Tromsø is a low, small island linked to the mainland by bridge and to the next, bigger island by a similar bridge. It is a land of tough fishermen and seafarers – Amundsen chose all his crews from Tromsø and started all his voyages from there.

But why did I chose Tromsø? Because it is the most northerly botanic garden in the world – I wanted to see some gardening at the very extremes of light.

When I was there in the first week of July, there was bright light for twenty-four hours a day. Broad daylight at one, two and three in the morning. People sitting outside, chatting and sunbathing, in the middle of the night. It is the strangest thing. On July 24th, five minutes of dark creeps in at either end of the day and by September 21st they are back in line with Britain. By the beginning of December there is pitch darkness twenty-four hours a day until February when the light starts creeping back into the sky for a few minutes each day. A place of unimaginable extremes of light.

So, for the first time in two weeks of travelling through Europe in high summer, I found some good weather with bright sunshine, iridescent blue sky and 20°C heat. But this, I learn, is a heat wave – the average July temperature is 12°C. At the Botanic Garden they were watering the alpine plants to cool them down.

The garden is very new, only opening in 1994, and by international standards is modest, with, excluding the wood, almost 5 acres of cultivated ground. The cold and moist climate of Tromsø, moderated by a branch of the Gulf Stream that makes for relatively mild winters (the January average is –4.4°C) and cool summers (the July average is +11.7°C), makes it much easier to cultivate many Arctic and alpine plants outdoors than in most other botanic gardens. This is particularly the case with plants originating from moist areas, such as the monsoon-influenced parts of the Himalayas and the neighbouring mountains of China as well as local plants from the Arctic.

It has a unique atmosphere too. There is no need to fix a time to visit the Botanic Garden as it is open twenty-four hours a day, seven days a week, fifty-two weeks a year. People do come and visit at two and three in the morning in the summer. There are no walls, fences or gates. This openness translates into a spirit of complete generosity inside the garden. It feels as public as the midnight sun and as accessible.

After a night where sleep felt like an enforced rest on a sunny afternoon, I went after breakfast to the Botanic Garden, still locked into my concept of appropriate opening times. I approached from the top, through a track leading from the university, with a ski jump surreally breaking through the forest into the clear blue skyline, into birch woods.

These woods – mainly birch but also some sorbus – are part of the Botanic

THE WOODLAND FLOOR IS AMAZINGLY DELICATE – SEEMINGLY NOT BASHED IN ANY WAY BY WIND AND RAIN OR CRUSHING HUMAN TREAD.

Garden and amongst the loveliest things I have ever seen. They are glorious, like the very best of an English May day but with a much higher light level and an incredible green lushness. The wood is under snow many feet deep for six months of the year. This protects and insulates it and provides moisture when it melts. The soil is very acidic, poor and damp and the trees grow slowly and thinly so do not shade out the flowers, which grow so profusely that it is like a meadow in a wood. I noted down *Geranium sylvaticum* (wood cranesbill), buttercup, grasses, the bunchberry, *Cornus canadensis*, geums, alchemilla and meadowsweet (*Filipendula ulmaria*) Every inch of the woodland floor is covered in flowers and grasses, all shining in the light. It is also amazingly delicate – seemingly not bashed in any way by wind and rain or crushing human tread. This alone is worth travelling so far to see.

Where the wood breaks and opens into the garden proper there is a sudden glade of meconopsis, the bluest of all blue flowers. There is *Meconopsis grandis*, *M.* x *sheldonii* and *M. betonicifolia*, being grown in open-bottomed pots as an experiment to try to stop the birch roots invading and taking the few nutrients that there are out of the soil.

To learn more about the garden I went and met the curator, Arve Elvebakk. I asked how they coped with the extremes of the Arctic climate and lack of light. 'Winter,' he said, 'is seven to eight months. Which can be difficult for gardeners but alpine plants love this. It rests them and the snow that lies from October to May protects them although climate change means that the snow melts earlier than it used to. For two months in the middle of winter we never come into the garden. We prepare our catalogues and the database, preparing guides and things like that. Where we are sitting now is covered by almost 5 ft of snow. The best month is June. Midnight sun lasts until mid-August then winter comes. At that point Arctic plants need more red light than darkness to stimulate dormancy.

*I was amazed to see the alpine meadows were foaming with cow parsley (*Anthriscus sylvestris*). In the front is pink-purple* Silene dioica *and the yellow flowers in between are the common buttercup.*

'But it is really very mild here. At the same latitude in Greenland, for example, we could grow practically nothing. It is amazing that we can grow so many Himalayan plants without adaptation to the climate when you think just how much further south the Himalayas are.'

Certainly as I walk around there are familiar plants growing with a kind of springy exuberance but out of the season with which I associate them. So *Rosa glauca*, lilac and cow parsley – all which I associate with May or even April – are at their best in early July. It is for me a second spring and it feels like a second chance.

The garden is essentially a large rock garden and, I confess, these are not usually my kind of thing. But under the razor blue sky and intensity of light, they make a new sense as though this is the language of the place. They fit. Again and again throughout my travels I have been struck by the importance of context. The right plant in the right place is what defines beauty in a garden and to start with you have to always go back to where plants originate from and see how they grow in their natural habitat. This cannot be cheated.

I then go and meet Brynhild Mørkyed, curator at the museum, who has been collecting plants from local households in northern Norway that were otherwise being lost because they are only grown in domestic households. The wives would grow a few flowers in a tiny patch of garden and when daughters left home to be married the young bride would take some plants to set up and start their own garden or to add to the existing garden in her husband's family home. This was the only way the plants were spread around and no one really knows how they got hold of many of the plants in the first place.

Brynhild has 560 different plants in the collection, all collected from northern Norway – an incredible variety of domestic plants. For example *Ranunculus acris* 'Flore Pleno' (gold button) had completely disappeared from most gardens and only survived from old stock in Tromsø gardens because it had simply been weeded out elsewhere – although old people remember it growing in gardens.

She told me how the indigenous Sami people developed ingenious ways of preserving plants, storing green growth in bladders and stomachs and this would have seen them through the winter. The wild mountain angelica is very much smaller than the garden variety in the UK, and the Sami would eat angelica stems as a vegetable in summer, use the stems as flutes in winter and smoke the dried roots. There was *Allium victoralis* which is a stunner and was grown by the Vikings for food, like a mild garlic. She herself collected meadowsweet, chives, caraway, angelica, bistort and sorrel – all are native plants – from the nearby fields.

Finally she showed me rosenrot – *Rhodiola rosea* – the roots of which were used as viagra – although when questioned it was always claimed to be for cattle use only but probably, she thought, by villagers too 'in the private room'.

So I flew back to the grey rain of home, 1,000 miles south. Apparently the weather turned in Tromsø the day after I left, but for just a few days I had a glimpse of life in unbroken light. It had been a fascinating trip to see how gardens manage history, myth, the cult of personality and extremes of weather. Above all, I came back certain that, although I love visiting gardens rich with history, the price is nearly always true creativity. A garden can only really thrive as a work of art when it is in a state of constant flux – as soon as a garden becomes any kind of memorial then that thrilling sense of a work of art in progress is lost.

Following pages
My trip to the Yellow Mountains in Huangshan was the only time I saw the sun in my entire trip but it was the heart of everything I saw in Chinese gardens.

The pines in the mountains grow straight out of the rock on the sheer slopes, looking exactly like what the Japanese call *bonsai* and the Chinese *penjing*. In fact it is the other way round – these artifices are directly inspired by and aspiring to the natural growth in the Yellow Mountains.

2 The Mountains of the Mind

China and Japan

China

As a student and young man I spent some time trying to understand Eastern religions and Zen Buddhism in particular. I was not successful. The hardest problem was one of language. Too much was lost in translation. I could see from photographs that the Zen gardens had an articulacy which I wanted to respond to but felt clumsy to express. I knew that Zen came to Japan from China and that any journey towards understanding the Japanese Zen gardens had to begin with a visit to see Chinese gardens.

So I arrived in Shanghai on a cold March day. Of all the places in the world, this seemed the most exotic, the most foreign. Nothing can prepare you for the scale of China. Everything exceeds expectation. I got a taxi to Suzhou (pronounced 'Sue-Joe') and was staggered by the amount of clipped and trained trees and shrubs lining the motorway. They went for mile after mile in their hundreds of thousands. Later I was to see whole towns built around nurseries growing these trees. Motorways, railways and factories are being built in every direction, yet amongst them will be buffaloes pulling ploughs and small villages living as they have done for generations. Chinese civilisation was ancient when the West was in the Dark Ages, yet the very, very old and the utterly modern seem to coexist without angst.

Suzhou is a city built on canals, famous for its textiles and mellifluous dialect. The old city is unspoilt and charming and it has a reputation as having the finest collection of historic gardens in China. I planned to visit two, The Humble Administrator's Garden and The Lion Grove. I also took a trip to Huangshan to visit the *Huangshan*, or Yellow Mountains. Not only are these extraordinarily beautiful but they also unlock a door to the understanding of Chinese gardens and thereby, I reasoned, the Zen gardens of Japan.

The mountains are in the southern part of Anhui province and have seventy-two peaks in 60 square miles. They are called the Yellow Mountains because in AD 747 Emperor Li Ongji believed that the Yellow Emperor Xuanyuan became an immortal there, so he changed their name to *Huangshan*, meaning yellow. This matters because the mountains are revered for more than their beauty. They inspire right-mindedness and spiritual purity. Poets, painters, calligraphers and philosophers have always been drawn to them. The resulting paintings in particular went on to inspire gardens. Chinese paintings can look fantastical and symbolic but when you visit the Yellow Mountains you realise that they never exceed the truth. The real mountains are beyond all exaggeration. I cannot recommend a visit to them too highly and if you are to come close to understanding Chinese gardens then it is essential. The views are life-changing. The pines in the mountains grow straight out of the rock on the sheer slopes, looking exactly like what the Japanese call *bonsai* and the Chinese *penjing*. In fact it is the other way round – these artifices are directly inspired by and aspiring to the natural growth in the Yellow Mountains.

The point is that every aspect of a Chinese garden aspires to capture this harmonious balance of nature, the yin and yang poised at the moment before the fall. Our Western gardens seem lush and cluttered by comparison and yet also extraordinarily empty. On the other hand, Chinese gardens can seem austere to the point of incomprehensibility, and Japanese Zen gardens even more so.

The Humble Administrator's Garden

Suzhou, Jiangsu Province

Above The wonderfully named 'Good for Both Families' pavilion overlooks both the western and central garden and refers to the period when the garden was divided.
Opposite In Chinese gardens the reflections in the water are just as important as the actual objects and plants that make them.
Previous page The shapes formed by the pine trees and peaks of the Yellow Mountains have provided inspiration for hundreds of generations of Chinese poets and artists.

DURING THE REIGN of the Emperor Zhengde, between 1506 and 1521, the site of what is now the Humble Administrator's Garden in Suzhou was occupied by a temple. But it was appropriated by a tax collector called Wang Xianchen who turned it into his private villa, complete with garden. The house and garden then changed hands repeatedly over the next few centuries, with alterations and additions made to the garden, so what remains today is an amalgam built around the core of the early sixteenth-century garden.

The site was originally a swamp and when Wang Xianchen first constructed the garden he used the water to create lakes, making islands with the spoil. The garden was the same size as it is today but simpler, although containing pavilions and trees as well as the carefully contrived water and stones. In the latter stages of the Ming Dynasty (1368–1650), about a hundred years after the garden was built, it was divided into three sections with the western and central parts becoming the villas of government officials. However, when the Ming Dynasty was replaced by the Qing Dynasty (pronounced 'ching'), the garden was repaired and modified, especially in the early years of the eighteenth century. About seventy years later, under the Emperor Qianlong, it was divided into two parts – the western end becoming Shu Youan, the Book of Study Gardens, and the eastern becoming Fu Yuan, the Restored Garden. What the modern visitor sees is essentially this late Qing stage of the garden, although it was not until 1949 that the eastern portion was joined to the centre. The buildings are all original but have been – and are being – heavily restored.

We arrived at 6 am on a very grey, cold day, just as the darkness became struggling half-light, giving us an hour or so to film before the first of the incessant stream of visitors came in. A gentle rain was falling constantly. The stones and white walls, marbled with algae and damp, almost merged into the damp mist. The buildings loomed out and then disappeared and the entire garden never quite took on an outlined physical substance, despite the huge stones everywhere. There are hundreds of pots, each on a stone pedestal, containing tree *penjing*, the art of creating entire miniature landscapes in pots through carefully contained and controlled trees and stones.

As with everything in China, you start to look for significance and meaning where in the West you would merely admire. Nothing in a Chinese garden is irrelevant. So the monkey grass (*Ophiopogon japonicus* – closely related to the black *O. planiscapus* found all over British gardens) provides the yin to the yang of the stones that it is planted amongst. Stone is always yang. Water is always yin. Both are always necessary.

The first section of the garden, the eastern end, feels like a public park funnelling you forward towards the central section. I wanted to linger but my guide almost manhandled me on so that we would have time in the central section before the crowds arrived. We strode past pines lapped with moss, and magnolias trying to break bud. Huge stones are set like sculptures along the way, the more holes and contortions the better. Thousands of dwarf azaleas in pots are being placed for a spring festival. Their colour is as rude and loud as the incessant firecrackers that the Chinese cannot resist. In fact, the Chinese love noise of all kinds. But the azaleas serve to reinforce the monochromy of the garden and the extraordinary subtlety that it contains. My eyes narrow their range and deepen their focus.

Pots of red azaleas put out for a festival make a temporary splash of colour in an otherwise green and grey garden.

The paths that we race along are in themselves wonderful, all mosaicked stone with a deceptively simple intricacy. That phrase pops up in my notebooks again and again. The walls are all white and topped with beautifully tiled roofs; the colour of the tiles signify rank – yellow is used for imperial palaces and temples, green for princes and grey for humility. The walls all have the marbled appearance of the best paper, the garden becoming three-dimensional against their backdrop. This combines to create great intensity – nature is distilled constantly in search of its essence. Every branch of every tree is shaped, considered and trained so that it looks to have arrived at this moment entirely by chance. Confucianism teaches order and duty, Taoism simplicity and restraint. Both of these huge philosophies are to be found in a single branch in the Chinese garden. Of course this is never just gardening. In China calligraphy, poetry, chess, philosophy, Confucianism, Taoism and music are all part of the creative process of making a garden.

All walls have lattice openings to glimpse the view ahead. Every style of lattice has meaning. Or so I am told. It is like walking through the streets of Suzhou, a babble of speech in an entirely strange tongue. There is nothing for it but to let the mind go and just take it in. There is more water than land and the paths negotiate the ponds like a maze. Like Suzhou itself with its labyrinth of canals, the Humble Administrator's Garden is a garden of buildings buttressed by water. As you go through to the central area, passing almost a street of large pavilions flanking the water, a glimpse of a pagoda is seen across the water, rising high into the mist. The two sections of the garden are divided by a walled passageway and the entrance consists of double doors with a screen immediately in front of them. This is good feng shui. Tension is built. Proper conduct implied. This is not just to make the visitor behave with servility but to help them to establish the right attitude. The Humble Administrator's Garden is a strolling garden, and the idea is that you walk through it both bringing and acquiring the right frame of mind. Gardens are somewhere to contemplate, write poetry in, to reach beauty of soul as well as art.

Through the doors there is a wonderful little pavilion with each wall pierced by a large circular opening that is half door, half window. Each of these moon gates symbolises perfection and frames an aspect that relates to a season, with spring looking over the fresh blossom, summer onto the water with its lotus flowers, autumn with moonlight on the bamboos and finally winter facing the snow-covered tiles of the passageway. It is an exquisite, perfect building.

There are far more rocks than plants and they are tended with the same reverence of the rarest specimen in a botanical garden. Rocks are revered. One man apparently adopted one as his brother. I met a Mr Wei who is a rock expert and we sat drinking the ubiquitous green tea to shelter from the rain whilst he showed me a few of his collection, each carefully wrapped in layers of cloth. All look a bit like something animate but the best should suggest rather than resemble. Ideally every work of art in China should leave space for the mind to interpret and travel 'between like and dislike' as Mr Wei put it.

I am learning that everything is designed to be glimpsed. Haziness is much valued, with hints and suggestions a better route than signposts or straight lines. Everything should be framed or set against a backdrop to create a complete tableau or picture – even if this is tiny or very simple.

Then the crowds poured in – 3,000 a day, every day, over a million a year – all in groups led by a guide with a loudspeaker strapped to their chest. The noise was astonishing, like a flock of hungry starlings under umbrellas with a dozen tannoy systems. But that is China. Noisy, beautiful, mysterious, poetic and with a deep, deep love of rocks.

The Lion Grove Garden

Suzhou, Jiangsu Province

THE LION GROVE GARDEN was originally created in 1342 by Weize, a famous monk, who wished to make a garden to remind himself of his former home, the Lion Rock on Tianmu Mountain. The entire garden is therefore designed to look like something (a mountain) that looks like something else (a lion). Gnarled, pitted, holed and contorted rocks pile on top of each other at every turn and every one is supposed to suggest a lion or some part of its anatomy (although at times I had to peer hard to even begin to see a resemblance). In many ways the rocks are like the crowds that pour through it: they speak loudly all at once, all speaking in Lion.

Lion Grove was created as a temple garden and Mr Wei, the rock master, elaborated on its creation for me. The story goes that Weize's teacher rode a lion to the site of the garden where it lay down and refused to move. When it shook its mane, hairs flew out and where they touched the ground each one turned into a lion cub. The monk, understandably astonished at this manifestation of the lion as a kind of dandelion, regarded this as a sign. As one might.

Every stone in this garden is revered and chosen for its likeness to a lion or a part of its anatomy.

The garden is approximately 2.5 acres and contains twenty-two pavilions and over seventy displays of carefully chosen rocks and bamboos or steles. It was initially famous as a retreat for painters and calligraphers but over the centuries fell into decline until it was bought in 1918 by a Mr Pei and given to the state when the Communists took over. Apparently it survived desecration through the simple expedient of shutting its doors.

I enter through a small, perfectly-proportioned court that led to the guest hall. It is the first of a series of enclosed spaces that draw you into the garden incrementally, the buildings larger than the spaces that they enclose. In the next court a *Magnolia* x *soulangeana* is opening its white petals against grey rocks. A cherry is in bud. It is an intimate space. All the stone in this garden comes from nearby Lake Taiu, which provides rock particularly prized for its holes, as the chemical composition of the lake eroded the limestone irregularly thus creating the fantastic shapes and the uniform grey colouring of the stone.

Narrow borders of stones and bamboo are set against each wall to create idealised landscapes; the whitewash of the walls is particularly prized for the stains, fading paint and mould – all encouraged as part of the composition.

Then you turn through a quatrefoil doorway that frames an absurdly life-like stone shaped like a lion's head, to see a vast pile of stones, layer of grey contortion heaped upon twisted, bony rock. This – and you can only see a small part of it to begin with – is the stone mountain built as a maze, symbolising the journey of life, where the traveller – that's you and me – enters fearfully, gets thoroughly lost, is amazed but eventually finds that they arrive exactly where they are.

It is fabulous. A wonderfully kitsch extravaganza whose seed – visually at least – falls from the same plant as the Victorian stumpery or the Georgian grotto. This is not to denigrate or belittle it at all. In its own way it is sublime, and twisting and shuffling through it (albeit negotiating the constant throng of visitors) is good fun. The millions of hands, grasping at rocks as corners are turned and narrow steps climbed, have worn newels of the limestone shinily smooth. It is very beautiful.

Rocks are very yang, of course, and have to be balanced by water, which is very yin, and so you come out of the rocky maze to an open pool banked by tiers of these rocks that double themselves in the black water. The stones are all individuals. The effect is massive but, as ever, nothing is casual. Each one is chosen.

On the open side of the pond are more buildings containing a display of paintings, calligraphy and, tellingly, the most prized possession of all, a cut slab of marble whose colorations suggest a range of mountains. It is a reminder that everything returns to the mountains and that they are the source of inspiration for natural harmony and beauty. To capture that essence in a garden, even in one single *penjing* tree or a tableau of pine, bamboo and stone just 3 ft wide and set against a stained wall – is the goal of every Chinese garden, and without understanding that then it is all merely fascinatingly strange, stretching the notion of gardening far across the cultural horizon. Bring the Yellow Mountains into the garden and it becomes the transcendental spirit of nature and humanity in perfect harmony. And even the most horticulturally blinkered Westerner would agree that that is the ultimate reason for gardening.

THE STONES ARE ALL INDIVIDUALS. THE EFFECT IS MASSIVE BUT, AS EVER, NOTHING IS CASUAL. EACH ONE IS CHOSEN.

The New Summer Palace

Beijing

I TRAVELLED TO BEIJING to see the final garden in China, the New Summer Palace, which was made for the Emperor as a summer retreat from the heat and noise of the Forbidden City. The two were linked by a canal so the Emperor and his family could progress in an easy and stately fashion between them.

As summer homes go, Yi He Yuan is impressive. It is huge. Enormous. The palace is like a small town and the garden runs to over 700 acres. Its history is, by Western standards, unimaginably long. An imperial palace and garden had existed on the site for over 850 years but the gardens that became the Summer Palace date from the Jin Dynasty (1115–1234). In the early fourteenth century, Kubla Khan 'a stately pleasure dome did decree… And there were gardens bright with sinuous rills/where blossomed many an incense-bearing tree' and he also enlarged the lake and made canals to bring water from the western hills. In 1750 the Emperor Qian Long built the Garden of Clear Ripples and expanded the lake, hiring 10,000 labourers to dig it out and turn it into a peach-shape to celebrate his mother's sixtieth birthday (the peach in China is a symbol of longevity). He then used the new lake for practising naval manoeuvres in.

The exquisite curve of the Jade Belt Bridge marks the division between the canal that led from the Forbidden City in the centre of Beijing and the grounds of the Summer Palace.

But in 1860 the Palace was looted and burned by the allied English and French troops and fell into decay. When the lake was dredged, 200 bombs were found from that war. The Dowager Empress Cixi (pronounced 'chi-chi') had the Palace rebuilt in 1886 to celebrate her own sixtieth birthday (clearly it was felt necessary to make dramatic gestures when you turned sixty – a box of choco-

THE TOTAL VIEW – THE OBJECT ALONG WITH ITS REFLECTION – IS THE COMPLETE THING. YOU CANNOT SEPARATE THE TWO.

lates and a card were never going to do). Amongst her many additions and alterations to the Palace was the marble boat – a copy of which is in the Lion Grove Garden in Suzhou. This was partly done as a justification for the expense of her work for, she claimed, that she was doing it all to set up a naval academy there, although the only ship that the Navy got was the marble tea pavilion shaped like a paddle steamer – possibly the ugliest building that I saw during my brief stay in China. But I can forgive her the excesses of a marble steamer and the appropriation of state funds as the result is a wonderful garden rather than warships.

The garden is an accretion of centuries of use and misuse, big in both space and concept. Whereas Suzhou had been wet and cold, Beijing was cold and very dry, thick with pollution, fog, smog and haze which, although not pleasant, gave the Summer Palace a ghostly beauty, but meant that I literally never saw the horizon. Despite all of its vastness, it remained shadowy and insubstantial all day long.

Clearly a 700 acre garden cannot be encapsulated in a single visit, not least if it is shrouded in enveloping mist. But the memory of it is unforgettable, even if it is made up of snatched sketches. Once you negotiate the 15,000 visitors that go there every day (over 5 million people visit the garden every year – all numbers in China exceed experience), the entrance is dominated by a vast stone of longevity that stands beneath a pine – taking one straight to the naturalism of the Yellow Mountains. Clearly even the imperial family

I stopped and stared at the artists writing carefully calligraphed poems in water on the black slates of the paving. They might have lasted only a few minutes, but they were still art.

revered nature. Walking round to the lakeside, men stood painting calligraphic messages in water on the black slate paving. Some passers-by stopped and read the poems they were writing, some admired their calligraphic style. I stopped in my tracks, astonished by these figures in the mist – making pieces of art that faded within minutes of being drawn.

The garden was fading in the pearly light, yet revealing more of itself. Willows hung over the water, their reflections as strong as the real things. Willow pattern came alive. Sun would have spoilt it – made it all too tangible.

The stones on their plinths are bigger here, better, and clearly literally, majestic. Cixi's palace is bright green, red and blue, the tiles an imperial yellow or gold and it has a lacquered newness that is rather disconcerting. But it is only just over a hundred years old, which brings it into a very Western scale of time. By the end of the nineteenth century the court had atrophied into a series of arcane rituals that consumed every waking hour. The energy of an earlier age was lost. But it does mean that the remaining palaces are untouched and strangely pedestrian, as much well-kept railway station as imperial palace.

The garden, however, remains imperially magnificent in every detail. Even on this vast scale the aesthetic pervades every branch, every stone, every new view. The lake holds the reflection of pavilions, islands and the bare trees of the pearly March day. The total view – the object along with its reflection – is the complete thing. You cannot separate the two.

Walking round the lake (which in itself is quite a hike), I notice that even quite small trees are trained and supported with large bamboo poles that are often more substantial than the trees themselves. All growth is carefully formed and trained and prepared in order that it might appear perfectly natural. It is hard to know if the Chinese see the irony in this.

Finally, as I leave, the sun peeks through the haze, an orange ember smouldering briefly. The composition is complete for a moment before the mist tucks it all away again, the evening draws in and I make the tortuous trip through Beijing's clogged traffic and prepare for the following day's journey on to Japan.

The hazy reflections of the willow trees and island pavilion in the murky grey water of the lake are ethereal and intrinsically entwined – the yin and yang in perfect balance.

Japan

Most people have an idea of what a 'Japanese' garden is like and have seen a version in Europe. It will have rocks and gravel, moss and bamboo, there will be a little bridge and a stone lantern and camellias, hostas, a willow and some kind of hard-pruned tree representing bonsai. This is, of course, a caricature of Japanese gardens but like all caricatures it contains distorted elements of the truth.

Gardens came to Japan from China in AD 607, when the Japanese envoy to China, Ono ni Imoko was received by the Emperor Sui Yang Ti. Imoko returned to Japan with, amongst many other many cultural influences, the hill and pond garden. Until then gardens as such did not really exist in Japan although one aspect of Shintoism was a deification of nature whereby a tree or rock could be worshipped and celebrated as something holy, something still very evident in modern Japan.

Through Chinese and Korean immigration, gardens developed through the centuries until, between 800 and 1185, a distinct Japanese style evolved, with the gardens of the wealthy and aristocracy admired and designed as 'stroll' gardens, and always including a pond. They were created as a display that was intended to entertain and impress. But then Zen Buddhism came to Japan from China (although it originated in India) and from 1200, gardens changed from a place of entertainment and relaxation to one of contemplation. Zen was taken up enthusiastically by the samurai, the military caste, and the dry garden, or *karesansui*, designed and developed by monks as an aid to contemplation and expression of Zen enlightenment, became the first truly Japanese style of garden. Most of the *karesansui* today are attached to temples or abbots' lodgings and are still tended by monks.

The two key principles of the guiding Zen aesthetic are *wabi*, which stimulates the mind and emotions to contemplate the essence of reality, and *sabi*, which stimulates the senses. Rusticity, melancholy, naturalness and age were highly valued and dominated the aesthetic in gardens as in all artistic expression.

The tea ceremony arrived in the late sixteenth century and was also taken up enthusiastically by the samurai. The gardens attached to the teahouses were based upon ideals of modesty, simplicity and restraint and were an important part of the mood setting for the ceremony.

My own interests in Zen and gardens means that inevitably it is this style that I wanted to see in Japan. And if you want to see the Zen gardens you have to go to Kyoto. This was the imperial city and capital of Japan until 1868 and there are still over 2,000 temples and shrines there, although they were all very nearly completely destroyed in the Second World War as Kyoto had been designated by the Americans as a target for one of the atom bombs. Fortunately, it was spared due to the lobbying of the American Secretary of State for War, Harry Stimson, who had visited the city and realised its exceptional cultural richness, and so diverted the bomb to Nagasaki. One can see that the citizens of Nagasaki might have mixed feelings about that.

So I left Beijing bound for Kyoto to see a select group of the hundreds of its Zen gardens, with the experience of China, and the Yellow Mountains in particular, hopefully equipping me to come a little closer to the bewildering but beautiful emptiness of Zen.

Ryoan-ji

Kyoto

I CAME TO RYOAN-JI at dawn. This meant rising at 4.30 am and driving for an hour to be there by 6 am as the light opened out onto the temple, but it seemed an appropriate hour and process to view the garden in the right frame of mind. There is a sense of reverence here that transfers itself to any visitor, however cynical. Although Ryoan-ji is a temple of which the garden is just a part, this reverence does not come so much from sensitivity to others' beliefs but from the materials of the place itself. Everything, from the clipped azaleas and hesitant cherry blossom in the car park, with branches supported by bamboo struts tied with black rope (the dye just so, the rhythm of binding exact), has an authority, a stillness and dignity that invites contemplation and quiet respect.

This can be a hurdle to understanding or even enjoyment. Westerners come to Ryoan-ji with such expectations and such an ardent hope for *satori* – that moment of enlightenment when everything in this clumsy world falls into place with the easy exactness of stones in raked gravel – that most come away confused or disappointed.

It is small. There is not all that much there. It is just some rocks, gravel and moss. It is really not much at all. But that, of course, is the point.

The site is very old. The first known temple on the location was built in AD 938 and the large pond from that period remains. The temple was destroyed in the Onin War and then rebuilt and occupied by Zen monks until it burnt down in 1488. It was then rebuilt again in 1499, along with the present garden. We casually ingest these dates but the sheer age of the Zen gardens in Kyoto takes some absorbing. It makes our Western garden history look callow. The temple burnt down again in 1789 and was rebuilt in a much grander style and then there was another fire in 1797. What we visit now has not changed since that date.

It is not certain who designed the garden at Ryoan-ji, although some attribute it to the great master Soami, but there is another school that says it was probably made and put together by professional workers, *sensui kawaramono* ('riverbank workers as gardeners'), assisted by the Zen monks. The lack of preciousness of ownership in something so minutely exact and measured is something that I like the idea of and seems somehow apt.

The (barefoot) approach is through rooms and halls of the most beautiful golden wood. Milky morning light falls through paper screen walls. No clutter. Emptying the mind.

Then into the garden, entering from the veranda in one corner. In the many pictures I had scrutinised of Ryoan-ji I had not seen how the temple buildings are part of the garden. One side of the temple opens via the veranda directly onto it and you can only see the garden from that elevated space. The garden and building are all of a piece – the colour of the wood exactly that of the tiles coping the enclosing wall. The paint of the walls can best be described as raked gravel colour. The golden, much weather-stained garden wall is the colour of the mats on the floor of the open rooms. There is no divide. On the walls (made

The rocks rise out of the carefully raked gravel in a seemingly arbitrary manner, but it is the spaces between them that are key. They are placed so that, when looking at the garden from any angle, only fourteen are visible at one time. In the Buddhist world the number fifteen denotes completeness, so only through reaching enlightenment would you be able to see all at once.

of moveable screens) of the chambers are paintings of the Yellow Mountains. The connection is umbilical.

And what of the garden itself? It is fifteen rocks, some surrounded by a small pool of moss, set in raked gravel and enclosed on two sides by a wall with a deeply pitched and tiled capping, on one side by a temple building and on the fourth side by a newer wall and small building. That's it. No annuals, decking, lawns, herbaceous borders, shrubbery, vegetable patch, meadows, pots or parterre. Nothing much at all. Just rocks, gravel and moss arranged flawlessly. Nothing to do except rake the gravel every month or so. A lot of space.

The space is the thing itself. Space becomes the strongest element in the garden. We all define what things are by what they are not as much as anything else, and in a garden the gap between two trees or plants in a border will tell you as much about the plants as their physical selves.

Nothing is more profound or beautiful to the enlightened Zen mind than emptiness and the Japanese have learnt how to fill a garden with emptiness better than anyone else. As anyone that has tried to grapple with Zen knows only too well, the Western mind has great problems with this. But every gardener has experienced moments that in any culture translate into enlightenment.

Karesansui (dry gardens) were not made as contemplative aids to enlightenment but were created by those that had attained enlightenment and so tried to express that experience in their gardens. This raises the gardens to art as well as humanising what might otherwise seem impenetrable.

The garden is perhaps 20 yards by 10. I had two and a half hours there before the public started streaming in with school trip chatter and a thousand cameras (taking pictures not of the garden but of them at the garden). It was nowhere near long enough. I needed much more time to see it all. I cannot explain why this is except that the space seemed huge and that there seemed to be so much to consider.

Ryoan-ji is certainly one of the great gardens of the world. I do not know what it means. It is just some rocks, gravel and moss. It is really not much at all. That is enough.

Isshidan, Ryogen-in
Daitokuji Compound, Kyoto

RYOGEN-IN IS ONE OF THE earliest surviving temples of the vast Daitokuji compound in Kyoto. Daitokuji has twenty-four temples, the earliest of which was built in 1319, most of which have gardens. Ryogen-in was begun in 1499 and completed in 1505, and contains five separate gardens including the tiny ToteKiKo, which claims to be the smallest stone and gravel garden in Japan – which, in the land of the miniature and endlessly precise, is saying something. But then, despite the whole temple site being no more than the size of a suburban back garden, the gardens of Ryogen-in have so much to say. I had to drag myself away from there to keep up with the schedule. I came to Kyoto striving to find and understand the spirit of Zen. I left empty handed of course, although I suspect that in that empty hand I was holding the answer. Certainly nowhere seemed to be closer to the spirit than Ryogen-in.

You enter into the temple with its outer garden of manicured trees, moss and bamboo. So far as expected. Impressive, beautiful but what the garden visitor to Kyoto soon learns to expect. Walk around the entire temple complex at Daitokuji and there will be a hundred glimpses and glances of such gardens.

But the five gardens inside the temple, where you enter with stockinged feet on broad grey boards, are each jewels beyond price. I had thought of grouping them together as one and they do interact clearly as a group roughly based around each face of the central hall of the temple. But their proximity to each other in no way lessens the integrity or power of each. If I had more space I would include all five here, including the perfect Kodatei which, to quote the handwritten placard by it, is 'the stone garden of A-un which represents the truth of the universe. "A-un" means exhale and inhale, heaven and earth, positive and negative, male and female. These are inseparable from each other and show the truth of the universe and the essence of Zen.' But then if I had more space I would have included dozens of extra gardens from all over the world. So I will include three of the five and hope that they will inspire you to go there yourself and rightfully relish the other two as well.

The first that you see is Isshidan – superficially similar in many ways to Ryoan-ji. There is an earth-coloured clay wall capped with ochre-painted tiles, groups of stone set in raked gravel and moss, with the temple lying along one of the long sides. Another of those Japanese gravel and rock gardens.

But that would be like lumping in Hidcote and Hampton Court as one manifestation of English horticulture. For a start there are historical details that make a lot of difference. The garden was originally created when the temple was built at the beginning of the sixteenth century, but was substantially remade in 1980 when its main tree, which was over 700 years old, died. The present priest, Katsudo, reconstructed the garden. This modernity seems to me to be very exciting. It is more than just a careful historical remodelling or reconstruction. It is a new work in its own right and yet seamlessly fits into a historical monument and style.

Everything about it is more muscular and imposing than Ryoan-ji. The white gravel (it is, in fact, a sticky, stony sand) representing the sea is raked into much more vigorous and deep rills, with clear dividing lines like low banks marking them out. The stones are bigger and the moss more obviously delineated. You are also more aware of the neighbouring buildings as opposed to the trees that are the sole backdrop to Ryoan-ji.

But it is alike in that it is a samurai Zen garden of contemplation with a ravishing sense of space and of objects poised in that space. Nothing feels at all contained or restrained. Its simplicity opens out seemingly endlessly. The stones and moss are very figurative aids to this, representing a *kameshima*, or tortoise island, and a *tsurushima*, or crane island. The large stones in the middle represent Mount Horai.

The tortoise and crane are both symbols of long life and happiness in Japanese culture. The crane because it takes the crane 1,000 years to fly to the sun and the tortoise because it does not grow a tail until it is 500 years old. Mount Horai is a mythological group of mountains where the ancient and immortal Chinese sages are supposed to have lived. It does not take a huge leap of association to see that the very tangible Yellow Mountains and Mount Horai share the same mythological and cultural space.

The *hojo*, or meditation hall, which is the oldest extant in Japan, is open to the garden and the two are clearly all of a piece with the garden supplying subjects for contemplation.

A quick look on the internet reveals many references from travellers to Kyoto, such as 'visited Ryogen-in and meditated…' along with a photo. What are you supposed to think when you studiously sit and meditate? Nothing. The garden is an aid in exactly the same way that a Hindu may use a mantra. But it cannot take you anywhere at all except to an awareness of the precise moment – now.

The rocks are larger, the gravel rills deeper, and the buildings closer together than they are at Ryoan-ji, yet Isshidan still induces a feeling of spaciousness and calm.

Ryugintei, Ryogen-in

Daitokuji Compound, Kyoto

RYUGINTEI, OR THE SHINING DRAGON GARDEN, is the oldest garden in the whole Daitokuji temple complex and is said to have been made by the great Zen master Soami (who is also perhaps the creator of Ryoan-ji). Where gravel is used in the other gardens, moss takes its place in Ryugintei. In some ways, this is a problem as the greens have a familiarity that breeds a touch of contempt. The gravel gardens are hard and take concentration to get into. The moss is initially more accessible, more cajoling and therefore seemingly less pregnant with meaning. That sort of comment, when dealing with Zen, is asking for a sharp rebuff but I can only be honest with my initial reaction. However a little information shows how wrong you (I) can be.

The garden is very small, some 30 ft by 13, and yet miniature in a way that the other dry gardens are not. It reminded me of the gardens on a dinner plate that we used to make when I was a child for the local village flower show. The effect is to make the garden seem much bigger than it actually is. The moss becomes hills and valleys viewed from the air. The tree and low bushes are – of course – pruned and bonzaied to seem agelessly huge until you compare them to the building behind and realise that it is perhaps 15 ft tall. The gradations in the moss are as subtle as paint in a Rothko painting (I am sure that Japanese Zen monks would put the comparison the other way round) and add layer upon layer of complexity to it. Like a Rothko, the more that you contemplate the garden, the more it reveals in colour and texture.

The garden might be miniature but it sets out to represent the biggest of all possible worlds. The stone in the centre of the garden, emerging from the sheet of moss, is intended to represent *shumizen*, the core of the Buddhist universe. This universe is supposed to consist of eight seas and nine mountains.

The camellia in Japan is a symbol of success, luxury and tastefulness and was particularly beloved by the samurai who admired its glorious yet short life, the fully formed flower falling to ground in a blaze of glory. Yet this affection was apparently not shared by the common people who saw it as representing bad luck, a floral symbol of the heads that the samurai were expert at lopping. When I was at Ryugintei a single bloom was lying on a stone beneath the clipped camellia hedge, its unsullied flower neatly separated from the body of the plant.

So this little garden, seemingly so modest, encompasses Buddhism, Zen, the universe, samurai and bonsai.

Opposite A single camellia bloom lay on a stone in the corner of the garden – a plant admired and revered by the samurai, yet thought unlucky by the common people. Below The horizontal branches of the tree have been carefully pruned to reflect the planes of the wall and building behind, contrasting with the irregularity of the stones and round clumps of moss.

ToteKiKo, Ryogen-in

Daitokuji Compound, Kyoto

TOTEKIKO, ALSO AT DAITOKUJI, is two of my paces wide and nine long, and sits in a space between two buildings that is barely wider than a corridor or side passage. The eaves of the buildings almost entirely overhang the space leaving a gap of perhaps 2 ft of overhead light coming down onto it, although light comes from either end. It is not isolated or preciously set to one side but created as part of the progression around the main temple building and consists entirely of five rocks set in gravel that is raked around them. The gravel continues underneath the wooden walkways, from which you gaze down upon the garden, at either side and at both ends. It is supremely, breathtakingly lovely and in every respect flawless – one of the great gardens of the world.

The boards – as old as the temple buildings – are exceptionally wide and exactly the width of each line of raked gravel. The colour of the wood is in exact harmony with the stone. The walkway is part of the garden. The buildings are part of the garden as, you realise, are you – the gazer.

The small hand-painted sign says 'ToteKiKo: The smallest stone garden in Japan. The main point of this garden is the sandy ripple on the right. It shows the truth that the stronger the power of the stone thrown into the water is, the larger the ripple is.' Which is both very straightforward and suitably gnomic.

The rocks are not still. One pair rises out of the gravel free of raking or ripples whilst the pair at the other end have a powerful circular swirl around them, albeit not individually. Their effect is solo. Two thirds of the way along is a single stone set flat and flush with the gravel with an equally powerful movement of gravel ringing around it. This, it seems, has been thrown the strongest.

The gravel ripples spread out under the buildings – how do they do that? There is something extraordinarily earthy and breathily human about squatting down under the walkways to rake the gravel there. The Zen monk who showed me around, with a kind of muscular cheerfulness that was devoid of the least hint of sanctimoniousness or piety, told me, with a broad smile, that he watered the gravel and rocks every day unless it was raining. Was that a joke, some kind of Zen riddle or statement of practical care? Zen fosters that kind of anxiety in the over-keen Western mind. He also told me that the garden represented the way that every action has a reaction and a consequence so that even the smallest gesture of kindness has an endless effect and that life is made up entirely of such small actions. Thus you should try and do the right thing in every way because it will always have an effect. At this point Zen refrains from spelling out what the 'right' thing is – much to the dismay of the Western mind that likes its spirituality delivered by rote – but contemplating a beautiful garden is as good a place to start as any.

Above and opposite
The smallest garden at Ryogen-in, ToteKiKo is full of Zen symbolism and totally perfect in its simplicity.

IT IS SUPREMELY, BREATHTAKINGLY LOVELY, AND IN EVERY RESPECT FLAWLESS – ONE OF THE GREAT GARDENS OF THE WORLD.

Urasenke

Kyoto

Above *Water is carefully sprinkled onto the paths prior to the tea ceremonies, not only to emphasise their beauty, but also so that their slipperiness will help the participant focus and empty their minds.*
Opposite *The Japanese revere the old and embrace the modern. In some ways this is reflected in their gardens – all plants are carefully pruned to hold them in a taut dynamic of longevity and renewal.*

AFTER THE INCREDIBLY PURE and almost inarticulate ascetic of Ryoan-ji and Ryogen-in, I wanted to visit a tea garden. As part of my attempts to study Zen I had attended tea ceremonies in the past and tried hard to adopt the right frame of mind although I confess I never felt anything less than achingly uncomfortable – observant rather than participant. But the ceremonies I undertook were without one vital feature and preparation. This was the garden and approach to the tea house through it. To get closer to Zen I wanted to visit a tea garden and undertake another tea ceremony.

Tea was an important part of Zen that was introduced to Japan, about 300 years after Buddhism, from China. In the twelfth century powdered green tea was introduced and was first used in religious rituals in Buddhist monasteries. The samurai took this up along with other aspects of Zen and the tea ceremony evolved as a ritual of its own. The ceremony developed its own huts, typically four and a half *tatami* mats big and with a thatched roof.

The most influential figure in this development came in the sixteenth century when a man called Sen Rikyu codified the ritual, introducing the tiny crawl-through doorway that showed that whatever their rank, all people were equal within the tea room. Rikyu developed the concept of *chado*, which is based upon *wa* (harmony), *kei* (respect), *sei* (purity) and *jaku* (tranquillity). Around the tea house a garden would be made that embodied and helped induce these four principals. These tea gardens were called *roji*. They were designed as a passage to lead to the building that you could admire and that would induce the right purifying frame of mind.

The Western mind can best understand the tea ceremony as a form of meditation, and the view of the garden is part of that process. Just as the tea houses are carefully rustic, so the garden is likely to be deliberately gentle and unimposing, expressing the same spirit of *wabi*, or poverty, as the ceremony itself. The trees and shrubs are carefully planted to create veils or layers of views, often with larger trees, stones or bushes in the foreground and smaller ones at the margins, creating the impression, in what is almost inevitably likely to be a limited space, of infinite horizons.

Like the ceremony itself, every branch, stone or bush is contrived and controlled minutely to attain exactly the desired effect – which is that of a completely natural landscape. Shintoism determines that there is absolute parity between man and nature – including inanimate objects like stones and water. Any natural feature can be worshipped, thus the reverence for special stones, cherry blossom, maple leaf, moss, and gravel as water. The reverence for gardens is real. All work is determined towards the end of capturing the essence of the plant, stone and place itself.

The path to the tea house will always be winding or zigzagged and made of irregular slabs or wooden blocks. Before the ceremony the Tea Master will carefully wet the stones of the path, the better for the guests to appreciate their natural beauty. That this made the slabs slippery and awkward was considered a virtue because it helped concentrate the mind on the approach to the ceremony – or else you would fall flat on your backside. By making you slow down and forcing you to concentrate fully on the matter in hand – walking – you were emptying yourself of extraneous mind-clutter. The path was

Even the home-made brushes that are used to sweep the paths are made of bamboo. They look effortlessly charming although, as ever in Japan, nothing is unintentional.

marked by objects of contemplation to create the sense of pilgrimage. Unlike the Zen gravel gardens, these markers are unlikely to be stone groups or water features. They might be a bush or a stone in amongst moss.

So I went to Urasenke, the home of *chado*. This is the oldest surviving tea garden in Japan. The first thing that I noticed upon entering the roofed gateway was an overwhelming greenness. The path is constrained and flanked by bamboos, azaleas and pines, with moss on the ground. There is a ginkgo that was planted in 1650. It is the only surviving plant from the original garden which was made 400 years ago – older than the oldest surviving British garden by a hundred years.

A gardener went by, brushing every leaf, twig and dust from the earthen path ahead. The Japanese understand that all gardening is simultaneously a celebration and perversion of nature. In Britain we have a tendency to use the garden as a stage for the performance of the gardener as much as the plants. 'Good' gardeners will achieve obviously difficult and spectacular results. But in Japanese gardens man works ceaselessly in order that no work should appear to have taken place at all.

Bamboo is everywhere. There are bamboo gutters, gates, tree and branch supports, well lids and ladles. There are bamboo plants growing too. There are twelve wells in the garden, some for drinking and some just for damping paths and some for watering plants. The best well has the purest water which can only be collected at the 'best' time.

I had expected ritual but had not appreciated the depth and extent to which it is enacted. It felt a bit like trying to do a Scottish reel with experts without knowing the steps – making me feel oafish and inadequate and yet fascinated.

The garden, like all tea gardens, is divided into an outer and inner garden. Between the two is a middle gate where my host – the Grand Master Zabosai Soshitsu Sen XVI – comes and greets me before taking me to the tea room. In fact, there are thirteen tea houses in the garden as each grandmaster would build a new tea house ranging in size from one and three-quarter to twelve mats. The garden mazes around them but all in tiny spaces. Size is not an issue and anyway, modesty is essential. Paths that are not to be followed are marked by a rock tied by the same thick black twine I saw at Ryoan-ji. They alone, on their stepping stone and surrounded by moss, are works of elegant art.

The buildings are deliberately modest and need constant repair. They are all orientated to the south to get maximum light. The roofs are thatched, with gutters of bamboo and walls of paper, wood or plaster.

Every twig is shaped, pruned and tweaked in order that it might be just so. The 'just so' is intended to be admirably natural which is confusing to our romantic Western minds. Yet Zen celebrates accident and uncontrolled incident. It might be that you need to have that sense of complete control in order that you can let it go.

And it cannot be underexaggerated how particular is the attention to detail. Everything visible matters and a lot that is not. The goal is elegance, simplicity, modesty and dignity in every leaf, twig and stone. Quirkiness and self expression are not an option. Yet the Japanese have a love of the imperfect and celebrate this in ceramics, paintings, clothes, the stain on the plaster of a wall, the way moss spreads or light falls. None of the many stone water bowls at Urasenke were round or regular. All were ravishingly beautiful. The Western mind struggles with all this. It does not resolve itself.

I will gloss over the tea ceremony. Suffice to say I was more uncomfortable than ever before and, I am deeply ashamed to admit, I got the giggles. *Sartori* had never seemed further away.

Tofukuji

Kyoto

TOFUKUJI IS THE HEAD TEMPLE of the Rinzai sect of Zen Buddhism. It was built in 1236. The original building was burnt down but rebuilt in the fifteenth century and despite some later fire damage it remains one of the great surviving medieval temples in Kyoto. The *hojo*, or main hall, was rebuilt in 1890, and in 1939 Mirei Shigemori, a friend of the Abbot, was commissioned to design the gardens. Shigemori was a highly educated and cultured man, familiar with Western arts and ideas and he wanted to encapsulate the Zen spirit and ideals within a contemporary garden. It is important to stress how revolutionary and explosive an idea this was. In the 1930s, Japan was a deeply conservative country, and gardens, especially temple gardens, were not considered to be open to that kind of interpretation.

Although he was a modern designer, Shigemori was steeped in the traditions of Zen temple gardens. He wanted to create something that was new and related to idioms of the twentieth century and yet not to lose any of the traditional elements. I met and spoke to his grandson Chisao Shigemori, himself a garden designer. He told me that his grandfather had come up with the concept of eight 'thought gardens', linked by the big idea of Buddhism. This would relate to the eight-fold path of Buddhist enlightenment or the eight thoughts of Buddha. He had drawn the garden that he envisaged again and again until he was happy with it and then set about choosing the materials that best fitted.

Although to the uninformed Western eye the garden seems conventional, it created a huge stir. The Abbot and the monks understood it but many of the public hated it. The garden was vilified because it was thought that it introduced Western techniques into sacred temple space. It is now accepted as a major Japanese garden but its importance is much because it broke open what had been essentially a closed conceptual shop.

This is one of the most modern of temple gardens. The use of large stones lying on their side was considered radical and shocking at the time.

You approach the garden across a wooden walkway that spans raked gravel opening out on the long side of the *hojo* into a large dry gravel and stone garden. The stones are huge – modern cranes and transport made this much more possible – and unusually numerous and, most shocking of all to the traditionalists, many are lying on their sides instead of vertically. This might seem slight but it had never been done before. Well, there seem to be worse crimes, and they have great presence and dynamism. The stones are set in very traditionally raked gravel, although Shigemori intended it, according to his grandson, to be raked in a much more complex pattern of overlapping circles. However, the monks, who have to re-rake it every two or three months, were unable to make the circles and so they abandoned this aspect of his design for a straight up and down pattern. The gravel comes from the bed of one river between Kyoto and Tokyo, and has sand and a clay binding agent that means it will hold its raked shape except in the very worst weather.

This large garden represents four islands, or changes or thoughts, and the four phases of the garden change as it moves down to the other end of the hall, the stones giving way to five mounds or islands of moss. Like the stones these mounds are distinctly larger than other Zen gardens, almost real islands, with a bonzaied but substantial pine on one.

The next garden turns the corner of the building and changes completely, moss replacing the gravel, with azaleas clipped flat-topped and square evolving into a chequer pattern out of the gravel. This looks very modern, minimal and easy on the Western eye – although it is based upon a traditional Chinese pattern called *seiden*. Good but not life changing. You then go round to the back of the building to what I consider to be both great art and great gardening. The theme of the chequerboard moves from clipped azaleas to moss, with stone making up the other part of the pattern. As the squares move on along the building as part of the sixth thought of Buddha, they seem to dissolve and float away with the moss becoming closer together, the stone disappearing and, with incredible attention to detail and skill, the moss itself becoming shorter, thinner and sparser until that too more or less fades away into gravel. This is genius.

At the other end of the building is a garden of the constellations where traditional stones are replaced by seven carved stones (originally foundation stones of the former temple building), representing the main stars of Ursa Major. They are set in gravel that again merges into moss with trees and a clipped hedge. On its own, this last section would be fabulous but after the supreme triumph of the moss squares everything else is bound to be an anticlimax.

The whole thing is a major work, operatic in scale compared to the quartet of Ryoan-ji or the solo pipe of ToteKiKo. It is big both conceptually and physically and I found it magnificent.

I left Kyoto to catch the bullet train to Tokyo and go home. It had been an extraordinary, once in a lifetime trip, intense, fascinating, and a genuine insight into the concepts that form Chinese and Japanese gardens. Infinite care is taken to create the perfect accident. The Yellow Mountains changed and informed everything for me in China but you have to have a knowledge of Confucius, Tao, I Ching, LaoTzu and the endless vein of superstition to really get to grips with their gardens.

Japan was very different and much more accessible in many superficial ways. However Zen remains tough. There is no easy answer – but perhaps no hard one either. Intellect is the wrong tool to understand Zen or its gardens. There is nothing to know and nothing to say beyond the responsibility of every action and the clear awareness of every moment. The gardens are rock, moss and gravel. You are here. That is all.

Above *The seven round stones are carefully positioned to represent the stars of Ursa Major.*
Opposite *A stunning combination of art and gardening, the chequerboard of stone and moss becomes increasingly irregular until it dwindles away entirely into the gravel at the far end of the garden.*
Following pages *Mexico has thousands of square miles of desert which have their own stark beauty.*

It is a strange, beautiful, fierce country ... a place utterly different to anything I had experienced before.

3 The Power and the Glory

Mexico and Cuba

Mexico

I arrived in Mexico and Cuba in the New Year, having been home only briefly over Christmas, and was still fairly jet-lagged. After a night in Mexico City I went down to Oaxaca (pronounced 'wha-haka') in the south. Waiting to travel with me were a number of very short, very Indian looking people, the men in cowboy hats. They had the faces of people in Incan or Aztec hieroglyphs. I had been to Mexico City before but it was at that moment that I woke out of my jaded traveller mode and realised that I was coming to a place utterly different to anything that I had experienced before. I didn't know what I expected to find. Darkness. Blood. Extreme ecstasy of life. The combination of Catholicism and Maya could be a wild brew. In a garden? Who knows.

Looking down from the air is a wonderful introduction to any landscape. You can read it, half map, half film, playing out below. The pleasure of observing from the air in a cloudless sky is, of course, one that one rarely experiences in Northern Europe. Patchworks of fields are a cliché but it happens to be exactly the right description in this case. Volcanic landscapes like this or New Zealand have that curiously knobbly, smoothed profile – all lumps and bumps, clefts and creases without any geological rhythm or undercurrent. Thinking about it, the landscape from the air looks just like the larva-smothered bodies at Pompeii. Or the bodies look just like the landscape.

Suddenly there is a rather shocking green plain. Where does the water come from? What is being grown and who for? Exquisite terracing scallops round the hills like contour lines, the fields running like rivers between them. An orange-pink flushes into the landscape – sandstone?

Oaxaca is in a high valley, about 5,000 ft above sea level, with mountains all around. Foreign Office advice is to avoid the place because of riots. The streets, intense with houses painted rich blues, apricot, yellows and deep blood reds, are dignified and quiet. It is bright, hot and clear.

For a day we drive round the region, getting the feel of the place. Oaxaca has a hugely rich biodiversity as well as ethnic groups and languages. The Zapotec and Mixtec are the largest Indian tribes but there are, I am told, sixteen ethnic groups and no less than 157 languages in the Oaxaca region; half the population still speaks an indigenous dialect. This is the land where mescal is made from Agave (and valued as infinitely superior to tequila, which comes from the north of Mexico), where there are more varieties of hallucinogenic cacti than anywhere else in the world and where the cochineal beetle is found. It is a strange, beautiful, fierce country.

On the way we stop off at the town of Santa Maria del Tule to see the largest tree in the world. This is the Tule tree or Montezuma Cypress (*Taxodium mucronatum*) in the churchyard there. It is at least 2,000 years old, an extraordinary thing, buttressed and unexpectedly massive, each branch the size of a large oak tree, the trunk 165 ft in circumference.

We go on 6,000 ft up the mountain to Monte Alban, the Zapotec capital between AD 200 and 900. It is an astonishing, awesome site. There are temples, market squares, observatories and human sacrifice platforms all in stone with high, steep steps, set on a flat plateau carved into the top of the mountain and overlooking the valleys. For over 700 years this was the centre of a sophisticated, powerful culture but it was abandoned by AD 1000. No one knows why. As it grew dark we went back down to Oaxaca and the sun set in a raging, burning sky.

The Ethnobotanical Garden

Oaxaca

Above *The magnificent Ethnobotanical Garden embodies the essence of the Oaxacan landscape. It is a thrilling and beautiful garden, if initially strange to the northern European eye.*
Opposite *At the heart of the garden, tall columns of organ cacti* (Pachycereus marginatus) *create a palisade protecting other trees and cacti of the region.*
Previous page *The Tule tree, or Montezuma Cypress* (Taxodium mucronatum)*, is the largest tree in the world.*

THE CHURCH OF SANTO DOMINGO was a short walk from our hotel in Oaxaca. This was the church of the convent that was founded in the late sixteenth century after Cortez, who was made Marquis of Oaxaca in 1529, asked the Dominicans to send over friars to establish convents to convert the Indians. The display and ritual – and no doubt the fury and deathliness – of Catholicism appealed to the duality of the Indian culture, where life and death were always present in everything, and they were, it seems, fairly willing converts.

The church itself is vast and astonishingly ornate and rich with a solid wall of gold behind the altar. Gold is everywhere. Even the light falls in golden shafts like gauzy ingots. To create this temple of wealth and power, the conquistadors systematically flattened all the Aztec buildings and monuments that they could find, using the materials for their own buildings, so the church is constructed from both pagan and Christian foundations.

The church was a Dominican convent from 1608 to 1857 but was then turned into a barracks and was wrecked and looted. The museum and the monastery remained the property of the army until 1994, when a plan was drawn up to build an hotel and car park on the 6-acre site. However, a popular petition prevented that and the decision was made to restore the convent. Work began on the Botanic Garden in 1997. So what we see now is a new, modern botanic garden, dedicated to plants of the Oaxaca region. A local artist, Luis Zarate, who had never designed a garden before, was chosen to design the layout.

It is a staggeringly beautiful garden, the beauty aided by the backdrop of the convent buildings, all of which have been skilfully included in the design. I found it difficult at first – like sitting next to a very beautiful person at dinner and taking a while to find mutual interests. It is self-consciously modern and not remotely soft or even very accessible. But it is fascinating. You need bring nothing of yourself or your own experience to it, yet you will certainly take much away with you. It has nothing in common, whether in design or plant material, with anything from a northern, temperate zone. Once I surrendered to its strangeness and otherness, I found it increasingly seductive.

The garden is loosely divided into different areas housing different types of plant and there is no set route through it. Indeed, some of the paths reach dead ends and others zig zag back on themselves. The scale varies from a large expanse of gravel with very low, scrubby bushes, small cacti and agaves to large trees – but it is also spiny and harsh. It is not a place to idly brush your hand against plants as you pass.

The centrepiece is defined by squared-off hedges of cactus. They are literally fantastic, quite unlike any living material I had ever seen. They are like organ pipes, each one fluted and seemingly unsupported, all different heights and the tallest reaching perhaps 20 ft. Inside the space they defined was a tangle of some prickly pear type of cacti. This transcends mere skilful planting and becomes land art. In fact, the works of art that appear in the garden, carved stone and wood, narrow rills about 10 inches wide running the entire width of the site, ochre coloured stones whose edges stop inches from identical russet coloured ones, tiny agaves planted throughout them both save in the empty channel between the two colours – these works appear amongst the botanical

planting without any sense of self-consciousness or division between art, plants and scientific research. It has an incredible harmony, created from a clear identity and sense of purpose devoted to this specific region.

A square of large columnar cacti are mulched with flat limestone. This looks thrillingly beautiful. Better than any border I have ever seen. I realise that when I see wonderful plantings or landscapes I feel physical elation. I want to jump, laugh, cry.

If you were to arrive here straight from Northern Europe, fed on a diet of National Trust gardens and the Royal Horticultural Society, the Ethnobotanical Garden might seem artificial and intimidatingly unnatural. But travel in the region at all and you realise that the essence of Oaxacan landscape, art and culture is all here. This could not possibly have been created by an outsider. How many public gardens can that be said of?

The construction of the garden was a huge undertaking. The army left it full of rusting equipment and rubble but it was cleared and rebuilt with complete popular support as an expression of local identity. Perhaps this is something that does not have the same resonance in Europe, but in Mexico it is a powerful political expression running through a garden.

The entrance courtyard is simple, even austere with cacti climbing the wall to the street and a single guaje tree in the yard. This, like all the trees in the garden, was brought in as a mature specimen from the surrounding hills. I spoke to Luis Zarate and asked him if he, given his work as a painter, created the garden as a work of art?

'No. I thought first of the plants and the buildings and worked to these. With every delivery of plants I would be here waiting for them and place them according to their size and quality. But first I went and saw every single plant growing in the wild.'

What about the cacti hedge?

'This is normal. I simply copied what the peasants use. It makes a very good barrier.'

He showed me a particularly gnarled and scarred cactus, growing out of a pile of rock, like the bole of an ancient tree. 'This was rescued from being bulldozed – in fact many of the plants here were.'

I asked him about the paths and their (slightly annoying, no one instinctively walks in right angles) zig-zag designs. 'These were taken from Aztec designs and patterns and pre-hispanic geometric shapes.' Every aspect of the design is intended to reflect the place it is grounded in.

I then met Alejandro de Avila, the technical director of the garden. 'The point of the garden,' he told me, 'is to combine the culture of 2,000 years with plants and the living culture of Oaxaca. We want to show plants as part of our culture and history in all their uses and forms rather than just as botanical specimens.'

He said that the garden is running desperately short of money. 'The government does not care. The staff have been stripped to the bone. But this garden is a local passion. It is a communal effort and must be allowed to stay.' Not surprisingly, he is an angry, worried man, seeing the lure of a five-star hotel on the site as still being very tempting for the local governors. Personally, I think that it would be a huge crime if the garden were not to be celebrated and nurtured, let alone bulldozed.

IT HAS AN INCREDIBLE HARMONY, CREATED FROM A CLEAR IDENTITY AND SENSE OF PURPOSE DEVOTED TO THIS SPECIFIC REGION.

Casa Barragan
Mexico City

WE TRAVELLED BACK NORTH to Mexico City to visit the work of Luis Barragan, one of the greatest twentieth-century architects, who also regarded himself as a garden designer. In truth, he saw no difference between the two – both were living spaces and he applied his design principals equally to both. The result is a uniquely striking fluidity of design between indoors and out, house and garden.

Barragan was born to a wealthy family in Guadalajara in 1902 and grew up on a large ranch on their country estate in Michoacán. He qualified as an engineer but found himself increasingly drawn to architecture although he never formally trained as such. Throughout his lifetime, this lack of formal qualifications resulted in many of the profession denigrating his work as 'amateur', although it did not stop him winning the Pritzker Architecture Prize in 1980 – the highest honour for any architect.

The entrance yard of Luis Barragan's own house and garden carries the familiar signature of his work: the high white walls are lightly draped with ivy and a cluster of terracotta pots stand beside a small black pool. A deceptively modest introduction to what follows.

In the early 1920s, Barragan spent two years travelling in Europe, and was strongly influenced by the writings of Ferdinand Bac, a French landscape architect. In the 1940s he slowly began to evolve his own style, using large volumes and in particular colour to control mood, light and a sense of emotional architecture. He began to dabble – extremely successfully – in property development and this financed his architecture for the rest of his life. The significance of this was that he only ever designed buildings and gardens when, where and how he wanted. The result was a purely artistic body of work.

I went to Casa Barragan first, the house that he built for himself in 1947. It is tucked away in a side street and from the outside is an unprepossessing, industrial-looking building. This was consistent with Barragan's beliefs that a house should be a refuge from the world and that its exterior should be plain and modest.

Once inside, the first thing that struck me were the extraordinary use of both volume and colour. These things are the key to Barragan's work both inside and out. You enter the house and go out into a small courtyard with high – very high – walls and a mass of terracotta pots. None contains any plants. There is a small rectangular pool of black water and ivy or something similar hangs down the wall above it. It is dark and, rather worryingly seeing that we have travelled a long way to get here, a bit dreary.

We go through a door into a small, almost entirely overgrown back garden. I experience a slight sense of panic. The director and I look at each other. Is this it? There is a large plate glass window – almost a wall – through to a beautiful room. The shadows from the plants play through the glass, shaping themselves into shifting patterns inside and outside the room equally. From out here in the garden the inside space looks richly inviting.

We go inside. The house has a kind of luminous monastic richness. The furniture is simple, strong – all designed by Barragan. The walls are mostly white but some are livid yellow or pink. Narrow stairs lead to a slim door onto the roof. I am hit by brilliant, resounding colour. The roof garden is a completely empty space. Yet it is filled with colour and shade from the high walls that go right round it.

I met the friend and pupil of Barragan (who died in 1988), Mario Schjetnan, himself a world-renowned landscape designer and teacher, and we sat on that roof talking about his mentor.

'With Barragan,' Mario said, 'there is always a sequence of spaces. You start by compressing and intensifying space and then it opens out and releases you into a big space with a piece of water, a yard or a piece of sky. Anticipation, compression, surprise. It is about emotions and their release.'

I asked about the huge walls in this house and in others that I had seen pictures of. 'Barragan believed that houses should be private – open but not overlooked. He took great trouble with these walls and the position of windows and doors. He would place the opening to line up with the landscape or garden – not the other way round. And he would often have the walls taken down and rebuilt slightly different or with a slightly altered texture. He was very particular.'

Were they always so intensely coloured? 'The use of colour developed later in his life. The flat landscape of the savannah of Mexico influenced him. The yellowish dirt, the grassland, the sky, the cacti. These all influenced him.'

How did he work? 'He said creation is a madness. It is a sequence of putting together spaces. He used to say "It is like a movie. I think of a garden like a script. How do you approach it? Where do you sit? I don't start by drawing. I start by imagining. I start to imagine spaces and the script, then I do sketches and then finally to plan." He also used to work with models a lot. It was not a process of methodology and logic. He worked more like a painter.'

His painterly qualities are evident at every turn. The colours of the walls are immensely strong but not instantly recognisable. You find yourself mixing words in your head like paints on a palette to describe them. This is because they were mixed by Barragan himself, as were all the colours that he used in his buildings. One wall is an orange-brown, the same tone as the terracotta tiles on the ground. Others include a pink so strong and so blue that it shimmers, still outrageously pink but almost mauve, almost violet. Another wall is white. The sky is bright, unsullied blue. It seems to be a deliberate part of the composition although I am later told that we were extremely lucky – it is very rare for a January day in smog-filled Mexico City to be so clear. Against the end wall, backing onto the garden down below, some trees appear and plants hang down leaving a darker pink shadow.

That's it. I would not wish to change or add a thing. Barragan was a deeply religious, spiritual man and his work reflects that side of him. This house, with its simple, cell-like bedroom and little dining room where he ate alone, culminates up here on the roof, wide open to the sky, the enormous walls making a generous space seem even larger and yet private, unoverlooked. The colours are gorgeous, flamboyant, shimmering, sensuous. Yet they do not undermine or lessen the simplicity or spirituality.

Is it a garden? Of course. It is a sublime, brilliant piece of gardening. To quote Burle Marx, 'a garden is nature organised by man for man'. Barragan has used his genius to organise those most elusive aspects of all – light and space through the medium of colour.

Opposite Slabs of bold, brilliant colour – terracotta, pink, blue and white – are juxtaposed to create Luis Barrragan's distinctive style of landscaping. Below I chat with Mario Schjetnan who explains the emotional impact of Barragan's work.

Casa Galvez

Mexico City

THE HOTEL THAT I STAYED in Mexico City – one of a huge chain – had Barragan-influenced walls that were great slabs of colour. They looked terrible, like an underground car park using up a job lot of paint. But this only heightened my respect for his real work. The difference between getting it very right and hopelessly wrong is often tiny – even on huge walls.

The day after visiting Barragan's own home, we went to a house and garden that he had designed for a client, Casa Galvez. This too was built at the end of the 1940s and is lived in by a family who have accepted it as a complete, untouchable work of art. Everything in the house, the colour of the walls inside and out, the furniture, the planting, is by Barragan. Changing it would be sacrilege but it is also an odd experience, like living inside a Picasso or doing the gardening in costume.

But it is an undoubted masterpiece. It is not open to the public so to be allowed to spend an entire day there was a huge privilege. It pulls together all the aspects of Barragan's work: colour, space, form and detail.

From the outside, the house is hidden behind a white wall, with the door on a platform with a simple pink, overhanging portico. The door opens to reveal more of the same pink and at once inside private and outside street space are tied in together. It is a typical Barragan ploy and as strikingly effective as always.

The entrance yard is very simple and pure: monochromatic white with dark brown broken stone – almost mosaic – flooring. The same terracotta pots as at his own house, with their tiny necks and plump bodies are lined up in ranks. A high white wall blocks the eye line. The touch of pink on the wall behind you pulses. All is low-key anticipation.

Go to the end of this little yard and turn round and what had appeared to be a sombre space explodes into colour. It is a savagely transforming moment. So this is what Mario had explained to me: anticipation, compression and surprise.

The high wall turns out to be a right angle painted the pink of the wall leading to the front door. All you see is that furious colour. This rectangular space is filled by a pool of black water and a glass wall with more of the pink inside. Nothing could be more dramatic and yet this is utterly private.

Inside, the house is carved into blocks of coloured space. Colour is used with a confidence that is almost despotic. To live like this needs great wealth and great assurance. Perhaps the two go hand in hand. Light bounces off the water, onto the exterior wall, through the glass of the window, into the room, onto the pink wall and back through the window again. If it sounds pretentious, grandiose and unreal then it is all of those things. And it is remarkably, breathtakingly, beautiful.

The back garden is an open, generous place. The pink continues through the house and out the other side, right down one length of the garden but is

THE PLANTING IS LOOSE AND EXUBERANT BUT SERVES THE COLOURS AND FORMS OF THE STRUCTURE.

joined there by a bright mustard-yellow wall, the white of the house, the green of the grass and a large slab of blue on what must be a neighbouring building at the end of the garden. The paving is lava-black inside and out.

Round a corner is a wall that is as high as a building, whose sole purpose is to compress the space it encloses, blocking the view from outside and framing and backing it from the interior. It is garden space that can only be seen, only exists from inside the building.

The levels outside are carefully manipulated and altered with steps and low retaining walls. Apparently, when Barragan started work on the site it was markedly sloping but he removed all slopes so that the huge planes of vertical walls are matched with horizontal planes of grass and paving. The low retaining walls mimic the shadows of the house and boundary walls. These shadows are always there, just as the sun has always been there during my visit. This could not work in cloud-covered Britain. The colours would appear hysterical and gaudy under a grey sky.

The planting is loose and exuberant but serves the colours and forms of the structure well. There is a large fig in the front courtyard, its branches bare when I was there in January but I imagine that it provides important shade and volume in the scorching summer months. There are no plants dotted around – they would look as absurd as scatter cushions would inside. The bougainvillea is exactly the colour of the walls. A dead tree is retained and a path goes formally round it. Why, I ask did Barragan not remove the tree? It was alive when he made the garden, I am told, then it died and he liked it so it remains. The branches have been cut back to the trunk. It is like an armless torso, a woody Venus de Milo.

Everything is big. The ideas are big. Barragan himself was big – 6 ft 5 inches. You come away feeling enhanced and enlarged. It inspires you to be bold, to have conviction and to realise that a garden can be created just from a really substantial structure, together with colour, volume, water and light.

The back garden of Casa Galvez has been kept exactly as Luis Barragan designed it in the 1940s.

Las Pozas

Xilitla

FROM MEXICO WE FLEW up to Tampico and then took a four hour drive north to the jungle town of Xilitla. As we headed north the landscape got lusher and the hills steeper. Whereas Tampico is a swampy, coastal outhouse of American consumerism – the road lined with every form of barrel-scraping cut price commercialism – Xilitla (pronounced 'ix-itla') is a straggling town of pick-ups, hens picking hopefully at the dirt road and the jungle leaning in on it. The streets are peopled with men in anoraks and white straw cowboy hats, with racks of bright plastic flowers and a damp coldness that is a huge shock after the heat of Oaxaca and Mexico City. It is a strange place. But it is not one tenth as strange as the garden made here by the English eccentric and millionaire Edward James.

Las Pozas ('The Pools') is just outside Xilitla. Edward James came here in 1948, travelling in Mexico with a friend and looking for a home for his growing collection of orchids. When they came to the pools with their huge waterfall, the friend stripped off and swam, then lay on a rock to dry in the sun. As he did so a cloud of blue butterflies flew round him and landed on his wet skin, covering his entire body. James, by then a famous collector of surrealist paintings, took this as a sign, and on the strength of it bought around 250 acres of land around the pools, of which about fifty are actively gardened and open to the public today. It is a vast site that takes a full day to explore.

Las Pozas, Edward James's fanciful vision of surrealism in a garden form, is created along the banks of a river.

Surrealism is central to understanding James and therefore the garden. He was born to immense wealth in 1907 and endured the upbringing that Edwardian privilege and limitless resources imposed. Money remained his prison and genie for the rest of his life. It bought him freedom and yet bound him to mistrust. Surrealism exactly suited the perpetual adolescent chaos that accompanied his extensive education at Eton and Oxford. His homosexuality increased his alienation and yet also his hunger for liberation. He adored animals of all kinds and travelled with a kind of mobile menagerie. I was told that by the end of his life there were 2,500 ducks at Las Pozas.

By the Second World War James had become one of the most important patrons of surrealism, and as their stock rose so did his wealth. Surrealism is nothing if not the unfettering of dreams and this lack of inhibition or regulation coupled with almost limitless wealth grew and flowered in the green valleys of the Xilitla jungle.

It would and could not have happened in many other places. Mexico then, as now, was without building regulations of any kind. It was not judgemental about personal behaviour in the way that Europe and America were. As the current owner, James's godson, Plutarco Gastelum, says, Mexicans have building in their genes, going back to the temples and palaces of Monte Albán and Chichinitza. There was also a willing, numerous and cheap labour force glad of the work. They were completely undaunted by the scale or scope of James's imagination. At one stage he had over 150 people working full time in the garden and over a hundred were employed permanently for over two decades.

The workers may not have been daunted but the scale of the garden, both physically and conceptually, is hardly to be imagined. Plutarcho told me that he now employs fifty people whose sole job is to cut back the jungle to stop it taking over the garden. The furious energy of the jungle is like a fire. One of the reasons that James could

afford his follies to be so extreme was that he knew the jungle would temper them – and inevitably one day consume them, just as it has consumed the Aztec cities.

The garden started conventionally enough as a home for his collection of orchids and I was taken behind the scenes, or actually up an enormously long, steep flight of steps climbing perhaps 1,600 ft up into the dripping jungle, to their home, a walled garden now almost entirely swallowed up by the jungle.

Despite the location and the unfinished building (everything at Las Pozas is unfinished although I was never sure if this was a sign of James's capriciousness or a deliberate nod towards the fluidity and lack of resolution of the surreal image), it is curiously formal and reminiscent of an abandoned English walled garden. James's family home, West Dean in Sussex, still famous for its immaculately maintained, walled kitchen garden with its nine glass houses and perfect discipline, is not conceptually so very far removed.

But in 1962, disaster struck. One of the rare but regular jungle frosts destroyed his entire orchid collection, which by then included over 1,800 specimens. They were irreplaceable. It was after this that he began to base his garden on concrete flowers, albeit ones of his dreams. At least they were hardy to all the weather that the jungle could offer – whilst we were there it went from 35ºC and 90 per cent humidity to 10ºC and pouring rain.

For thirty years James worked with the same carpenter who translated his sketches into wooden formers, into which concrete was poured to create the twisting fantasies in the jungle. Walls and steps were built into these dream buildings – all precarious, devious and adorned with pillars and entrances that mimic and compliment the bamboos and monstrous foliage that surround them. All is arbitrary, organic in form and playful. Many of the constructions housed aviaries and animals and some of these have been converted into guest houses that can be hired by the night. There is certainly no better way to get inside the garden and the mind that made it.

By turn, as you probe into the recesses of the green space – the sky only occasionally glimpsed through the branches – it can seem like a crazy palace, an Aztec temple, a Surreal World theme park, a sculpture park or a series of eighteenth-century follies. In fact, this last comparison is, I think, the most apt. For all his modernism, Edward James is a figure straight out of Valdek, or the Gothick milord indulging his whims like a cross between a rock star and country squire. Are these Eschler's stairs, going nowhere except the subconscious, in the jungle any stranger than the ruined cathedrals or removed village amongst the comfortable rural landscape at Stowe? What are the ponds and walks and wonderfully unsafe footbridges linking aviaries of parakeets or cages of ocelots other than the drives of Claremont or Stourhead with their temples, grottos and ha-has?

I stayed for three nights there in one of the converted buildings. Below my bedroom the river fell down the valley with its constant watery whirr. In front and above the jungle rose on what seemed to be a vertical wall of the ravine. Epiphytes and bromeliads sprouted astonishingly from an orange tree whose fruits were tantalisingly out of reach. A concrete house with no walls, roof or hint of reason other than its strange beauty was partly hidden through the undergrowth. Steps and paths wound towards buildings that lurched out of the jungle like a dream. It is gardening through the looking glass, where the subconscious rises to the surface and takes literal concrete form.

Las Pozas is untrammelled, unedited, unfettered, unbalanced and completely unworldly. It is a folly, the manifestation of the coincidence of enormous wealth, a particular education, oppressed sexuality, a skilful, abundant, cheap workforce, a local culture that was remarkably enthusiastic and uncensorious and above all, of the Mexican jungle.

The Floating Gardens of Xochimilco

Mexico City

WHEN THE SPANISH ARRIVED in the Valley of Mexico in 1521 they reported back a vast area of 'floating' gardens set in the middle of a huge lake. In fact the gardens, or chinampas, are man-made islands set in the lake. We know that they are at least 1,000 years old and despite a century of neglect they still survive, albeit only to a fraction of their original extent, and as such they are the oldest surviving gardens in the world.

The Xochimilcas (pronounced 'sojgi-milka') founded their city at the southern end of the valley, over 6,900 ft above sea level. The land is dominated by huge lakes and undrained marshland so they fed themselves by creating the chinampas. Each acre could support eight people – roughly one family – and they vary from a half to 2 acres in size. Each family would maintain a number of them around the lake, meaning a huge surplus of food was produced. The chinampas are still tended by family groups, with the young men still working on them, 1,000 years of experience and growing skills in their blood.

The chinampas are made by layering mud and vegetation until it rises proud of the water, and are held in place by a kind of basket of posts and willows planted all around them until eventually the roots bind into the soil of both the island and the lake bottom, holding the whole thing together. It is a kind of enormous, permanent compost heap and is fantastically fertile and productive.

I set off to see them by boat, taken across the black, flat waters in a punt. The area is strictly part of Greater Mexico City, but as soon as I settled back to jerk across the water, I could have been a hundred miles from the city centre. Iron blue and grey herons and impossibly white egrets stood sentinel every few yards. The water is still, flat and black, reflecting everything more truly than the thing itself. Double trees, river edge, birds, me peering over the edge. The edges of the chinampas are revetted with posts and the ever

The Floating Gardens of Xochimilco are man-made islands with extremely fertile soil that produces continuous crops of vegetables and flowers.

fastigiate willows, the roots meshed around the chinampas and the branches providing shade from the sun and shelter from the fierce spring winds. Boats full of orange flowers are slowly punted down the black mirrored waters, the boatmen walksing the shaft of the pole down the length of the boat as it grips the black mud of the black bottom.

Everywhere, just before the festival of the Day of the Dead on November 2nd, are marigolds, *Tagetes erecta*, or, for the Aztecs, cempoalxchitl, growing in tangerine-coloured fields. Orange is the Aztec colour of the dead – they believe the dead can recognise it better than any other colour – so on the Day of the Dead every grave and home is decked in a blaze of orange marigolds to welcome home the returning departed.

The water between the chinampas is a series of ditches, dykes and canals and I constantly had to remind myself of the astonishing fact that all this is man-made, built on and in a vast lake. It is an extraordinarily calm and calming place. Willow trees, locally known as Ahuejote (Salix bonplandiana) overhang the canals to hold the soil in place.

Unlike modern horticulture these resurrection flowers do not sit in carefully weeded soil but rise out of a mass of lush grass and weeds so the effect is of the most astonishing orange meadow. It is surreal, breathtaking and yet part of the balance of the place. They are everywhere, and at every turn a figure or two is cutting the flowers. The marigolds are surprisingly stemmy and tall and gathering them is quite a performance. It is done with a machete, stripping the leaves and making bundles to take to the market.

The raised beds are made by adding more shining black silt from the lake bottom. Once it drys a little, it is raked level and then divided into squares by a machete. These vary in size depending on what is grown, with up to 18,000 such squares in each raised bed. A group of men were patiently making a thumb divot in each of the squares, then carefully placing a coriander seed in each divot. I was shown how the blocks slowly separate as they dry and the seedlings grow until they are big enough for the blocks to be individually lifted, roots meshed within, and transplanted at wider spacing to another area to be grown on. This is the system that has fed successive empires for millennia. They never add any fertiliser, weed killers, pesticides or fungicides. The marigolds serve to keep 'the plague' – in all its various horticultural forms – at bay. Each raised bed can provide six crops a year with a two week rest between harvesting and sowing the new crop. All organic material is composted and a new layer of silt added before each crop so that the raised beds are renewed and refreshed and are, in effect, mini chinampas.

Over the centuries the basic quartet of plants has always been the same, all interacting and benefiting each other symbiotically. These are corn (maize), beans, squashes and chillies. The beans and squashes climb the willows and any other trees and the chillies are another ward against 'plague'. The flowers fit in and around this constant quartet.

Throughout the latter part of the twentieth century, pollution from the city destroyed much of the bird, aquatic and human way of life. The vast area of tens of thousands of acres that remained under production well into the last century dwindled to just some 850 acres and these only remained partly due to the work of a pressure group, and partly from the unlikely intervention of the army who, apparently, saw the area as an important source of fresh water and foresaw riots caused by future water shortages.

However they have been preserved, the chinampas of Xochimilco are a unique, completely special place, powerfully charged with the battery of 1,000 years of growing its particular mix of food for the living and flowers for the dead. They must be treasured, not just as a monument to an ancient past but because the skill and simplicity of the growing culture has so much to tell us for our overcrowded, overheated future.

Cuba

From Mexico City, we went to Cuba. I had been wanting to visit Cuba for many years and it seemed that time was running out. Fidel Castro was gravely ill and, in the view widely held in the West, on the point of death. Regime change was imminent. Cuba was about to change drastically. It had proved tricky to get permits to film there and negotiations by the BBC took many months. They were a bit suspicious of our motives. Why would we send a film crew to film their gardens? But having got there, they could not have been more helpful or friendly.

Havana is like no other city. It is beautiful, ruined, imperious, earthy, archaic, easily the sexiest place on this earth. The people of Cuba are as racially diverse as any nation – every colour of skin and hair, shape and size is to be seen on every street. The only common factor is that the women are exceptionally beautiful and the men tall and handsome. The streets of derelict, crumbling eighteenth- and nineteenth-century Spanish houses (Cuba was a Spanish colony from 1492–1902) are busy with people, not traffic. Most vehicles are pre-1959 and lovingly repaired – anyone with a motor vehicle in 1959, when Castro took over, was allowed to keep it but since then only very few party members are dispensed cars. People cadge lifts off strangers at every junction. It is a city that does not seem at first impression to consume or spend money. There are few if any shops to be seen. No restaurants or cafés. But people were extraordinarily generous to us, sharing what little that they had.

However, the people have to eat and this need created a second revolution in the early 1990s. After the fall of the Soviet Union in 1990, Cuba's sugar sales, which had been heavily subsidised by the Russians, fell to almost zero and their oil imports, also from the Russians, dried up. Practically overnight they were left without money, fuel, fertilisers, medicines or power. The population, especially the cities, began to starve. Now Cuba is not a third world country. Its education and health services are superb. But because of the American blockade they simply did not have the raw materials they needed to feed themselves.

So began what they call the 'Special Period' of 1990–94. Every scrap of spare land within Havana was cultivated for produce by making raised beds, often using the materials from the fallen buildings that had originaly occupied the plot. All crops were grown organically through necessity. There was no fuel, so practically no machinery. Oxen were bred and old men who remembered working with them trained others in how to use them. These sites, called *organiponicos*, specialised in vegetables and herbs for medicines. The staple crops were grown in the countryside. People came to work on organiponicos from all walks of life, pooling their skills and resources. In 2005 there were 300,000 people in Havana alone working on the land. More than 90 per cent of Havana's fruit and vegetables are grown within the boundaries of the city on over 7,000 separate organiponicos, covering over 80,000 acres.

Spurned by the West and abandoned by the Soviets, Cuba has managed to make a role model that we can learn a huge amount from. It was these organiponicos and gardens in Havana that I wanted to visit, to see how they were doing it and what exactly we can take from them for our own cities back home.

Organiponico Vivero Alamar

Havana

Above *Tools are mended and reused until they can no longer be repaired, then parts are cannabalised for other tools.*
Previous page *The charm of Havana – a street of dilapidated eighteenth- and nine-teenth-century Spanish style houses still manage to remain beautiful.*

AN ELDERLY MAN, wearing a waistcoat over his bare torso, ragged trousers and large Wellington boots is protected from the blazing sun by a large straw hat. An enormous cigar is clenched in his mouth and stays there as he steadily hoes a long row of beetroot, occasionally stopping to draw with slow satisfaction. A dozen other figures of all ages work in the same field of raised beds. The earth is bright orange. I stand in an earthen yard watching three women boil a huge pot over a wooden fire, a pile of firewood all hacked with axes lies waiting to fuel it. Beyond the vegetable plot a road is busy with buses and rickety, monstrously overloaded old lorries. Tower blocks fill the horizon.

This is Organiponico Vivero Alamar at 8 am and it is one of the most sophisticated, inspiring vegetable gardens I have ever been to. My eyes are as big as saucers. It is a place of precise and measured control and yet held together with ingenuity, patience and unremitting hard slog, producing superb organic vegetables. I feel completely at home.

The organiponico started ten years ago without its creators really knowing what they were doing. There were four of them and none had any experience of growing anything. For the first few years they were completely stretched, physically and intellectually, and every day consisted more of solving problems than growing things – although that was the root of their problems. They had a large site – 10 acres in total, although none of it was cultivated. Now it has fourteen full time employees and 116 workers, all from the local community. It is a self-financing and self-sustaining cooperative that feeds itself first, then the families of the workers and then the rest of the community.

It is a highly organised set up, and over the week that I am in Havana I come to realise that the Cubans are a remarkably focussed, organised people despite the incredibly laid back, almost louche, atmosphere of Havana. There is real physical energy in the air rather than the exhausted frenetic activity of most modern cities.

As well as the vegetables all growing in raised beds, Organiponico Alamar has an area for processing juices and dried produce, a nursery that raises 3.5 million seedlings every year, all immaculately grown in plugs ready for planting out, a maintenance area which has practically no tools but somehow mends and repairs everything, from hoes to their delivery lorry to the two-wheel tractor given to them by a German benefactor. Everything is reused and mended until it cannot be mended any more and then the component parts are cannibalised to create or fix something else. Absolutely nothing is wasted. There is a dining hut where every worker has a truly delicious lunch cooked outside over the open wood fire, a large area devoted to the production of compost and a bamboo pyramid where workers can sit and recharge their inner batteries. Who is to say that it does not work?

In fact it is a very unhippy, very down to earth, scientifically measured place. It is not perfect. The work is long and hard. The raised beds for example, are all made anew by hand.

IT IS A DEEPLY INSPIRING PLACE. AS WELL AS SUPERB VEGETABLES, THEY GROW PLANTS FOR PHYSICAL, MENTAL AND SPIRITUAL HEALTH.

The Organiponicos not only provide fruit and vegetables for the local community, I believe *that they are also the model for a sustainable future in the post-oil world.*

*Using just home-made
compost, each bed has
six crop rotations a
year, and grows every-
thing from lettuces,
carrots, tomatoes,
chard, avocados and
cucumbers to culinary
and medicinal herbs.*

I have done this in a small garden. Believe me, it is hard, hard work. Here, they do it on 10 acres in tropical temperatures. The pay is very low although much higher than office equivalents. A doctor can earn more in Cuba hoeing vegetables than treating the sick. A young man with a good engineering degree plants cabbages in order to earn enough to live.

But it is a deeply inspiring place. As well as superb vegetables, they grow plants for physical, mental and spiritual health. They take this very seriously and regard our neglect of plant use for health as curiously backward and ignorant. It is. They really understand how plants grow and their relationship with them is much more intimate than that of the average British grower. It has to be. Their lives rather than their livelihoods depend upon it.

Each raised bed has six rotations per year before it is remade. Sevn pounds of worm compost are added per foot per year. That is the sum of their fertilisation. They make 200 tons of worm compost each year, starting as long compost heaps, all turned by hand and then going into concrete troughs where the 'ordinary' garden compost is refined down by worm activity. All weeds and organic material are cleared and composted, including green manure. Nothing is dug or ploughed in. Under the Cuban sun they turn fresh composting material into the final product in ninety days, and thinly apply it as a surface mulch.

In amongst the raised beds were fruit trees – including the noni, whose squishy, slightly translucent fruit smells exactly like a very ripe stilton. Visitors are offered it as an example of something disgusting – of course the BBC film crew and myself inhaled long and deeply, thinking of home and Christmas.

At one end of the plot the stalls open up and the day's produce is on sale. Local people, all on foot, come and buy fresh vegetables. Tomorrow they will come again. This is as much their garden as anyone's.

Huerto Alberto Rojas

Havana

HUERTO IS SPANISH for 'kitchen garden' or 'orchard' and, unlike organiponicos, they existed within Havana before the Special Period. I went into a backstreet in the middle of Old Havana to visit Alberto Rojas and his huerto, looked after entirely by himself.

The garden is behind a high block wall and metal gates fronting onto the street. An old man and his granddaughter sit on the pavement watching us. A 1950s motorbike with sidecar draws up and a man gets off carrying a bunch of flowers and rings a doorbell hopefully. The balconies lean out across the street. A cockerel calls loudly. It is Sunday, early. Havana is still sleeping.

Alberto greets us and lets us in. He is white haired, stocky, could be a European. I don't speak a word of Spanish and he has no English. We smile and shake hands and then both simultaneously speak in our own languages. An interpreter picks up the pieces.

The site is still flanked by crumbling tall walls of the building that was once there but is now filled by raised beds edged with roofing tiles. Along the edges are a clump of bananas, apples, peach trees, a papaya, vine, oranges and some chickens in the corner, explaining the cockerel. The enormously high buildings on either side make it seem like a secret walled garden, but the broken chair by the gate, the wheelie bins for compost, the little pile of metal that might come in useful are more like an allotment. A meticulously organised, productive allotment. The high walls are the secret, Alberto told me.

Not a weed in sight in Alberto Rojas's highly productive kitchen garden. Neighbours provide kitchen waste for compost and in return are given vegetables or compost for their plants.

Alberto Rojas has tended his 'borrowed' garden for twenty years.

It protects the garden from the sun by creating good shade. It is a beautiful morning but I have to remind myself that Havana can get blastingly hot.

The huerto began twenty years ago on the site of a collapsed building. Alberto's brother-in-law and sister, Nieves, lived in a flat of a house that backed onto it but they did not have direct access to it. Although they did not own the land, Alberto helped them to clear it, removing lorry loads of rubble before making raised beds. The topsoil was brought in by wheelbarrows and the odd lorry load as and when some became available. Then his brother-in-law died and Alberto carried on looking after the garden. They still do not own it. It is just a patch of unused ground.

Through an interpreter Alberto told me that he changes the topsoil every two or three years. I ask where he gets it from. The answer, rather astonishingly, was the Canadians help him with topsoil and seed. I never found out if this was a particular arrangement that he, Alberto, had come to with the Canadian government or a Canadian charity. He composts everything possible and buys in rice husks to bulk that compost out. I poke about in the bins. There is paper, coffee beans, sawdust. Whilst we were there local people came by with buckets of kitchen waste that they added to the compost. All the compost goes back onto the raised beds as a mulch. There is no digging.

All the beds are full but most have been recently planted. There is not a weed in the garden. The beds are planted with peppers, tomatoes, onions, lots of each. There is no attempt at the vegetable virtuosity you might see in the garden of an experienced British gardener. They grow what will store and keep well and, critically, what others would like to have, so while there is only a small selection growing, there is plenty of it.

Alberto likes sharing with the community in a number of ways. People come and give him their kitchen waste not only in return for vegetables, but for compost for their pot plants. Later that day I see an elderly woman lower a bucket full of peelings down to the ground on a long rope. It is taken to Alberto and bought back full of rich, crumbly compost, tied to the rope and she hauls it up to the third floor and her balcony filled with pot plants. He sells some of the vegetables to help pay for the garden but gives away medicinal herbs and he also shares his garden by showing people the space. There are not many plants in this part of Havana. Children come in here to see what they look like. Whilst we were there, people were continually popping in and out. The sense of privacy from the high walls is an illusion. The gates are open and it is clearly part of the street. In many ways this is the opposite to a Luis Barragan garden – utilitarian, open, scruffy, poor, and above all open to the life of the city that it is part of. Anyway, the concept of privacy in Havana is not the same as it is in Europe. Walk down the street and you will be invited into a house for an orange juice. People share what they have. Mostly it is their time.

Alberto said that he had gardened organically even before the Special Period. 'It is better that way.' It seems that in Cuba the organic movement replaces chemicals with organic alternatives rather than bypassing them altogether. So there is much talk, as there was at the organiponico, of home-made fumigants, fungicides and pesticides.

We go back to Alberto's sister's flat, overlooking the far end of the huerto, and share a lunch we have brought. The flat is roomy, sparse but clean and comfy. An old television sits in the corner with 'Made in Russia' on the front. I go to the balcony and look across the street to the houses just feet away. A couple are in bed. They wave at me. We sit on the balcony under a vine, eating our sandwiches and Alberto's tomatoes and drinking a glass of home-made wine. I show Alberto pictures of my garden and my wife. The wine is cloudy and syrupy-sweet but we drink and toast each other's gardens, families and future.

Huerto Angelito

Havana

I VISITED A NUMBER OF ORGANIPONICOS and huertos around Havana. It is hard to avoid them. They are everywhere. There was one run-down site, Huerto Solar Rojo, with grand mansions crumbling on either side – presumably it too had once been a mansion and grand – that only grew herbs for medicinal use. It was tended by a retired army officer. He said that he had been an illiterate peasant but thirty years in the army had educated him. But when he left the army he knew absolutely nothing about growing plants. He had to start from scratch both with himself and the site. The herbs were tied in bunches and laid out by the entrance on a couple of shelves. Locals used it as their pharmacy. I was particularly impressed by the worm compost that he nurtured in an old bath, draining the liquid from the plughole.

Another organiponico was on an open street corner in an area of modern tower blocks. The raised beds were edged in used asbestos guttering and were being carefully painted white when I was there. Two large tanks were in the corner of this most urban of organiponicos and had written on them '¡viva Fidel!' And 'Si por Cuba'. A busy block-built stall was right on the street so that this most inner city, poor area had their organically grown vegetables available to them literally within minutes of coming from the ground and not a single piece of machinery was involved in their production, transportation or consumption.

Maria Los Angeles's garden is unusual in Havana – she grows plants for their beauty as well as their usefulness, enlisting the aid of every spare container.

But the final garden I went to in Havana was not just focused on food production. It belonged to a woman called Maria Los Angeles in Old Havana. Old Havana is a place of wonderful buildings and streets that have had no money spent on them for decades. It is literally falling down and yet the streets are used and clean and every building is occupied. Any that actually do collapse are cleared and used as organiponicos. This means that the area has a faded, abandoned beauty and great dignity. But there is no money, and all the unromantic problems – human, social, and structural – that go with that.

Maria's garden is on one of these derelict sites but the exceptional aspect of it is that she grows plants for their beauty as much as for their usefulness. This is not to say that it conforms to a British notion of a beautiful garden or would win a prize in a best-kept village competition. The front is a tangle of corrugated iron blocking off the street, and when you go through the door there is a path of various stones laid on top of the earth leading to the back. Rubble lies between the plants. There is the ubiquitous noni tree and the cheesy fruits lie squashed at its base. But there are flowers. Bougainvillea in a corner. A rose with a couple of pink flowers. A jasmine. A couple of ferns rest in the deep shade of the wall. And what I can only vaguely recognise as an assortment of houseplants grown for their foliage. I don't like them. It would not be my choice. But her urgent desire for colour and texture over the imperative of food is bubbling and joyous. At the back of the garden she has lettuce, garlic, coriander and basil growing in containers. A banana tree arches over and the leaves give some shade. There were times she said, when the bananas it produced were all that they had to eat. Anything that will hold soil and retain water is press ganged into use for this. An old coffee pot, cooking oil cans, polystyrene packaging. There is a lavatory, sinks and, rather oddly even amongst this collection, a lifejacket container.

There is no need to patronise her or her garden. It is not beautiful. Necessity means that she still has to grow more fruit, vegetables and herbs than she would choose. She longs to fill the space with colour and scent. Her soul needs these things. Her garden is a sanctuary for her, a spiritual solace as well as a provider of physical sustenance.

Now I don't think that Maria's garden is in any way more admirable or closer to a concept of a 'true' garden just because she grows some plants purely for their beauty and the pleasure that they give her as well as others for physical sustenance. But it was interesting to see a garden in the very poorest part of the poorest area of Havana where the human need for spiritual nourishment was expressed in a garden, especially in a city that has so ruthlessly and brilliantly tackled the desperate demands for physical sustenance. In some ways, Maria's garden is a hint that a softer, more feminine approach to gardens might evolve in Cuba.

It is also interesting because it is such an exception. There is nowhere else in the world that has organised its food production so effectively through gardens. I came away from Cuba hugely inspired by this – as well as full of admiration for the intelligence and dignity of the Cuban people. The huertos and organiponicos are a shining example of the future for the Western world. Impoverishment and blockade have forced the Cubans to turn a crisis into a model of the future that we all face. Even in the middle of a large city, with practically no money and no resources, they are producing fresh, seasonal, organic fruit and vegetables by and for very local communities working together. I saw nothing in Havana that led me to believe that the communities were less happy or satisfied than those in London or Paris. The infrastructure desperately needs cash and lots of it but the people have worked out a model for the future of this planet – in their gardens.

Above Maria's garden may be small, but it is still her sanctuary, and she is justifiably proud of it.
Opposite Materials from derelict building sites are used to create raised beds in this inner-city organiponico. Considering the health risk from using old asbestos pipes for the edging is a luxury Cubans cannot afford.
Following pages The Sítio, Roberto Burle Marx's garden near Rio de Janeiro, began as a testing ground for Brazilian native plants.

If I have only learnt one thing from my travels
around the world, it is that no garden is an island.
Context is everything.

4 Live Energy

South America

South America

My trip to the Amazon started with a slightly unfortunate twist when I managed to pick up the wrong suitcase at Sao Paolo airport before going up to the Amazon at Manaus. To the intense amusement of the film crew, some poor Indian woman was now sariless and my only clothes for a week in the Amazon were a cotton suit, and the shirt, socks and pants that I had left London with.

Manaus is a frontier town made mad with opera house and electronic factories, the latter supplying a stream of vast container ships that look as incongruous as whales would wallowing up the Severn in England. Vultures sit rubber-necking on the buildings and we were watched on the dockside as we filmed by prostitutes and their pimps, and children that could smell our Western affluence. The dockside is packed with steamers which in turn are filled with hammocks occupied by men and women talking, arms flung over the side. Light drops away but the heat remains.

At dawn the next morning we motored down to the point where the Rio Negro and the Solimoes meet. The Rio Negro is, as its name suggests, slow, deep and dark, whereas the Solimoes is alkaline, quick, shallow and a buff, chalky brown from the muddy sediment that it accumulates from the Andes as it flows from its Peruvian source. The Negro is deep and stained with acidic organic matter from the jungle floor. Because of this pH difference the two run side by side for a while, taking about 10 miles to mix completely and become the single Amazon before flowing for another 1,000 miles to the sea. It is an astonishing sight, dark and milk chocolate ebbing against each other, only slightly blurring at the edges as they meet.

All three rivers, Solimoes, Negro and Amazon are breathtaking. For a start they are unimaginably huge. At its widest point the Amazon is 25 miles wide and even in the dry season it is 6 miles across. There are beaches to rival the Caribbean. At one point I looked over to the distant shore some miles away to be told that it was in fact an island and on the other side of it was the Solimoes – also four or five miles across. Think big and perhaps you might nibble at the edge of imagining. It is also stunningly hot. Coming to the tropics for the first time it was a bit of a culture shock. Life almost erupts from empty air in the Amazon. All the statistics are superlatives. There are more fish in the Rio Negro than the Atlantic, and more species of tree in a single acre of rainforest than in the whole of North America.

But for my first garden visit in the Amazon I did not set foot on land at all but instead boarded a small canoe with an outboard and headed gently down the Amazon for an hour so to a small group of houseboats.

The Floating Gardens of the Amazon

The Amazon Rainforest, Brazil

Above The gardens are moored to house rafts to accommodate the rise and fall of the Amazon which can vary up to 30 ft between the rainy and dry seasons. *Previous page* Setting off to visit my first garden which was actually on the Amazon.

IT WAS THE DRY SEASON but felt unbelievably hot to me having arrived from an autumnal England just a day before. The jungle that pushes hard up to the river edge did not appear at all tropical, but much more like an enlarged, vaguely unreal European wood. But vultures spiralled overhead and buffaloes grazed the grassy margins. The occasional dash of a parrot threw colour into the air. Along the side of the river a group of pigs were foraging through the mud. There was mud aplenty because the river was low – dangerously so apparently – at least 30 ft below its flood height and set to get lower before the rains were due, still many months away. In 2005 many of the side rivers dried up, stranding the tribes that relied on them as their routes in and out of the rain-forest, and meaning that their supplies had to be brought in by helicopters flying down the dry riverbeds. The same could happen again. Climate change – caused as much by the deforestation of the rainforest as anything else – is making matters much worse.

However, as our little canoe motored on, we came to a group of what looked like shacks or huts, floating on the water. There was a floating petrol pump and a shop or two. Dogs barked as we passed, standing as close to the water's edge as they dared. Many of these houses were little more than a roof with hanging plastic sheets for walls, but some were elaborate with verandas, painted walls and fences. And there were gardens. Real, planted gardens with flowers, fruits, vegetables and even trees. As we pulled closer to one, it was clear that it was being towed behind the house rafts on its own raft made from logs, or in many cases in unusable boat hulls, often supported across timbers. To most visiting Western eyes, including my own, it had great beauty, but nothing seemed to be done for creative effect. Nothing was tidied or custom-made. If something worked at all, then it worked well. Everything was random, ragged and completely functional.

A small boy, perhaps eight or nine years old, passed us in a canoe towing twenty vast tree logs lashed together. A man and a dog stood on them, walking up and down the tree trunks as though it were a pavement. The river is a busy street and these house-boats are a village. People were calling to one another across the water and visits were constantly being made between the boats by canoes manned by children looking scarcely old enough to ride a bicycle, handling them with incredible dexterity and skill. There was a sense of unhurried business. Bright orange and electric blue butterflies as big as thrushes tottered unsteadily by on oversize wings.

We stopped at a small shop. An open window revealed shelves neatly and brightly stacked with cooking oil, white rum, toothpaste, razors, sweets, tins and packets of food and bags of crisps. Sacks of flour were stacked in the kitchen and front room. There were no ceilings and everything was made of wood from the forest. The kitchen gleamed with scoured pans on the wall. Fish, caught by a net a few yards from the house were drying in the sun.

The owner, Sebastiana, led us to see her garden. Out the back, growing out

IT HAD GREAT BEAUTY, BUT NOTHING SEEMED TO BE DONE FOR CREATIVE EFFECT. NOTHING WAS TIDIED OR CUSTOM-MADE.

Soil is ferried to the gardens from the shore and put into any avail- able container – in this case, an old, disused boat hull.

of rickety, rotting wooden containers half-submerged in the warm, olive water was an exotic orchard of cashews, carimbola with their flanged fruits, banana, lemons, pineapple, guava and passion fruit. They were rooted in thirty sacks of soil that Sebastiana fetches, bucket by bucket, from the shore, mixed with cow manure. Twice a day she splashes water from the river onto the roots using an old aluminium cooking pot.

I had never tasted carimbola and foolishly said as much. So Sebastiana picked one and washed it in the river and passed it to me. Good manners meant I could not refuse although I was very aware that the water was sewer, mortuary and general drain for the village. It tasted very good and there were, as it turned out, no ill effects. That was to come later courtesy of a Rio restaurant.

Any idea of a floating horticultural idyll was rather spoilt by the news that Sebastiana was about to move to a seventh-storey flat in Manaus. It was the only place that her husband could find any work. I asked her what she would do about the garden? 'Take it with me,' she said, and I had a happy image of the garden floating like a balloon from the balcony. Did she have a favourite plant? I expected one of the more productive fruit trees but she led me to the side of the houseboat and a scrawny bougainvillea struggling in a cut-off plastic jar. 'It cheers me up,' she said.

I visited three or four more of these floating gardens, one that specialised in roses of all things, each grown in an old cooking oil can, and another that included a good sized sow and her piglets and a very bad tempered parrot trying to snooze in the shade of the pigsty. Best were the wooden canoes planted with melons, oranges, onions and peppers.

As we made the two-hour canoe trip back to our boat, we retraced our steps past the villages with their floating back gardens. They are almost entirely practical, a means of adding to an otherwise very limited diet. But there is a poetry to them too which is relished by their owners just as much as our sophisticated passing eye. The need to grow things and celebrate their beauty is elemental, even on a river that is slowly dwindling in the dry season in the middle of the Amazon rainforest.

The Black Earth

The Amazon Rainforest, Brazil

CHOOSING THIS AS ONE of my eighty gardens is a bit of a cheat insomuch as it is not really a garden, or at least it is much more than just a garden. But it seems to me so significant, and so fascinating in dealing with the question of how the Amazon rain forest can be cultivated in a sustainable manner for the future that it has to be included, not least because the divide between gardening and agriculture is wafer-thin in most parts of the world. In many cases, it is up to gardeners to repair much of the damage caused by farmers and to engage with the unavoidable environmental problems that are so urgently pressing upon us all.

This is the story of the *terra preta* or Black Earth of the Amazon rainforest. The soil of the rainforest is by and large extremely thin and nutrient deficient. The fecundity is maintained only by the heat, animal activity, fungi, termites and bacteria converting waste, moisture and constant leaf fall to compost astonishingly quickly to provide nutrients for plants. Despite the scale of growth, it is, in fact, a very delicate balance and most of the nutrients never spend any time in the soil.

When the rainforest is cleared for agriculture the big timber is removed and the remainder is set alight – the traditional 'slash and burn' process. For the first year or two the ash provides extra nutrients and crops grow well, but the soil is quickly exhausted and typically abandoned after about three years. It then takes some fifty years to be able to produce more crops and about 200 for the forest to regrow.

The terra preta, *or Black Earth, dotted around the Amazon rainforest, provides inspiration for a new method of sustainable permaculture which could replace the traditional 'slash and burn' process. Unlike the rest of the forest, the fertile black soil here will support sustainable papaya crops.*

But a tiny proportion of the rainforest – just 0.2 per cent – has been found to have a layer of exceptionally deep, rich black soil. This is the *terra preta*. One fifth of 1 per cent is a tiny amount but given the size of Amazonia it adds up to over 12 million acres – an area more than twice the size of Wales. Archaeological excavation has found pottery and other artefacts in this black soil going back to prehistoric periods and, as it is mapped in very small units clustered around long-inhabited tributaries of the Amazon, it is believed to have slowly built up over centuries. In other words it has been made by, and has supported, tribes continuously over a very long period.

The film crew and I went to see one of these excavated sites, taking a canoe to a ferry transporting villagers, with their fruits, chickens and labour, to the skyscrapers of Manaus, and then going by van to the Costa d'Laranjal on the banks of the Amazon.

The area was surrounded on three sides by thick forest, but was rich with papayas, bananas, mangoes and oranges, together with crops. The dig itself was on the site of a smallholding that had been continuously cultivated by the same family for generations. There was a large rectangular pit dug into the bright ochre soil, showing a deep chocolate layer of soil from just below the surface at a depth of about 5 ft. Terracotta pottery was clearly visible 4 ft deep. This layer of soil explained the fertility evident in the growth all around us despite continuous cultivation.

The dark soil was undoubtedly caused by the burning of wood there and there are large pieces of charcoal in the soil layer to prove this. Although work is still underway, recent research seems to explain the difference between the 'slash and burn' land and the *terra preta*.

In modern, conventional clearance, 'slash and burn' fires are lit indiscriminately and always in the dry season. They rage at furious heats, reducing the material to grey ash, which in turn provides an immediate supply of nutrients for the subsequent crop.

In the *terra preta* the site is chosen carefully, trying to include as many palms, which burn slowly and at a low heat. The firing is always done in the rainy season, again encouraging a relatively low, smouldering heat. This means that carbon and charcoal are produced rather than ash, acting as a sponge for the nutrients, and locking them into the soil over a long period. Because it is the rainy season the available nutrients are washed gradually into the soil – and held by the charcoal – rather than being washed away into the river as it would be if the fire created ash in the dry season.

After the first crop the villagers pile all their organic human, animal and vegetable waste onto the surface of the soil as a mulch where it decomposes very fast. Another crop is planted and when this is cleared the ground is left fallow for one or two years. The resulting, very vigorous vegetation is cut and again left as a mulch to rot down before another crop is taken from it.

This cycle can be repeated endlessly with the carbon from the initial fire holding nutrients in the soil for take-up by plants at a much slower rate than the rainforest. It is a kind of permaculture developed to a high degree of sophistication by the people who have lived in the rainforest for millennia, and which I saw being continued with much success.

As I write and you read, thousands of acres of Amazonian rainforest are being plundered every day for the growing of crops such as soya to feed Western cattle to produce beef burgers or supermarket 'prime cuts'. Thousands more are being cleared for feeding a growing Brazilian nation. But there does seem to be another, sustainable way, the way of *terra preta*, the Black Earth.

Baku's Garden

Satere Mawe Village, Manaus, Brazil

THERE ARE STILL PLENTY of indigenous people in the Amazon using a sustainable form of horticulture to grow food and medicinal herbs and I had the opportunity to visit one of them, the Satere Mawe, where the matriarch, a tiny terrifying figure called Baku, has what is probably the smallest and least obviously distinguished garden in this book. I loved it though and it is completely fascinating.

The Satere Mawe village is by the river – in the rainy season the water comes right to the village edge and you step from the boat to the buildings. When I visited, in the dry season, it was a ten-minute walk from the shrunken water's edge, through the thick forest, past cathedral-buttressed trees. It is self-consciously a traditional settlement, carefully maintained by the villagers, who receive almost all their finance from tourists visiting from Manaus. They wear grass skirts and painted bodies during the working day but behind the huts are new bicycles and washing lines strung with Manchester United and Brazil football shirts.

None of this is any more phoney or cynical than a Cotswold pub hanging horse brasses in the lounge bar. They have to live. And it is the real thing all right, just the real thing on self-conscious display.

The village is composed of huts made out of wood, with palm leaves woven into mats for the walls and roof thatch. There is a sense that it is entirely and organically borrowed from the jungle, that it would revert to more forest floor litter in a matter of months if left.

The smallest and possibly the most modest garden in this book is nevertheless entirely in tune with its surroundings.

Above '*Spoiled wood*', consisting of dead wood, leaves and twigs, is burned slowly and the ash used to enrich the acidic soil.
Opposite *The growing conditions in the Amazon are so fertile that Baku can tear a twig from a tree, stick it in the ground and it will be growing from its own roots in a few days.*

Baku took us over to a corner where a small fire was smouldering. Through an interpreter I asked what she was doing. I was told that she was burning 'spoiled wood' so that she could put the ashes onto the soil to feed her plants. 'Spoiled wood' turned out to be dead and rotting wood, plus leaves and twigs to keep the fire going. The resulting ash is used to 'sweeten' the soil – to counter its inherent acidity.

She took some ash in her hands, added an equal measure of rotted organic matter and mixed it with one hand exactly as my mother would blend dry pastry. When she was happy with the mixture she took it into the little fenced garden and sprinkled it around the plants like a simple mulch.

I asked her why she made this garden. For pleasure? Practicality? 'What garden?' she replied. 'Er, this one, that the two of us and the film crew are squeezed into, the one with the rows of plants.' 'This is not a garden,' she replied rather fiercely. 'This is just where I grow my medicines.' She seems not to understand the word or even the concept of a garden. It is, for her, just a gathered or ordered part of the jungle. We agree to differ on the semantics or else this would be 'Around The World In 79 Gardens Plus The Bit Of The Jungle Where Baku Grows Her Medicines'. Doesn't quite have the same ring to it.

I asked her how she propagated her plants. She answered that she gathered all her materials from the forest. She just breaks off a branch and then puts it in the soil and it makes roots. There is a little bundle of broken branches on the ground, some quite thick and which, in *Gardener's World* terms, would be hopelessly unsuitable as cutting material. I ask her how long ago she had gathered it. Two days. Looking closely I see that there are already a few new roots growing. The truth is that the Amazonian rainforest is like a hot mist propagator, where almost anything will grow, all the time.

She says that she knows every plant in the jungle, that everything she could possibly need is just a few minutes' walk away. This garden is simply an ordering of that, to keep certain plants close to hand. Here is a plant to combat worms. This one next to it is called, I think, 'shut-up'. 'Shut up? What is it for?' 'For people who ask too many questions,' she says, staring intently at me without a smile as the translator passes the message on.

I leave the village with mixed feelings. Clearly it is a tourist display, and as such not 'real', yet the villagers are real enough and they are doing no harm whilst maintaining an intimacy with the rainforest. Baku's knowledge is being passed on, even if it is only to passing TV crews. The village children ran down to the river with us, racing ahead to clamber onto branches and wave goodbye to our canoes. It is a display infinitely more spontaneous and charming than the 'traditional' song and dance put on for us a little earlier. They are still waving as we disappear round the bend of the river. There is a slight pang of loss, knowing that I will never see them or be there again. The job is done. We move on. But Baku's garden (sorry Baku, not-garden) seems the right model to take away: small, in tune with the world growing around her, useful and effortlessly beautiful too.

It was an hour's canoe journey back to the boat, as dusk fell around us. We were all exhausted by filming since dawn in the extreme heat. Kingfishers the size of pigeons darted to take the fish that popped ceaselessly. Three macaws flew overhead with remarkable grace. As the light dimmed suddenly, thousands of bats appeared out of the trees and zigzagged across the water inches from the canoe. Bats as big as blackbirds and as silkily acrobatic as swallows. This tested me for a moment – I have a phobia about bats – but as I was in a little canoe in the middle of a small river leading to the Amazon, at least thirty minutes from the boat, there was little I could do but watch in wonder until the darkness was so complete that even the riverbank could not be seen.

Copacabana Promenade

Rio de Janeiro, Brazil

THERE ARE FEW GARDENS best seen from the twenty-seventh floor of a hotel. But then there are very few gardens that bear any resemblance to Roberto Burle Marx's promenade at Rio's Copacabana beach. Its dimensions are huge and odd, 2.5 miles long and no more than 160 ft wide at its broadest point – a width that also includes six lanes of traffic. But a garden it surely is, as municipal and as public as bedding on a round-about. The tower blocks are the key. From twenty floors up the miles of coloured paving and clumps of trees become a brocade of front garden for the anonymous buildings.

The day that we visited, the weather conspired against us. The idea had been to film the beautiful, tanned, thonged creatures of Rio posing and parading on the famous beach, but it was grey and wet and the entire beach was empty. In fact, it meant that the clean sweep of sand around the bay became a borrowed part of the view that is rarely able to be appreciated without the dots of bodies.

Before the city edged down to the beach and the tower blocks made an unbroken pallisade along the seafront, Copacabana was apparently a quiet neighbourhood of houses and gardens with a natural progression to the shore. So, in an attempt to recapture something of that transition, at the end of the 1960s land was reclaimed from the sea and the Avenue Atlantica constructed, sweeping round the bay. In 1970 Burle Marx was commissioned to design what is, in effect, an esplanade. His response was what amounts to a 2.5 mile long painting using black, white and red Portuguese stone mosaic, a stone used throughout Rio because it expands and contracts in the heat without cracking.

Burle Marx knew from the outset that pedestrians and motorists would only see the details, not the context of the larger picture, but that the entire design would be visible from the rooftops. On the ground the detail is real, with stones making various textures of mosaic, and small segments as complete and contained as cameos within the larger picture. It is a piece of art as surely as any painting, using the city, sea and seafront. I stood for an hour or so in the rain and never grew remotely bored with the way that the shapes and volumes in the stone worked around me, whilst not really having any idea of what they looked like. Perhaps that is how the birds must feel about our back gardens.

Seen from above, the promenade has huge, energetic charm. Waves and lines are marked out in the same road paint as road markings, tarmac and paint echoing the wavy stone pavement. The corners of roads entering into the Avenue Atlantica from the city are as curved and rounded as a Brazilian bottom. Cars and walkers with bright umbrellas become as much part of the design as plants might be in a conventional garden.

On the day I was there the green of the trees shone wet and bright, adding a three-dimensional element, shimmering above the hieroglyphs on the ground. Chosen for the ability to survive the fierce, salty Atlantic gales, on sunny days *Cocos nucifera*, *Paritium tiliaceum*, *Mimusops coriacea*, *Clusia fluminensis*, *Coccoloba wiffera*, *Ficus* and *Terminalia catappa* shade the benches for the resters and watchers, whilst the inevitable joggers and i-podded walkers march up and down in search of the perfect body.

What is most extraordinary is that Burle Marx, an obsessive plantsman, could turn his skills to such confident abstract painting on such a vast scale with such apparent ease. I cannot think of any garden designer in history who could have done the same.

Above *Roberto Burle Marx chose plants such as these* Cocos nucifero *at the Museum of Modern Art in Rio de Janeiro as much for their ability to survive Atlantic gales as for the way they looked.*
Opposite *Burle Marx is one of the gardening geniuses of the twentieth century who broke free from the pervading European influences and created a style that was uniquely Brazilian yet had universal appeal. His extraordinarily ambitious designs flanking Copacabana Beach in Rio de Janeiro are a joyous celebration of that idiom.*

The Sítio

Santo Antônio da Bico, Rio de Janeiro, Brazil

Above Roberto Burle Marx was among the first garden designers to appreciate and use native Brazilian plants. His testing ground outside Rio de Janeiro now contains 3,500 species. *Opposite* The vast kapok tree, Ceiba pentandra, *is known as* sumaumeira *in Brazil. The size of its trunk, roots and leaves is truly staggering.*

ROBERTO BURLE MARX is unquestionably Brazil's greatest garden designer and arguably one of the few really important garden designers in history. Yet I approached his own garden, The Sítio, with some trepidation. What I had seen of his work, in books and magazines, left me cold. I didn't get it. But I have found that it is best to suspend judgement as far as possible until you see the work with your own eyes. Pictures may not lie exactly but they certainly exaggerate.

I need not have worried. If I came to Brazil with doubts, I left as an overawed convert. Burle Marx was a great artist. He is also one of the few, very few, artists to have spanned the worlds of painting, botany, design and architecture. He was a polymath, and spoke Portuguese, Spanish, English, French, German and Italian fluently. He was an urban planner, a painter, musician, designer of houses, stage sets and jewellery amongst almost everything else. Gardens, and above all plants, were just one element woven into his life and he seems to have been entirely devoid of the artistic and horticultural parochialism that dogs most European gardeners.

Burle Marx was born in 1909 in São Paulo, to a German father and Brazilian mother. The family was wealthy and he grew up in a highly cultured household, moving to Rio de Janeiro in 1913. As a teenager he developed serious problems with his eyes and remained very short sighted for the rest of his life. In 1928 he was sent to Berlin for treatment and at the Botanical Gardens of Dahlen he saw, for the first time, Brazilian plants used in a deliberately ornamental way. This staggered him. Back in Rio, gardens were entirely influenced by European plants – native species were considered unsophisticated and not really worthy of using in a garden. When he returned to Brazil in the early 1930s, he was determined to garden with native species, although at that time he was studying painting.

In 1932 he designed his first garden professionally, using only Brazilian native plants. By his death he had completed over 2,000 more. When he started work no one else was using tropical plants as part of Brazilian gardens and if they were used at all, they would be imported from Europe. He was passionate about preserving the ecology of Brazil. He would hear about some act of destruction of the rainforest and rush off with a team of volunteers to rescue as many plants as possible. In this process he collected over 3,000 species of which twenty were discovered by him. Before Burle Marx, Brazilians viewed the rainforest as a chaotic, endlessly renewable resource. He was amongst the first to recognise its fragility and astonishing diversity of species. By applying this to gardens, he raised a national consciousness and by constantly campaigning and challenging the vested interests of the loggers and ranchers, he did as much as anyone has ever done to preserve the flora of Brazil.

In 1949 Burle Marx bought the Sítio, at Santo Antônio da Bico, about 40 miles outside Rio, to store his plant collection, and he lived there from 1973 until his death in 1994. It is huge, spreading to more than 100 acres and containing more than 3,500 species. To the visitor these statistics are daunting. But the

IT IS, AS BURLE MARX HIMSELF DEFINED A GARDEN, VERY MUCH NATURE ORGANISED BY MAN, FOR MAN.

first impression is exactly the opposite to that. It is so personalised, so quirkily idiosyncratic, that, once past the inevitable security guards, it is much more like visiting the home and garden of an artist than the paraded trophies of a member of the great and good. It reminded me more of an outdoor Kettle's Yard in Cambridge than a botanical garden, with its mixture of house, chapel, plants, stone, wood, sculptures, paintings, bowls and shells. Burle Marx was an obsessive collector, a trait that touched every aspect of his life as well as plants. If he wanted one he wanted as many different ones as possible. This obsessive collecting integrates here in his garden, each object individually fascinating and lovely.

Although Burle Marx was a garden and landscape designer, the Sítio was never designed. In fact, when I met one of his closest assistants, Haruyoshi Ono, he stressed that it was not a garden but a 'testing ground' for plants. He would collect plants, grow them at the Sítio to see how they behaved and grew best and then propagate from them to provide material for the gardens that he was designing professionally.

This distinction seemed to be important to them and I am sure that, in its intention at least, it is true. I am also sure that this is why it is a great garden. It transcends skilful design and grows organically, without much premeditation, but directed in every detail by the hand and eye of a great artist and designer and imbued at every turn with his idiosyncratic genius. The result to my eye is, unintentional as it may ironically be, carefree, spontaneous and a beautifully designed garden. Hoisted by his own genius.

Burle Marx's genius overspilled every medium and every occasion. He could not stop or help himself. He had an exuberance that is exactly mirrored in the Sítio with its astonishing fecundity. If you think back to the revelation that he had in Dahlen, that rather than aping an anodyne European version of gardens, the native Brazilian plants were the right medium for Brazilian gardens, you can see that he also tapped into the rhythm of Brazilian growth with its relentless energy and vigour. Now this can be overpowering and chaotic but the Sítio is never that. Apart from anything else the scale of its maintenance and the implied expenditure required are staggering. It is, as Burle Marx himself defined a garden, very much nature organised by man for man.

All the planting is in huge blocks and drifts with as many as hundreds of plants making a uniform mass. I was told that Burle Marx would often say that you have to put many plants together for people to see one, and it is surprising how the eye and general aesthetic will tolerate huge ranks of identical plants without becoming tired or bored by them.

The relationship between the details – the curve of a buttressed trunk or the placing of a sculpture or steps – and the massed effect of planting on a huge scale is tremendously satisfying. The site slopes steeply and has huge boulders and outcrops of rock as well as pools, huge trees and paths that curve and slink like the astonishing roots of yet another unknown tree snaking above the ground. I am a hopeless botanist and my knowledge of plants is limited to my own gardening experience but nowhere has ever made me feel more wonderfully submerged in my own ignorance as the Sítio. It ceased to be an intellectual experience and became something more visceral, fully formed if not informed.

Burle Marx's methods were always quixotic and involved a spontaneous reaction to an event, whether it be a piece of music or the news that a section of forest was about to have a road smashed through it. He would do things first and then discuss or even explain them later. When he returned from a plant collecting trip, he would stand in the Sítio with helpers placing plants and direct their movements like a conductor, rather than draw a plan or consider the planting for a while. The garden evolved through his whims and caprices and this redeems and elevates it above a mere collection or catalogue of plants.

Burle Marx loved chance in all its forms. So he would make gardens and even buildings around unplanned purchases, gifts or discoveries. One wall, assembled in a Mayan or Incan style and bristling with bromeliads, is made up of stones from a bank pulled down in Rio. A huge room was added to the house to accommodate a pair of doors.

He also loved entertaining and the garden has an area laid out for throwing parties on an heroic scale, which is apparently what he did every Sunday, holding an open house for artists, politicians, millionaires and assorted Brazilian luminaries, jostling for position around the table. It is significant that this area at the back of the house, with its huge paved spaces, a large glazed mural on one wall and a dramatic curtain of water falling from the concrete structure built to support the jade vine, should lead straight out into a planting evoking pure, lush green, native jungle growing at a rampant rate. It is artifice insomuch that it is as artfully created as the party place, but the two parts of Burle Marx's life are always in sight of each other.

I have not attempted to describe the Sítio. A hundred acres of intensive planting, full of species new to me, defies that. But it is as good a reason to travel to Rio de Janeiro as any other. Burle Marx gave the garden, including his art collection, library and artefacts to the state in 1985 and it became the Roberto Burle Marx Foundation. He lived on for another nine years, an uneasy partner to the inevitable bureaucratic restrictions that the government-run foundation imposed on him. He bought another piece of land next to the Sítio and continued his work there, becoming increasingly short-sighted and limited in movements. When he died on June 4th 1994, he was painting to the very end. Burle Marx's work is all over Rio and he is rightly heralded as one of the fathers of modern garden and landscape design. But if you want to get close to the heart of the man you must visit his testing ground, his not-garden, the Sítio.

Burle Marx loved to make gardens from the unexpected; in this case a wall assembled in a Mayan or Incan style and covered with bromeliads, is made of stones from a bank pulled down in Rio.

Dos Talas

Buenos Aires, Argentina

FROM RIO, I TRAVELLED SOUTH to Argentina. Sitting by a window I gazed into the clear sky as we crossed a vast open space of pampas in Uruguay until we passed the River Plate and finally reached Buenos Aires. Buenos Aires is very different to Rio. It is a big, open city with broad, leafy avenues reminiscent of Madrid or Paris. It feels familiar yet exciting and fresh. One of the men responsible for creating the way that Buenos Aires looks was a Frenchman, Charles Thays. Born in Paris in 1849 and trained as a landscape architect, he visited Argentina when he was forty and decided to live there. He was appointed 'Director of Parks and Walkways' in 1891 and almost single-handedly shaped the way that the city looks today.

I spent a day in the city walking round and visiting Thays' parks, adjusting to a very different atmosphere, climate and culture from Brazil. Tango dancers rehearsed in the park moving with a mannered exactness that was almost like tai-chi. A dog walker went confidently by with no less than fourteen dogs of every shape and size attached to him by leads. Best of all was the mind boggling vast gomero in St Paul's Square that was planted by Thays. With flanged buttresses to its trunks that splayed out into fins and lateral trunks that would not have shamed the trunk of a 500-year old oak tree, it is an astonishing, miraculous living thing.

But what I wanted to see was Thays' work outside Buenos Aires, in one of the estancias or ranches out in the pampas. So, after breakfast the next day, I piled into a minibus with the film crew and set out for the 125-mile drive to Dos Talas.

Dos Talas is one of over 800 estancias in Argentina and although it is representative of the type, it also has particularly superb gardens that were designed by Charles Thays in 1908. The house was built by one Pedro Luro who had a general store in the small town of Dolores. An estancia owner gave him the job of planting a eucalyptus forest on his land, offering a price per tree and then leaving for Europe. When he returned a few years later he found that Pedro Luro had planted so many trees that he could only pay him by handing over a portion of the estate – some 42,000 acres – which became the future Dos Talas. Pedro Luro left the estate to his daughter Agustina who commissioned Buenos Aires' top landscape architect of the time – who was of course Charles Thays – to design a 75- acre park to accompany a new house that she had had built.

The garden that Thays designed had a maze, rose gardens, a vast walled kitchen garden, boating lake and sixteen gardeners to tend it. The estancia is now reduced to a mere 3,500 acres of which Luis Elizalde farms a third and looks after the garden. It is much reduced in circumstances but is still in the same family and still, apparently, a splendid example of an estancia.

When we arrived, we drove down a long avenue of dead elms, bleached like bones in the southern sun. They are an amazing, purely sculptural sight. Approaching the house there is a whole pig roasting on an open wood fire beneath a large cedar of Lebanon. Argentina – indeed all South America – is not a country for squeamish vegetarians. Luis and Sara Elizalde greeted us and proceeded to treat us all like spe-

Opposite *Avenues of trees divide and protect the garden at Dos Talas from the pampas winds. I have never visited a garden with such large shelter belts – like a home counties estate on the edge of a Shetland heath.*
Below *The charismatic Luis Elizalde runs the farm and garden of the estancia.*

cial guests. Their hospitality was warm, lavish and friendly in a completely easy fashion. A tame deer nibbled at my trousers as we lunched under the tree. Chimangos, the noisy, garrulous eagle-like hawk of the pampas, flew overhead. At dawn and dusk they make as much noise as rooks before settling.

I took a stroll. The garden is remarkably English for all the unlikely menagerie, with vast trees set in great sweeps of grass. Cedars, Scots pine, deodar, elms, huge magnolias, palm trees all stand as superb specimens. The garden seemed enormous. It is.

The park is carved into great avenues, once obviously neatly hedged and clipped but now tall and meeting at the top so that they become dramatic tunnels like cathedral naves, dividing the woods into blocks. One opens out to a large brick pigeon house built like a folly, clearly intended for more serious meat eating. The ledges are Old Red Sandstone – the same stone as my house in Herefordshire – bought in especially from Switzerland. Bees crowded around one of the hundreds of empty pigeon holes.

The woods were fresh with a southern spring, with cow parsley and the smell of new mown grass an almost painful reminder of spring at home. The orchard was covered in blossom. A taste of out-of-season spring was both a delight and a torment. I moved on.

The bark of the plane trees glowed bright orange in the dusk. Watching the sun set over the lake it was not until I looked through binoculars that I could see how far the horizon stretched. Flamingos were noisy on the marshy pampas – an exotic reminder, if it were needed, of how very far from home I really was.

The next morning I was up early and walked around the park again before breakfast, taking with me Thays' original plan. The vegetable garden is a football pitch sized patch of mown grass but in the wood behind it I found an outgrown 'hedge' of 100 ft tall privet. It was completely beautiful and must have once been a low containing hedge at the back of the kitchen garden. It reminded me of the garden at Killruddery in Ireland when I first visited it some twenty years ago, the seventeenth-century yew and box hedging grown into woodland.

Originally the great squares of wood here at Dos Talas were planted with peach, apple and quince but all died through neglect. Now they have reverted to self-sown woodland of privet and acacia. This is a pity but still completely lovely.

The garden is halfway between a lost, abandoned world, where one stumbles upon ruins and treasures, and a modern take on what is sustainable and appropriate in a modern world. Luis, who learnt his English driving a yellow cab in New York and who daily flies his small plane over the estancia when not riding horses around the cattle, is incredibly hard working but realistic. He loves it and wishes to care for it but knows the limitations before him.

My own feeling is that gardens constantly change and adapt. The existence of a huge garden is in itself a kind of miracle set in the vast, vast expanse of pampas. The garden is a kind of mastery over this fertile yet hostile space, imposing a European culture upon it. The tree planting is both lovely and absolutely necessary to protect the garden from the pampas winds and I have never visited a garden with such large, or for that matter grand, shelter belts. It is like a home counties estate on the edge of a Shetland heath.

But Thays was good enough a designer to include the pampas. He plotted sunset and sunrise and left openings in his planting to view them across the pampas. The beef and the horses and even the light aircraft are part of the set up. Garden and pampas work together to create the estancia. If I needed further proof of this, it came when I asked Luis what his biggest garden pest is. 'Armadillos,' he replied.

Clara's Garden

Santiago, Chile

FLYING INTO CHILE from Argentina on a clear day is a dramatic experience. You cross the parched brown plains for a couple of hours and then suddenly, without preamble, the Andes soar up ahead, the snowline as clear as a tidemark. As you fly over them they become a series of sharp, glaciered wrinkles below you, each one an impassable peak, in a vast broad expanse – a 100-mile wide impenetrable barrier. Together with the Pacific Ocean on its west coast, the Atacama desert, which is the driest place on earth, in the north and the Antarctic in the south, it creates an hermetic seal for humans and animals and most plant life. Chile is effectively an island with a high degree of endemic species covering every type of condition other than tropical rainforest. Despite being nearly 3,000 miles from top to bottom it is no more than 150 miles at its widest point and mostly much less than that. This long strip of land makes for a stunningly beautiful country.

Having checked into a hotel in Santiago we were driven up into the Andes by our fixer Christian. Christian is a birder and falconer who breeds and flies peregrines and gyre falcons. In my eyes he could hardly have a greater claim for glamorous respect if he had won the World Cup or climbed Everest solo.

When you go east in Chile you climb. And climb. The road took us through valleys and gorges splashed bright orange with tens of thousands of the most zanily spelt of all flowers, the *Eschscholzia* or Californian poppy. We had parked at around 8,200 ft to film the mountains and yours truly looking wind-tousled and energetic, when Christian quietly pointed something out in the middle distance behind me. It was a pair of condors perched on a rock. One pulled away into the air, as big as a parasail and as easy as an eagle.

I wrote all this down in my little notebook which I invariably have with me, a fresh one for each trip, noted the eschscholzias and a black-chested buzzard eagle (Christian told me that), then we went back to the van and the lurching, winding spiral back to Santiago. The next day I hunted every-where for the notebook. Rob, the sound recordist, said that he had definitely seen it on a rock before we left the mountains. With a sickening gut-lurch I realised that I had almost certainly left it up there. It had all my notes for the whole of South America. Every experience, every plant, every name, every thought was in that book. I told Christian who thought for a moment then calmly rang a friend and set him off on the road for the three-hour drive to the point where we had parked, whilst we got on with filming.

The crew, whilst sympathetic at the loss of the notes, were looking at the track

Everything in Clara's garden has been recycled – from planks of wood to rusty sheets of corrugated iron. It's not conventionally beautiful but I like how it works.

record. All clothes lost on the first day, arriving in the Amazon with seven saris and my hand luggage, losing notebook with all material on nearly the last day. We still had another year of travelling ahead. Would I finish with any possessions at all? They tried all day not to laugh and failed dismally and ignobly in the attempt.

The taxi driver rang from the mountains to say he was at the parking spot. Where should he go? 'Park up and I will talk you through it,' Christian said. Thank God there was a signal for the phones. Then the taxi driver said that he had parked, got out of the car and directly ahead of him, no more than a yard away, was a black notebook on a rock. It was covered with an overnight dusting of snow. He picked it up and drove three hours back down. The pages before me now on my desk are still wrinkled with damp but it was miraculous luck.

That day, before driving north to see the garden of Juan Grimm, we visited a little garden attached to the low, single-storey building of a hacienda worker. It was tended by Clara who used every possible kind of receptacle for plants. This, apparently was a local tradition amongst the workers, who would in particular use kitchen utensils once they were no longer serviceable. So kettles, washing machine drums, tea pots, sauce-pans, a bidet, an old telly, a vacuum cleaner, a red drum, tyres, as well as tins, plastic food pots and paint pots, all were planted up and set outside the little house. The effect was a kind of lovingly tended, flowering scrapyard.

Nothing is wasted. Eggshells are all kept and ground to feed plants, cigarette stubs boiled up as a fungicide. Everything is used, recycled and reformed. The two spades have long handles clearly cut from a tree. They are both smooth with use.

The inevitable accompaniment to this is piles of materials waiting to be used, from wood for the outside stove to pots, rope, tubing, guttering etc. In England this would be seen as junk and untidiness. Clara accepts it as a valuable part of her garden and the plants happily grow through, in and around all this stuff.

There is no concept of design or arrangement. Things are grown where there is space. There is no grass but what soil there is – a patch a few yards square – is cultivated to grow vegetables. Bits of tin and wire make a chicken coop. The washing line lies over cabbages and compost. I am shown their avocado tree, heavy with hundreds of fruits. They are big, glossy and black – the best kind, Clara tells me proudly. She has lemons and oranges, a peach and two apple trees. A grape vine is beginning to produce tiny fruits on a pergola made from bits and pieces of wood.

Not a lot of weeding goes on. It is scruffy. You can hardly move around for all the bits and pieces piled and scattered about. But it is beautiful, vibrant and much loved.

Above *Aloe vera peeks out of an old tin in Clara's garden.* Opposite *Clara's garden is typical of many small, modest Chilean gardens tended with extra love and care. I stopped to look over the fence of another garden near to Clara's home.*

YOU CAN HARDLY MOVE AROUND FOR ALL THE BITS AND PIECES PILED AND SCATTERED ABOUT. BUT IT IS ALSO BEAUTIFUL, VIBRANT AND MUCH LOVED.

It is also expertly managed. The plants are all healthy, the fruit and vegetables all grow in abundance and are good to eat. It transforms and improves a life that does not have much by way of material possessions. It would not win any prizes in a flower show or best-kept village competition, but for my money it is a superb garden and Clara an expert gardener.

I left inspired and enriched and then found I was to be reunited with my notebook. All in all, a good day.

Juan Grimm's Garden

Los Villos, Santiago, Chile

WE HAD SPENT ALL DAY driving down the Pacific coast of Chile to film the native Chilean palm, *Jubaea chilensis*, which is now extremely rare. It is a fascinating plant, with the greatest longevity of any palm – living to over 2,000 years old. It grows extremely slowly but will eventually reach over 100 ft with thick trunks like elephant legs, and is the largest species of palm in the world. But it had rained incessantly all night and continued without break all that day. The palms were duly filmed in a puddled garden but my fascination was heavily diluted by the rain, and a trip into the hills to get them in their natural environment was thankfully aborted. The film crew, the kit and our clothing, right down to our underwear, was all soaked. A minibus packed tight with a soggy film crew three weeks from home is not a cheerful place. Because we had finished early we decided to go and recce the next day's location, the holiday home and garden of the landscape designer Juan Grimm at Los Villos, three hours north of Santiago. (Juan told me that Los Villos got its name from an English pirate called Lord Willow. The locals couldn't prounounce that so it became corrupted to Los Villos. It sounds far-fetched but a good story.)

Juan Grimm is almost unknown in Britain but he is undoubtably one of the world's best garden and landscape designers working today. I later discovered that, whilst he may not be a national name in Britain, he is revered in Australia and New Zealand and casually mentioning that I had spent a day with him in his garden increased my own credibility hugely.

We knew that Juan would not be there until the next day but we had met him on the motorway the previous night so we could hand on a pair of his trousers (it's a long story that I never really understood) and he knew we might pay a pre-shoot visit. The housekeeper had been primed.

Even on a wild day it was a stunningly spectacular place with the house cantilevered out over the rocks that dropped down to the sea, but we hoped that there was enough garden proper to expand upon the sensational position.

We need not have worried. The next day was gloriously warm and sunny and I spent all of it with Juan revelling in his garden.

The real point is so did Juan. So does and will anyone who ever comes here – every time. A lot of this is to do with the beauty of the house and the planting but it would be a stunning place to visit if there was no trace of man. That is the point of the garden. All of its meaning is in the context. The site was chosen and the house designed and built specifically for it. The planting does not turn away from the sea but embraces

Above *Juan Grimm is one of the world's leading garden and landscape designers and spending a day with him in his own garden was a lasting inspiration.*
Opposite *The garden is designed to gradually grow out of the rocks, up the hill and away from the sea. All the plants Juan Grimm has used are local to that particular area of the Pacific coast.*

THE RESULT IS ONE OF THE MOST BEAUTIFUL AND INSPIRING GARDENS ANYWHERE IN THE WORLD.

it, using the rocks and even the waves as part of the garden. It is a really big, ambitious concept. Yet to Juan it was obvious. There was no other way. All of his work, whether for private residents or large landscape projects, seeks to integrate the hand of man with the natural landscape and plants. This makes for a profoundly meaningful transformation and, in my opinion, some of the best landscape work on the planet.

Juan's garden was inspired by his visits as a child to the coast some 10 miles south of Los Villos. So all the plants on the seaward side of the garden are not just native to Chile but to the specific area of Los Molles. I went to that stretch of coast that evening, when the sun was setting over a fat rock wedged into the sea, noisy with sea lions, a few penguins and vultures skimming the coast. The shore was meadowed with cacti, alstroemerias, pua, wild fuchsias and a gentian-like flower I could not identify. Juan had absorbed a childhood of these plants and shore and sea and translated them into a garden. The result is one of the most beautiful and inspiring gardens anywhere in the world. One can imagine a completely satisfying day spent simply looking at the view. In fact, Juan says that he does not attempt to work there. 'It would be too distracting', yet clearly it is the fount of all of his work.

The genius is in the subtle gradation from shore to threshold, the garden evolving from water and encrusted rock to sleek modernity without ever missing a beat or betraying the spirit of that particular coastline. If I have only learnt one thing from my travels around the world it is that no garden is an island. Context is everything. A garden created as a stage set or show garden only has meaning in terms of what it is escaping from and thus must always end as a cul-de sac. The best gardens are open and wired directly into the climate, geology, flora and culture of the place. And no garden I visited was more directly tuned into its context than Juan Grimm's home at Los Villos.

Of course there are all kinds of conceptual issues for the visitor to deal with when a garden is so closely integrated with its surroundings. Where does the garden begin and end? What is horticulture and what just happy accident? The approach to the house, the building itself with its clean lines and planes of stone and glass and the planting down to the circular swimming pool are all accessible and easy enough to admire. But what of the rest? Is the lichen gardening? The rock pools? The pebbles washed up by the sea or even the drying tide on the rocks? Yes and yes and yes.

The plants on the rocks and around the rock pools near the sea are all natural. But Juan waters them all throughout the six baking, dry Chilean summer months and this encourages extra germination and growth. So the bromeliads, cacti and alstroemerias thrive and flower on the bare rocks. He moves plants – and stones and driftwood – and weeds and cuts the grasses back to stop them predominating. But his real skill is knowing when to do nothing. This is gardening of a very high order.

Gradually the rocks become covered by vegetation as you move away from the shore towards the house although the progression is seamless. He says that the house should be like another rock and every few years it is painted black to exactly match the colour of the lichen tidemark.

I asked him how he defines the difference between a garden and a natural landscape. 'Gardens,' he said, 'should always have a viewpoint. That is the one thing that makes them a garden. So a circle of trees in a wood becomes a garden or a seat positioned over a valley. My house is the viewpoint that creates this garden.' The approach to the house is almost entirely green, with the building tucked into this verdancy as a series of boxes broken by a huge stone wall. The sea is hidden. The green flows and swells like cloud topiary, a kind of tightly controlled bubbling of foliage. But as soon as you enter the building and look out, that greenness is overpowered by the blue of sea and sky. This is the view and the point of everything that frames it.

There are certain rules that Juan tries to follow. For example, all steps are hidden from the house so that you look out onto an unbroken landscape. This, of course, depends upon the quality of the landscape but essentially all paths and steps lead towards the house from the landscape and not the other way round, so that the connection of the viewer is immediate and without transition. I notice that all the paths are carefully softened by plants overflowing over their edges, so that in places the steps become treads between the plants rather than cutting through them.

Looking up to the house, either from the driveway on the land side or from the sea, it is all billows and mounds of vegetation, some natural, most clipped, providing structure. The landscape has no right angles at all and there are no hedges in the garden so the stone walls provide exactly the same crisp structure in the approach to the house that the house itself – all straight lines and right angles against a blue sky – does from the sea.

As you go through the glass door from the house you enter a walled space that is like another room of the house except that it has no ceiling and the floor is made of gravel. There is an open view to the sea but this is the same size as the big windows inside. The walls are identical to those inside the glass wall of the house and the plants and stone seem domestic, accessible. It is a brilliant transition, a seduction that is easy and natural but which otherwise could be a dramatic leap. The spiky leaves of a silvery *Puya* look wonderful but resist stroking – their looks suffice, especially with their pinky, magenta flowering stems, topped with artichoke-like heads bursting with violet flowers like electric pineapples.

The swimming pool is a circle edged with wooden boards, like a hole dropping down into the ocean. I am never sure about swimming pools, suspicious of the way that they can tip the sublime into the faintly ridiculous but this one sits comfortably within its ridiculously beautiful setting.

Juan is adamant that the single most important thing to know about any plant you are planning to grow in your garden is how it grows and propagates in the wild. If its seed is spread by wind then it should be planted in drifts rather than groups, whereas if the seed falls locally around the parent, then that is how it should be grouped in a garden. If the natural dispersal is in spirals then that is how he plants them in his gardens. This is the only way that you can achieve the integration and harmony with the landscape that is central to his design concept. Obviously to do this you must find out how your plants grow. His love of plants is very detailed and knowledgeable but as much for their sensual qualities as their botany. This is something that any gardener or designer in the British horticultural establishment would find hard to admit to. We are too often trapped in the science of horticulture and closed to its poetry. It is our loss.

Juan Grimm is not typical. He says that it is a very recent thing that Chileans are learning to value and use their native species in gardens. But, like the rest of South America, there is a palpable sense of something immensely creative happening. The combination of their extraordinary native flora and a creative tradition that springs from a South American identity is dynamic, and as exciting as anywhere in the world.

Following pages *Villa d'Este in Italy is dominated by water – there are over 250 waterfalls, fifty fountains and 255 jets, shooting several feet into the air. The eagle was part of the Este coat of arms and carvings of the birds decorate many of the fountains.*
Below *There cannot be a house in the world with a more spectacular position than Juan Grimm's home.*

I wanted to see how the two utterly different strands of civilisation, the Greco-Roman on the one hand and Islam on the other, expressed themselves in gardens and how they influence and affect the gardens of the twenty-first century.

5 Growing out of the Past

The Mediterranean

The Mediterranean

For anyone living in Northern Europe, the Mediterranean is our first choice of destination when we want sun, history and an entirely different landscape, flora and architecture. It is our neighbourly otherness, an easily accessible world that is different in almost every way to our own but not confusingly so. It is also the basis for our own civilisation with a huge Roman influence coming from Italy, the Islamic world – which is generally not acknowledged as having the influence that it does – coming via North Africa through Spain, and the Semitic and Greek civilisations also filtering through to our own.

But it is a huge area and range of cultures. In an ideal world I would have travelled literally around the Mediterranean basin in a circle, visiting gardens from Greece through Lebanon, Israel, Egypt, Libya, Morocco, Spain, France, Italy and perhaps the islands as well. If only. But that would have meant this book being called either *Round the Mediterranean in 80 Gardens* or perhaps *Round the World in 800 Gardens* and either way I would still be writing it in three years' time. It was just not logistically possible. Tough decisions had to be made. So I decided that what would interest me most was to see how the two utterly different strands of civilisation, the Greco-Roman on the one hand and Islam on the other, expressed themselves in gardens and how they influence and affect the gardens of the twenty-first century. Given the current tensions and misunderstandings between Christianity and Islam, this has an urgency that one would hardly associate with gardens. But they have been central to both cultures from their earliest days and we are fortunate that both have enriched and informed each other. It is not hard to find a glimmer of hope for our own civilisations there.

I began my trip by flying to Italy. When I told people this I was bombarded with suggestions of gardens that I had to visit. Everybody had their own shortlist but about six were included in all. I had time to visit just three. People who have never been involved in the process of filming are usually appalled at how slow it is and how long it takes. We worked flat out, never less than ten hours a day and often fourteen or fifteen, one day off every fortnight, and considered it a feat to have recorded enough for an hour's television in four weeks. Each garden took a minimum of two full days to film, often three, and travelling had to be fitted around this. So, given my line of enquiry, I decided to restrict myself to Hadrian's Villa, Villa Lante and Villa d'Este. I would then move on to Marrakech and visit the Islamic garden, the Aguedal, as well as Jacques Majorelle's modern garden – just because I like it. Finally I would take a train to Tangiers, cross the Straits of Gibraltar and go to the wonderful Islamic garden at the Alhambra at Granada, up to see the patio gardens in Córdoba and end my journey with a visit to the home of one of my heroes and one of the truly great living garden designers, Fernando Caruncho. There were huge gaps in that itinerary but nevertheless, as I set out, it felt like a pretty thrilling jaunt to me.

Hadrian's Villa

Tivoli, Rome, Italy

I LOVE ITALY. If I were to live anywhere in Europe outside my home, it would have to be in Italy. I love the food, the musical flow of the language, the climate, the landscape, the history, the art and architecture, the wine – did I mention the food? Apart from what we eat in my kitchen at home, it has the best food in the world. Going there is always a treat.

I was of a generation that learnt Latin at school from the age of eight. By the time we were twelve we were expected to be fluent in a language that had not been spoken in Britain for 1,500 years. The Romans left Britain completely in AD 436 yet their influence is still evident in every nook and cranny of modern British life from our language to our buildings, laws, roads and ways of thinking. However, ancient Roman monuments are few and far between in Britain and Roman gardens even rarer but in Italy archaeological sites are still everywhere and Villa Adriana – Hadrian's Villa – at Tivoli, just 15 miles outside Rome, is one of the largest and best preserved of them all. This was built as the Emperor Hadrian's retreat from Rome itself, although in the second half of his reign he also governed from there. It is called a 'Villa' but in reality it is a vast palace, on the size and scale of a small town. This is what struck me most when we arrived there. It is simply vast. The whole site is around 300 acres of which 100 acres have been excavated so far.

Hadrian, or Publius Aelius Traianus Hadrianus to give him his full name, ruled as emperor of the Roman Empire for twenty-one years from AD 117 to 138. He was born to a noble family and spent his childhood in Spain, although Trajan, the preceding emperor, took him under his wing and oversaw his subsequent military career. When Trajan died, Hadrian was named his successor, inheriting the Roman Empire at the peak of its power and wealth. It completely encircled the Mediterranean as well as modern Europe right across to the Black Sea and most of modern Turkey. Beneath him was a ruthlessly effective army and colonising system and unlimited wealth coming in from conquered territories. His power and wealth were unmatchable. On a personal level, he was learned and a patron of the arts. He built libraries, aqueducts, baths and theatres. More than half his reign was spent outside Italy, travelling through his empire and he visited Britain in AD 122 and initiated the building of Hadrian's Wall.

The scale of the site and ruins makes it hard to get an overview of what the villa must have been like in Hadrian's day but there is a model of it for visitors to see. This shows the strength of the axes and layout of the buildings linked always by avenues and lines of trees and water to make a coherent whole.

What is fascinating about this is how it might possibly be humanised. Magnificence is all very well when it comes to establishing power and authority but it does not fulfil the creative need for intimacy and a human scale. To be honest, this can't possibly be related to as a garden. However there are two parts of the villa that seem to be hugely influential.

The first is the Marine or Maritime Theatre. The theatre aspect has nothing to do with performance but refers to its construction. It is a round building with a moat running right round the inside of the walls that surround it. Fishes swim in the green water. Columns ring round both the inside and outside of the moat. Inside the moat is

Hadrian's Villa is also listed by UNESCO as a World Heritage site by virtue of its amazing combination of art and architecture, which, together with its gardens, represent a culture and civilisation that have long since gone.

The Serapeum has a peculiarly shaped dome which was sneeringly likened to a pumpkin. Hadrian never forgot the insult and the architect, Apollodorus of Damascus, was later exiled and executed.

a smaller building reached by crossing a bridge which was apparently a drawbridge in Hadrian's day. This meant that he could go in there and literally retreat from the rest of the world. So this little building – well, OK, grand, imperial, magnificent building that is relatively small compared with the enormous buildings all around it – was a moated retreat, within a building that was a private retreat within a villa that was a retreat from Rome. Now tawny grass grows on the ground of the circular ruin, the marble columns mostly stumps of themselves. But it is a strangely magical place, the sort of atmosphere where hushed voices seem appropriate and where you need time just to sit and take it all in – even though you are mostly unsure of what it is that you are absorbing.

The second part of the site that is particularly fascinating is the Canopus. This is a long rectangular lake, 131 yards long and 22 yards wide, flanked by steep wooded banks, with caryatids and statues, and once formed the open front of a covered walkway, with a building, the Serapeum, at the far end. It was built in a natural valley and was designed to mimic the Canopus canal that led from Alexandria to Canopus in the Nile Delta, where a temple was dedicated to Serapis.

Hadrian's Serapeum had a huge domed roof but was open to the water. It was used as a banqueting hall, with further guests arranged, according to their status, along the length of the Canopus. A complicated hydraulic system drew water up into the roof and created a sheet of water that fell between the diners inside the Serapaeum and the Canopus.

Now, of course, it is largely ruined, but just enough remains to give a hint both of the power and ingenuity of Hadrian's court as expressed in this water garden, for that is what it is, as well as the elegance and lightness of touch of it. The formality, ritual, symmetry and very controlled human organisation of space that acknowledges the spiritual world in many complex ways is all there still.

Apart from the insight into Roman imperial life at its peak, Hadrian's Villa, with its architecture, use of water and use of symbolism in buildings and statues, provided a model for Renaissance gardens that drew heavily upon Ancient Rome for sources and influences.

Villa d'Este

Tivoli, Rome, Italy

VILLA D'ESTE IS JUST A MILE or two down the road from Hadrian's Villa, up in the town of Tivoli itself. In fact Villa d'Este draws upon the much older buildings in more ways than one – not only does it get much inspiration but it also systematically nicked stones and even statues from there. It was built around an earlier Benedictine monastery in 1550 for Cardinal Ippolito d'Este, the son of Lucrezia Borgia and Alfonso d'Este and grandson of Pope Alexander VI. Ippolito d'Este was a bishop at the age of two, an archbishop at ten and a cardinal at thirty. The route to being pope seemed assured but he was defeated in this ambition by Julius III who effectively exiled d'Este by appointing him governor of Tivoli. This was supremely clever because Italian law stated that a governor could not leave his province. D'Este could see Rome on a clear day but could not physically go there. So for the remaining twenty years of his life he lived out his frustrated ambitions and dreams in Tivoli and expressed them in the creation of the garden.

Between 1550 and 1565 Pirro Ligorio, the papal architect, was hired to design and oversee the construction of the gardens. From the outset it was designed to rival the papal palace in Rome. The work to the garden was expanded and continued in the seventeenth century but in the eighteenth century the garden gradually decayed.

The Oval Fountain cascades down into a pool set against a rustic backdrop, with yet more small fountains inside the niches.

Villa d'Este is a place of exuberant water displays but my favourite is the most modest – the terrace of the Hundred Fountains.

It had a period of care in the nineteenth century but it was not until the 1920s, when it became the property of the Italian state, that proper restoration began and it was opened to the public. Maintenance and restoration work have continued since then, not least as a result of Allied bombing in 1944.

Ligorio's design was always intended to be overwhelmingly impressive, however rich and powerful the visitor might be. The garden was and is a combination of visceral magnificence, allegory, learning and history. He plundered the ruins of Hadrian's Villa and employed the best artists and craftsmen that money could buy.

The modern approach to the Villa d'Este from the town is modest, entering the courtyard sideways. The old convent building and the church are next door. But you were intended to come up to the house from the bottom of the garden, gradually rising up the steep slope with a crescendo of shock and awe as the garden revealed all its wonders to you, literally topped by the cardinal's palace. The reaction is to gasp and surrender to the power and ingenuity on display. It is 8 acres of lavish magnificence.

I came in from the bottom to experience the original reaction that the garden was designed to create. The entrance is grand but stylish and restrained. A high fountain is visible ahead but high flanking walls and an overhead canopy hide much of the view. The first thing I noticed was the murmur of water running in stone steps either side of the path. Two small grottoes, with rustic stonework tumble with water and ferns. The sound of the water slowly builds.

Then I came to the first formal water, the Rotunda of the Cypresses. It is still more or less modest within the terms of a grand palace. Two of the original cypresses remain, bent, broken-backed and lovely. Originally there were pavilions here but they are long gone.

The rotunda is on a flat piece of ground that is large and broad and it seems accessible – almost like a public park. But it is interesting that as soon as you go past the hedge dividing the fish ponds the whole garden shifts through a batch of gears. Everything is expanded beyond experience.

There are three rectangular fish ponds laid out in a series across the width of the garden and although a fourth was intended it was never built. They are lovely in themselves as well as practical for keeping the cardinal's household in fresh fish. One end of the terrace looks out over the landscape below but the other end dominates everything else. This is the Fountain of the Organ and the roar and spray of its water (deliciously cool on a hot day) overwhelm your senses – as, of course, they are intended to do. Water is the main theme of Villa d'Este and it is everywhere in the garden – there are reckoned to be 300 sluice gates, 255 waterfalls, 250 water jets, a hundred baths, sixty springs and fifty fountains – but this is its biggest watery showpiece. It reaches the basin at the bottom via six separate levels and has a series of powerful jets and fountains that operate vents in pipes and 'play' a tune. It all adds to the sense of theatre and performance that is at the centre of the garden. I watched as a sequence of lovers came and had their photographs taken in front of the fountain. It is clearly an Italian icon, a backdrop to pitch your life against.

The first steps (of many) rise ahead with cascades running down the bannisters to the next terrace with the Fountain of the Dragons and curved stairs sweeping round it up to the next level. The garden is very steep by now and each terrace high above the preceding one. But turn right along this terrace and you reach the Fountain of the Owl, which has been recently restored. Like all restorations it seems shockingly new – which is exactly as it was intended to be when made, although poor Cardinal d'Este can scarcely have seen it in its newness as he died in 1572 when it was still under construction. The garden took a long time and a huge sum of money to make – the engineering logistics must have been staggering. The Fountain of the Owl sends out dozens of jets of water into the courtyard when you step upon a hidden button on the ground, soaking innocent visitors from the sixteenth to the twenty-first century. A Baroque joke.

Back up to the next terrace, high above the entrance with views of distant fertile lands all around, you come to what I think is one of the world's great horticultural masterpieces, the Hundred Fountains. This runs the whole length of the terrace with a high bay hedge along the edge and a low box hedge at its base – in itself a good structural ploy – a mosaic path then a wide stone ledge or shelf against a rill running the entire length of the terrace, constantly filled by three levels of jets that pour into three stacked canals that flow down to the bottom one from the open mouths of gargoyles set into the retaining wall of the terrace above. This wall is covered in maidenhair fern. The Hundred Fountains spout up in the top layer of water. All these jets make a constant rumble and growl of water. It is simple enough but the repetition on such a scale is magnificent. It took five years to make and is 142 yards long. It is worth every moment and penny.

At one end of the terrace of the Hundred Fountains is the Rometta Fountain, but this was being repaired when I was there. However, at the other end is the Oval Fountain. This is set in a courtyard with the original plane trees, planted in 1575, and is curiously like a town square. It is dominated by the semi-circular fountain falling like a curtain into the large basin. I guess this is what Hadrian's Canopus must have been like – and the stone for it came from the same quarry. I was lucky enough to be allowed in behind this curtain of water, which of course would have been one of the main attractions for the private visitors to the garden. It is fun – a watery game.

The water for all this comes from the river and all the water displays in the garden are designed to work simultaneously without a single pump – although there is one now. The whole garden has the cumulative effect of a liquid firework display. I found myself almost audibly oohing and aahing as yet another fountain or hydrotechnics was revealed. This is exactly what you are meant to feel. D'Este is impressing his power, erudition, lineage and wealth onto you before you even step inside the Villa itself. The irony behind this is that the motivation behind this was the bitterness of frustrated power. If he had become pope he would certainly not have made this garden here. He might have made an excellent pope for all we know. But I am delighted that we have the garden instead.

Spouting gargoyles are hidden amongst the maidenhair fern of the Hundred Fountains.

Villa Lante

Bagnaia, Viterbo, Italy

Above *The* catena d'aqua *cascades down the long flight of steps, cooling the surrounding air as it goes.*
Opposite *Seen from the film crew's crane, the terrace is perfectly symmetrical, with the giant* Fontana dei Mori *in the centre of the large pool, which in turn is precisely in between the two casini, and separated from them by more carefully shaped box hedges.*

VILLA LANTE IS JUST on the edge of the impossibly picturesque town of Bagnaia, near Viterbo, about 100 miles north of Rome. The summer residence of the bishops of Viterbo was within the town walls, and at the end of the fifteenth century Cardinal Riario thought the palace too modest so built a villa on the hillside above the town. This was then redesigned in 1566 by Cardinal Gambara. The work is attributed to Giacomo Barozzi da Vignola although there is no contemporary documentation to support this. Part of the woods belonging to the old villa was turned into a formal garden with water flowing from a single fountain down through a series of pools, waterfalls, fountains and jets and only then draining into the town to become its drinking supply (although modern Bagnaia has its own separate supply).

It did not become known as Villa Lante until the villa was sold to the Duke of Lante in the seventeenth century, when it was already a hundred years old. In the nineteenth century the family, revived by an American heiress duchess, still lived at Lante in some style. In 1944 the gardens and buildings were heavily damaged by Allied bombing after the fall of Rome but in the late twentieth century the villa was acquired by Dr Angelo Cantoni, who completed a long programme of restoration.

It is generally acknowledged as the perfect archetype of the Italian Renaissance garden, exemplifying the central tenets of Renaissance artistic ideals. These were largely based upon a book called *De re aedificatoria libri X* (The Ten Books of Architecture), written by Leon Battista Alberti in 1485, which reawakened Italian architects to Roman and Greek theories of architecture. He evolved a theory of beauty in terms of mathematical symmetry and proportion. He wrote that 'everything that Nature produces is regulated by the law of harmony, and her chief concern is that everything should be perfect. Without harmony this could hardly be achieved, for the critical sympathy of the parts would be lost.'

This theory was widely taken up by Renaissance architects, and proportion and perspective were applied to both house and garden where they worked together as an entity and were linked to the landscape in a way that had not been done in earlier, more violent medieval periods when castles and towns were essentially fortified places and the outside landscape potentially hostile.

You approach the garden through the wandering streets of Bagnaia, having stopped for a cappuccino and bun in the square. Originally the entrance to the garden was from the top where the park was and I strongly advise you to resist going directly into the garden at the bottom, but instead to take the route up the side of the garden so that you too work your way down from the top.

Holm oaks and olives grow up within the colonnades so that stone and wood mirror each other. The garden is surrounded by trees and there is a distinct feeling of *A Midsummer Night's Dream* about the place – mysterious and wonderful things could and probably did happen here. Classical loggias with wall paintings of the Muses flank a grassy, square grotto backed by rusticated stonework with fern-filled niches spouting water into a basin. Green algae mirrors the green of the ferns. It is empty save for a sun that is already too hot for comfort. Then, wholly unexpected, water jets from the eaves of both flanking pavilions, filling the little court with a fine arching spray. Well, it wasn't

a surprise and probably doesn't happen for every visitor but we asked them to do it for the cameras. Certainly the cardinal's guests would have had the shower. Unlike the Owl Fountain at Villa d'Este, this is more of a watery performance than a prank. It certainly transforms the whole end of the garden and is very lovely. There is a sense of nature tamed but not crushed. It is not the enemy yet it must be kept firmly under control.

The garden only has one route. Follow the water. It goes to a hugely ornate Dolphin Fountain that is surrounded by stone seats against a box hedge and shaded by trees. Originally there was a lattice pavilion here but that has long disappeared. The water pours out of dozens of spouts as well as the fountain on top; busy, rushing, moving fast.

Thick green box hedges flank steps down the hill and in the middle of the steps is a *catena d'aqua*, an amazing cascade made from stone, raised up above the steps in a series of swirling arabesques. The water tumbles down but is contained and formalised. The green box is in great slabs at the side of it. The air as you walk down the steps is cooled by the water. It is a lovely conceit, water held solid as part of architecture and stone made liquid by the constant play and movement of the water.

It gets better. The water flows through the head of a giant crayfish, the symbol of Cardinal Gambara and you realise that the cascade is in fact its body. It tumbles into a large basin, the Fountain of the Giants, where two huge stone figures recline, representing the two great rivers the Tiber and the Arno. Below it is a huge stone table, nearly nineteen of my paces long with a rill running down its centre. Guests would dine here with dishes of fruit and desserts kept cool as they floated in the middle of the table. It is a theatrical masterpiece, not intimidating but inviting, the best possible setting for an outdoor party, inviting admiration rather than awe.

Down another level and another fountain and some misplaced nineteenth-century planting – this garden does not need flowers or colour. Stone, water, wood and foliage is entirely sufficient. There are greys, ochres, greens and the intense blue of the sky both

The large stone block was used as an al fresco dining table with dishes floating on the water in the central canal to keep them cool.

above and reflected in the water. More colour would merely add business to a garden that is wonderfully integral and complete.

But it is by no means finished. On this level are two almost identical casinos, perfectly cubed buildings that flank a descent down to the large bottom terrace. Originally there was just one of these, the second being added thirty years later. Below them is the square parterre, complicated box and yew geometry, infilled with red stone and sand, surrounding another, final, large fountain in the middle of a large square pool. The central area is reached by crossing four bridges, and a centre basin contains the *Fontana dei Mori* by Giambologna: four life-sized figures standing square around two lions; they hold the heraldic mountain surmounted by the star-shaped fountain jet, the Montalto coat of arms. The stone is blackened and the statue has long been known as 'the Four Moors' as a consequence.

This parterre seems typical of many that one sees, balanced and strong in concept and structure but in fact it is amongst the first ever made – the culmination of the entire garden with the town butted up to the wall at its far edge ready to receive the water now that the garden has finished with it.

The whole garden is balanced, controlled and harmonious yet without any sense of restriction or tightening of natural forces. It is a place at ease with itself. It is a place of comfortable, not to say, luxurious, peace. But unlike so many grand houses and gardens, I came away with a sense of generosity and enrichment.

It also sets the tone for almost all that has followed in northern European gardens right up to the present day. The mixture of balance, clear axes, a degree of integration with the surrounding countryside and habitation and yet seclusion from it, and above all a sense of the garden as part of a balanced cultural and intellectual life – something that everyone in Europe with money or aspiration to status has tried to emulate since the Renaissance.

However there was another equally strong influence in the Mediterranean that flowered long before the Renaissance. To see the roots of that I had to leave Italy and go to North Africa, to the Berber city of Marrakech.

The Aguedal

Marrakech, Morocco

The Aguedal is so vast that all the gardeners need bicycles to get around.

MARRAKECH IS CHANGING FAST. Ten years ago, when I first visited, it was well adapted to tourists, with superb hotels and restaurants, but it still felt like an African city. Camels and carts pulled by donkeys outnumbered cars. Almost everybody wore Arab dress, either the long, hooded burnous or jellaba and you felt that you were seeing a completely different culture. Now hotels are being thrown up everywhere, expensive cars fill the streets and Western dress is much more common. However, it is still a fascinating city and this new Westernisation is clearly good for some, although it ignores the virtues of a local culture and, in the case of Morocco, one that is incredibly old, rich and sophisticated. The original occupants of the country were the Berbers, which simply means not-arab, but in the seventh century the Arabs expanded west and introduced Islam and its highly conceptualised gardens.

Marrakech, 100 miles from the coast, in the plain below the Atlas Mountains, might seem an odd destination for an exploration of Mediterranean gardens. But it was hugely influential on the gardens of Spain and we also tend to undervalue the role that Islamic gardens had on the gardens of the rest of Europe. The city was founded in 1062 by the Almoravid Dynasty, rulers of the nomadic Sanhaja Berbers, and was primarily a city of gardens. Two-thirds of the medina – the central walled city – was orchard or garden and it remained that way until the 1920s.

One type of North African Islamic garden that became common was the aguedal – large fruit gardens laid out in conventional Islamic squares with irrigation channels dividing them. These were pleasure gardens and often had pavilions but their primary role was as an orchard and they were highly productive.

The Aguedal in Marrakech is the world's oldest unchanged garden. There was some restoration work done in the nineteenth century but everything that you see dates from the twelfth century. It is in the middle of the city, just south of the Royal Palace and open to the public on Thursdays and Sundays when people come and have picnics under the trees. There are lots of trees to sit under. It is essentially a series of orchards with a large tank of water at the centre. Really large. The 'tank' is a large lake, 200 of my paces square – roughly 10 acres. The water for it is bought in by canals from the Atlas Mountains, whose snowy peaks in the 40°C heat are just visible, 15 miles away. These canals were made nearly 1,000 years ago and still work as well as they did then. In medieval times the tank was the source of drinking water for the city, and before the Arab invasions of Europe the landlocked armies of Marrakech used it as a training ground for their ships.

The vastness of the Aguedal is perhaps best understood by the very beautiful exterior wall of peach-coloured mud, crenellated and revetted, that runs for almost 8 miles. This is typically Islamic in that, although fortified, it is modest and plain and does not hint at the luxury of water and fruit within.

There are many gateways and entrances but the main one is approached by a long, dusty earthen track and has a simple but very beautiful pavilion at the end, with date palms and cypresses. Everything is a bit scruffy, a bit neglected. There is no money. The pavilion was traditionally for viewing the garden from the shade of an upper floor. It needs repair, at least to stop it deteriorating further.

I found myself looking for signs of recognisable garden features but you have to abandon the European concept of what a garden should be. Here function has beauty. Water has intrinsic beauty and is an indicator of wealth. Fruit and fragrance have great beauty. Blossom is beautiful in itself but more so as the precursor of fruit. Everything has a usefulness that enhances its aesthetic attraction.

Go round beyond the pavilion and a causeway leads to a ramp up onto the walkway around the main tank. Irrigation channels run either side and these stretch out across the entire site. The water is a breathtaking sight. The planting of the orchard is based around fig, date, pomegranate, almond, citrus, apricot and olive trees. The citrus was introduced later from China but all the positions of the other fruit trees have remained unchanged since the garden was built 900 years ago – although the individual trees have obviously been replaced many times. I was lent a bike and cycled round the orchard blocks on the tracks dividing them, irrigation ditch along every one, mud walls dividing many. To pedal gently between apricot and pomegranate groves is an astonishingly beautiful experience and unlike anything I had seen before. It has none of the mercantile philistinism of a European commercial orchard and is yet a scale beyond any garden.

I was taken down to one side of the ramp and shown the incredibly well-preserved eleventh-century brick sluice system that channels the water from the tank into the irrigation ditches. They are still the only means of watering the garden. Like everything else it needs repair and were it in Europe it would be hailed as one of the great historical monuments. But then were it in Europe I would not be allowed to get down in the ditch and have a really good look at it without officialdom interfering. This brick irrigation system is one of the great monuments of the world and the guide told me that they only need the equivalent of £1 million to repair the water systems but he has no hope that the money will be forthcoming any time soon. The garden is of international cultural importance on a par with Versailles or Villa d'Este yet needs a fraction of the money that these places require just to maintain them. One cannot help but think that the West undervalues Islamic culture and is ignorant of it. We should be ashamed of ourselves.

The water tank at the centre of the garden is so huge that it used to be used for naval manoeuvres.

Jardin Marjorelle

Marrakech, Morocco

BEFORE I LEFT MARRAKECH to follow the path of Islamic gardens up into Spain I went to a twentieth-century garden that has had a huge influence on contemporary European gardens. It was a hot, clear morning and the medina, where I was staying in a small and lovely riyad, was surprisingly quiet. But then there is no traffic in there and traffic always makes everything worse.

Jardin Marjorelle is a relict from the 1920s and 30s when the French influence was at its peak in Marrakech. France made Morocco a protectorate in 1912 (Morocco did not become an independent kingdom until 1956) and wealthy, liberal French came to the city for its sun, culture and frankly relaxed attitude to sexual behaviour. One of these visitors was Jacques Marjorelle, a painter from Nancy who came there to improve his health in 1917 and stayed there until his death in 1962.

Jacques Marjorelle travelled in the Atlas Mountains and southern deserts and was struck by the Berber habit of outlining window frames and the interior of alcoves with a particular shade of deep, cobalt blue. He bought a plot of land in 1924 and built a house and studio there and in 1931 laid out the gardens and, significantly, painted the studio the same shade of Berber blue that he had seen in the Atlas Mountains. This was then an extremely radical thing to do and provided a unique backdrop to Marjorelle's collection of plants. He was an obsessive plant collector, financing plant hunting expeditions and specialising in cacti and succulents and palms – all of which dominate the garden.

Originally Marjorelle's garden was about twice the size of that the public has access to today, but what we now see is the heart of his plant collection. Normally the words 'plant collection' fill me with dread. They very, very rarely make good gardens. Jardin Marjorelle is the exception to the rule.

The garden is laid out along local Moroccan principles for agricultural land and riyads, which is to have small areas sunk below raised paths so that the beds can be flooded to irrigate them. The paths and edges to the beds are of painted concrete, with blue used for the edges and a rich, very Marrakech pinky-red for the surface of the plants. Pots are painted a brilliant lemon-yellow. The paints are all very matt so the pigment soaks up light, giving it extra intensity. In 1981 the French fashion designer Yves St Laurent bought the garden and added a shade of particularly unappealing green to the pots which is a mistake. It doesn't work because it dilutes the intensity of the yellow and blue and, because it is a combination of these two colours (although an actual mixture would give a very different green), it forces you to modify how you see them. It also modifies all the colours of the foliage.

But this is the only thing about the garden I didn't like. It is an exhilarating, exuberant, life-enhancing place. I visited on a cloudy day on my first trip to Marrakech and the colours were flat. This time, under a clear blue sky even the shadows glowed. When I was last there, in February, not only was it grey but the garden was dry and sparse. Now, in early summer, it was lush and the greenness of the foliage, even in this desert city, is essential to get the full experience.

It might have been added by Yves St Laurent, but personally I find that the green of the pots, here filled with a large Epiphyllum, *weakens the startling effect of the blue walls.*

The blue and the scale of how it is used are genuinely big ideas. Most of the garden is green on blue but a spray of bougainvillea flares bright pink against the blue of the studio wall. Shocking blue and shocking pink and there, by the steps into the studio, a vast, egg-shaped, shocking yellow pot filled with deep purple foliage. You feel like applauding out loud.

Around a square pool with a fountain in the centre cacti grow in every form and shape possible, all planted in the local pink gravelly sand. The glaucous green of the cacti are cool and balance the intensity of the paints. I have never been a huge fan of cacti as a gardener although when I have come across them in the desert they are always beautiful and often monumental. What makes them work as part of the garden here is not their variety – however fascinating that might be for cacti growers – but the scale in which they are planted. It is all of a piece with the garden as a rich, intense performance.

As well as as bananas, cycads, jacarandas, sago and date palms, the garden has dozens – scores – of hugely tall palms rocketing up free of the garden. They are the roof of the garden and these, along with the bamboos and the upright prickly columns of the cacti, are what give the garden its structure. There is a layout but you are never really aware of it. It might as well be one bed with concrete walkways in amongst it. But this vertical structure is like a garden laid on its side, transforming it into something more than a collection of plants with very bright paint into a tall cathedral of a garden with the intense colours like stained glass. Much is made of the Moroccan influence on Marjorelle but I suspect that the Catholic influence was as strong, albeit perhaps subconscious. Despite this the garden is curiously unspiritual. It is a garden of earthly delights rather than of the soul.

It is a crowded garden with an endless trail of trippers paying homage to the blue. Well, I was one of them, blocking their path with a film crew. But go early and get ahead of the crowds and just relish the playful intensity of it. Jacques Majorelle was an uninspired painter that made his garden his masterpiece. A thousand names are graffitied into the stems of the larger bamboos like Polynesian tattoos. Mine too now.

The Alhambra

Granada, Spain

The gardens at Generalife were designed as a sheltered summer retreat from the hurly-burly of the court in the main Alhambra palace.

I FIRST VISITED THE ALHAMBRA in February 2005. Sarah and I stayed for three whole days at the Parador in the grounds of the palace, and spent every daylight minute exploring the gardens and buildings. The weather was clear and bitterly cold and great lumps of ice floated in the canals and basins and the orange trees were yellow and curled in upon themselves and when we drove up the Sierra Nevada, just above Granada, the road was blocked with snow. Now, returning in midsummer it was a parched, even scorched landscape but the Alhambra, with its fountains and green hedges and trees, was blissfully cool.

The significance of the Alhambra in European gardens – as if being life-changingly beautiful and one of the great treasures of the earth is not enough – is that it represents the heyday and last bastion of Moorish rule in Europe. Granada was founded in the eighth century on the site of a Roman settlement and until 1234 it was part of Moorish Spain. The Christians then retook a huge chunk of northern Spain and Granada became the capital of the remaining Arab territories, now called the Kingdom of Granada. It flourished as a centre for learning and trade for the next 300 years, up to and beyond the final expulsion of the Moors from the European mainland. What we see now at the Alhambra was largely built in the late fourteenth century – consolidating 600 years of Islamic European culture. Although all the standing buildings have been hugely restored and repaired with varying degrees of embellishment and imagination, it remains one of the oldest Islamic gardens and the only medieval one extant in the West. It is also 300 years older than any garden remaining in Britain.

While the Christian Spanish destroyed most of the Arab cities of Seville, Toledo and Córdoba when they conquered them, the Alhambra was untouched save for an enormous church and the unfinished Renaissance palace building of Charles V. The Alhambra is not a palace or coherent garden. It is a fortified site containing a series of palaces, a military fort and, at one time, a medina with over 2,000 people working in a muddle of tiny streets. There were twenty-two sultans and they all made additions and changes to the site. From the outside, it is a large, bare fortress. But from the inside it is a small city linked by a series of exquisite gardens and buildings containing extraordinary riches.

To understand the Alhambra you have to set everything into the context of the Islamic faith and the notion of paradise as a garden. We metaphorically talk of a lovely garden being 'a little bit of paradise' but the Islamic gardens were specifically created to be just that. The exterior of the Alhambra is plain to the point of functional austerity but the interior of the buildings and the gardens that they are wrapped around are embellished and decorated to jewel-like intensity. The magic is that they also have dignity and profundity of space and form. They know when utter simplicity is everything.

Originally the connections between buildings and garden were umbilical and now hedging is used – almost exclusively box, myrtle and cypress – to delineate the positions of the walls of buildings no longer standing, although this tends to give the modern Alhambra a false sense of shared, public gardens. Originally this was never the case. Gardens lay concealed within the courtyards, places of private pleasure and as intimately connected to the buildings and their occupants as any of the rooms.

The Alhambra is a living reminder of Spain's Moorish past and also of the importance of the Islamic influence in Europe.

Water, of course, features everywhere. The timing of the buildings – mainly from the middle of the thirteenth century to the middle of the fourteenth – coincides with the development of irrigation. Andalucía is dry and cold in winter and hot and dry in summer. It seems an unbelievably harsh landscape. But the soil is very fertile and there are springs and rivers and when the soil is irrigated it is rich and productive. So harnessing the water for pleasure was the ultimate expression of power and control. If you have water and control over the supply then you have absolute power.

The extraordinary thing about the site is that it has no water of its own. All the water that fills dozens of ponds and innumerable rills and fountains is taken from the hill above the Generalife – the summer palace of the Islamic rulers across a valley from the Alhambra – and pumped into reservoirs before being channelled to the Alhambra. The water splashing down steps and through conduits cut into marble-floored rooms is a display of wealth that could not be more impressive had it been molten gold.

Seeing the Alhambra in midwinter was to see it austere and stripped of its finery. It was largely empty and I had total, unfettered twenty-four hour access. It will remain as one of the best garden experiences of my life. This time it was hot, crammed with tourists (it has over 2 million visitors every year) and the garden was lush and fulsome with growth. If before I had seen it in private, this was the full, sumptuous public performance.

The place is huge. Even having spent four days there now, I still feel as though there is more to see. But certain parts stand brightest in my memory. The Patio de Comares had been still, frozen on my last visit. Now, on a midsummer dusk, swifts were nesting in the intricate plaster fretwork and screaming round the courtyard by the hundred. The white marble of the paving shone like water. The water of the long central canal was black, reflecting shadows. The myrtle hedges had an immensely satisfying substance, one that I have encountered again and again around the world when a hedge is wider than its height. These long low ramparts of myrtle, now over a hundred years old, are as good examples as any I have seen. The Patio de Comares is very simple. In its Moorish heyday it would have had carpets hanging from windows, cushions on the ground, and there may have been orange and lemon trees in pots. Early fifteenth-century writings speak of the decadence of having oranges growing in the courtyard of the Comares Palace. This was because oranges – what we now call Seville oranges – were so bitter as to be practically inedible until sweet oranges were introduced from China in the sixteenth century. So they were grown simply for their fragrance and visual beauty. But the virtues of modesty in exteriors holds true. Inside the buildings the ornate richness is staggering. Outside, the luxury is one of coolness, privacy, light and water.

The Partal Palace gives us the best examples of an Islamic garden in Europe. The building is perfectly balanced with one side looking down over Granada and the other opening and reflecting fully into a large square pool. It is matchless, unimprovable. The water is fed into the pool from a series of higher tanks and rills, running sweetly through mosaicked cobbled paths, down the centre of steps into channels and then into the pool.

Then there is the Generalife. There is so much more physically in between but go there, see for yourself. Let me just give you a taste of the place. The Generalife can be seen from the main palace as a series of sculptural, architectural blocks of hedging on the other side of the valley with spires of cypress behind. It was the Sultan's hunting lodge with orchards and vegetable gardens for the palace. These are still there, still productive. From 1429 to 1921 it was private, held by the same family. Then in 1931 a new garden was made and in 1951 another. When I was there in summer 2006 a huge musical auditorium was being added to it. It sounds a sacrilege but it looks wonderful.

In essence it is a series of clipped cypress walks containing water features, rose beds, and the ornate, almost mosaicked, pebbled paths that thread through the whole of the 30-plus acre site. We tend to think of the cypress, *Cupressus sempervirens*, as a slim dark spire marking verticals on a bleached landscape but it also makes a really good clipped hedge – although global warming probably needs a few more years before it could be considered as suitable for northern European gardens. Because they tend to grow tall and fastigiated they make the perfect plant to mimic the walls of missing parts of the palace and to create green corridors, much narrower and taller than one is used to seeing in a garden. The spaces they enclose are all small too, with hedges often as high as the enclosed space is wide. It is a key lesson of good garden design and essential for shade in Andalucía.

The famous avenue of water spouts along the central canal in the garden court of the Generalife is very unlikely to be an original Moorish feature, beautiful as it certainly is. Too noisy. Generalife was a sensuous place for holidays, to escape the intrigue of court. The whole point of the original gardens was to create a place where colour, form and scent could be harmoniously savoured with the added backdrop of music. This was a vital element and the noise of fountains of any kind other than a discrete bubbling or splash would have competed with it. But the water running down the bannisters on the steps up to the mosque is original, dating back to the fourteenth century. As you walk up the steps to prayer the water cools the air and provides a means of washing your hands and face. Nothing could be simpler or, 700 years on, more entrancing.

There is so much here. So much to see, so much to say. But I leave on a section of the Alhambra that was never intended, and is not part of any historical past beyond the last few decades. This is the box nursery on the path up to Generalife, where perhaps an acre of box plants have been left to grow out into one undulating green landscape. Abstract, simple, and completely satisfying.

The Alhambra is a vast palace and this is one of many towers scattered through the complex of gardens.

The Patios of Córdoba

Córdoba, Spain

Every inch of the walls of the patio courtyards are covered in plants both clinging to the walls and growing in pots hanging from the stonework.

THE ROAD FROM GRANADA to Córdoba takes you deeper into a European Islamic past, one which is older in this part of Spain than Christianity. I kept this thought rolling round my mind as we drove north-west, the enormity of it and the paucity of our understanding of our Islamic heritage both staggering. Mind you, as you motor through mile upon mile of modern olive plantations and the semi-industrial landscape of monocultures and processing plants, it is easy to forget the detailed sophistication of Islamic agriculture.

Córdoba was founded by the Romans as the capital of the province of Hispania (where Hadrian came from) and was the capital of the Umayyad Dynasty and a centre of learning, especially for philosophy. In the eleventh century the Berber dynasty of the Almoravides and Almohades – who built Aguedal – reunified it and linked it to Morocco. In 1236, it was recaptured by the Catholic Spanish, followed ten years later by the other great Moorish city, Seville. The remaining Arab population fled to the Moorish stronghold of Granada, ruled from the Alhambra.

There are reports from the tenth century of thousands of gardens in and around Córdoba. There still are but the chief feature of them is that they are patio or courtyard gardens. As people came from the countryside to live in Córdoba, looking for work, especially from the nineteenth century, families would occupy a room or two of the large square buildings built around courtyards on three or four floors. Due to the level of overcrowding and the climate, these patios became communal living spaces where people washed, ate and entertained each other. They also became communal gardens with a few plants, nearly always in pots, and perhaps a tree for shade and a climber to grow up the inside of the walls.

In the late twentieth century these communal buildings became rarer as Spain became more affluent and more people could afford to live in self-contained homes. But many still choose to share their patios and many still treat the courtyard as their garden and spend an important part of their lives in that space.

Since 1932, in an effort to promote the patio gardens, there has been a contest to find the best patio garden. This has become a festival that lasts over a weekend and inspires great feats of horticultural display as well as much exuberant partying. We had timed our visit to coincide with this festival.

It was my first visit to Córdoba and the demands of visiting as many patios as possible – and filming them – meant that I did not see as much of it as I would have liked. It is a city I would love to return to. The idea of the festival is for people to walk round the city visiting as many patios as possible. Some are very small and intimate, others are grand. All are decked out in floral finery. Although you enter from the street by small doorways into an enclosed, almost monastic, space, there is a sense of the patios being part of street life. People go from one to the other. The doors are always open. In one that we visited the building had been bought communally by a group of friends, each with their own family. They were laying a large table in the patio when we arrived and shared a delicious meal with us. Wine was drunk. Pots of pelargonium hung from the wall – a common theme in almost all the patios – and a large jacaranda tree gave shade.

Another patio was one of the oldest in Córdoba, small, lived in and tended by an old woman who had grown up there as part of a large family, with pure white-painted walls and over a hundred pelargonium, each in a terracotta pot painted bright blue. Shades of Marjorelle.

We visited one patio at midnight. The gardens were open all night and people came from restaurants and bars, dropped in and admired them in the same way that they might visit an art gallery. This particular one was clearly acknowledged as a tour de force and there was a queue to enter. Men, women and children. When did you last see children queuing to see a garden? When did you last see British people doing something as a family, all ages unselfconsciously together, thoughtfully, respectfully celebrating their local heritage? And at midnight? Lights lit the plants. Petunias, pelargonium, ferns, banana, white jasmine, a bougainvillea. Warm midnight laced with scent. A band came down the street drawing a crowd behind, dancing, swaying and moving on to the next garden.

There was no sense of corporate branding or the city marketing this – although they do. The organising hand could not have been lighter. The patios displayed themselves because they felt worthy of display. A shared climate, culture and history make it possible and cohesive. And the extraordinary thing is that all the hundreds of patios do seem to make 'a' garden. I could have taken one at random to illustrate that but that would have been to have missed the point. They are the fruits of a community, both on an individual level and collectively. And they are marvellous.

Pelargoniums are a feature of all Córdoba patios jostling with each other for space in the courtyard and on the walls.

Casa Caruncho

Madrid, Spain

I HAVE A CONFESSION. A few years ago I arranged to go to Madrid to interview a garden designer whose work, although I had seen it only through pictures, I greatly admired. I planned to interview him for the newspaper that I then wrote for. He was, I assumed, a bright young thing who inhabited a world rather like the most famous fashion designers. It was November and all I could do to get dressed in the mornings. At the last moment I felt that I could not face either him, the journey or the brightness, the youth, the thingness. I cancelled the interview. Fernando Caruncho's office – for it was he – were polite and understanding. Another time perhaps.

Well, now I was in a train from Córdoba having had a few hours' sleep, heading for Madrid to see him at his home. This was that other time. I admired his work beyond measure. It seemed to combine a feeling for landscape, gardens, spirituality and philosophy that was immediately exciting and inspiring. He had that magic that transcended the merely attractive or interesting. This was art.

The train journey was more than just a means of transport, albeit an astonishingly comfortable, fast and efficient one. In Britain catching a train always seems a risky, rather random thing to do – a punctual, problem-free journey is the exception rather than the rule. This one was beautifully smooth, and took me from Islam, the Arab influence, the patios and their evolution, from the industrialisation of rural Spain, to the twenty-first century and a modern master. The changes in the landscape outside the train window were extraordinary. Between Granada and Córdoba there had been the most industrialised agricultural landscape I had ever seen. Now there was cork forest literally as far as the eye could see on both sides of the train. The ground beneath was grazed and growing under it a shimmer of lavender, like bluebells, in countless acres.

Madrid railway station alone is worth the journey, with a huge lush palm house made from the old railway concourse. Bananas, palms and ferns that you could walk through and sit and have a cup of coffee beneath – and of course the nineteenth-century cast-iron old station is exactly like Kew Palm House. Stunning. We got a taxi to Caruncho's house on the outskirts of Madrid.

The house is on an estate of large houses, very Californian. There was, oh horror, even a golf course. My heart sank. But I need not have worried. The house and its site were modest in scale but thrillingly beautiful in every detail. The exterior of the house is painted an ochreish orange and is windowless. It is warm, strong but closed, balanced between modesty and hostility. A courtyard with clipped hedges and a pool of clipped escallonia before it and large steps leading to a door. A canal of water runs along the base of the wall with spouts gently jetting into it. I ring the bell and Caruncho himself greets me. He is a warm, modest, handsome man and seems to be my age, perhaps a little older. Not young, not bright – although intellectually brilliant – and as much a fogey as me.

If I had thought the Islamic world had been left behind, I was wrong. Caruncho explains to me that the entrance courtyard, small and empty, with a rose-covered mesh wall and doors off on either side is based upon the idea of the Islamic entrance as a kind of half-way stage between outside and the home. Space is collapsed and made intimate.

The back of the house opens immediately onto a pond with sculptured contours of topiarised escallonia rising up to a summer house facing the main building.

The walls are painted the same colour as the outside. It is a box of apricot light. The mesh squares divide the garden beyond into a leafy grid.

We go left through the main living room and out onto a patio with room for a table and passageway, massive square columns, a mesh roof supporting wisteria and a large pond seemingly filling the entire space that the house wraps around. On the other side of the water is a bank, with a summer house on top of it facing the main building. Escallonia, clipped into flowing unbroken contours, covers

I liked Fernando Caruncho enormously and found we have a very similar outlook on garden design – we like to let the garden find itself, rather than impose a preconceived plan onto the land.

the bank. Everything is very simple, very strong and the effect is incredibly subtle.

We sit on the patio to talk, his twelve-year old son Pedro translating although in fact Caruncho's English is very good. He told me that he trained as a philosopher and when reading Euripides he realised that the Greeks made no difference between man and nature. A garden was a magical place to attract the gods. Modern gardens are protected places where God might be present. This is at the core of all good gardens.

He was also strongly influenced by the summers that he had spent with his grandparents at their house in Ronda where there was a magical view to the mountains. 'Views, the scent of summer and light have always been an obsession with me and at the centre of my work.'

He is intense, poetic, wistful and modest, and there is something almost very old-fashioned and slightly innocent about him. But he does not see himself as a creator. 'No. I am a facilitator. All gardens are inside people. That is where they begin and end. Everyone has their inner gardener. Gardens reach the inner gardener in everyone and bring them out.

'When I go to design a new garden I arrive without any plan or ideas. I spend perhaps a week before my first visit to the site preparing myself, but mentally, spiritually, not artistically. I listen to Bach, do not talk very much. I try to go as empty as possible and let the garden find me. Usually it takes about two to four hours until I find the garden. I am only a medium for this. Everything follows on from this.'

He is very matter of fact and modest about this. Without doubt he is one of the true geniuses of garden design but he says, 'All gardening is simple. Planting should be simple. All gardening should be fun. You must do what the poet Pope said – "consult the genius of the place". The invisible thing is always the most important part of a garden. If you use memory, communal history and your subconscious and try not to think, it will come. You have to let the hand do it alone.'

This is so exactly my own experience and belief that I am almost bouncing in my seat in agreement, but it is a million miles from the prosaic pragmatism of most British gardening. I point out that many would find this very intellectual or even abstract. 'But,' he says, 'it is important to tend the garden oneself. You have to have that intimacy with the plants, to really know how they grow before you can design with them.'

We walk round to the other side of the garden to the pavilion on top of the bank made from the spoil excavated for the pond. The height of the mound, the pavilion itself and the house across the water is carefully calibrated so that he can sit and see the mountains and landscape beyond the plain around Madrid. It is his childhood and the visions of the light on the mountains by his grandparents' house returning.

His own garden is restrained, smallish and refined right down. His obsession with the grid appears in the mesh he uses as screens both on walls and ceilings and in the shapes created by the architecture but it is not as evident here as in many of his commissioned works where a grid of pools, tiny fields, courtyards or flat-topped or undulating blocks of green recur again and again like a musical motif. He is famous for much larger, grander schemes such as the famous Mas de las Voltes with its grid of wheat and olives, cypresses and square pools, or Mas Floris, which extends to 25 acres.

I ask him how he works with his clients, how he compromises his beliefs with their requirements? He seems surprised at the question. 'I treat each garden as my own. They always accept it without modification. I never compromise on the design once I have found it.' And what of the subsequent upkeep? He said that all his clients – often enormously wealthy bankers and businessmen, for his gardens are not cheap – end up becoming gardeners themselves and guiding the spirit of the garden.

But then he adds, 'But the gardener must always be less than the garden.' Aware of the film crew and the way that British television has made icons of its TV gardeners I cringe a little, embarrassed and yet longing to go home to lose myself to my own garden, fired, inspired and enriched by this meeting. Which, after saying goodbye and taking taxi, plane and car, is exactly what I do.

On the flight home I consider the journey I have made. I have glimpsed into the extraordinary voluptuous riches of Ancient Rome at Hadrian's Villa, carried on by the Renaissance combination of power and clergy at Villa d'Este and made purer and simpler in the integral perfection of Villa Lante. The fruits of this certainly carry on into the twenty-first century in British gardening but without any of the classical symbolism that is so essential to these three gardens. We have lost all that. This means our gardens have influence without the spiritual core that drove these great Italian gardens.

The Islamic gardens are of a level of sophistication that we can scarcely emulate today. They do not have the weight of allusion behind them but an incredibly rich spiritual resonance that is reflected in very material ways – the handling of light, colour and space. Again, with our modern obsession with plant clutter we can seem to have learnt very little from that although I am sure it has influenced us more than we are aware or acknowledge. The patios have a vitality and communality that is entirely hopeful and that I have seen in allotments and in hanging baskets and window boxes on the streets of cities like Nottingham. But our grey and cold climate does not lend itself to communal, outdoor lives for much of the year.

Finally my visit to the great Fernando Caruncho was both inspiring because it reinforced the fact that gardens can be completely modern and also because it showed that without spirituality they become just an arrangement of plants. From Hadrian, through Berber Marrakech to the flowing euonymus contours of Caruncho's garden in Madrid, one thing that he said resonated with me all the way back to my own garden in Herefordshire and seemed as a result of this trip to be truer than ever: 'The invisible thing is always the most important part of a garden.'

Following pages
The Garden Vineyard on the Mornington Peninsula, outside Melbourne, Victoria, successfully combines British gardening tradition with a modern Australian use of native plants such as Rhagodia spinescens *and* Westringia fruticosa.

I wanted to see how the colonisation of the continent manifested itself in gardens and how that had evolved into modern, twenty-first century Australia.

6 Becoming Themselves

Australia and New Zealand

Australia

I had visited Australia a couple of times before, both with the BBC on filming trips. Neither were ostensibly about gardening but, even under the auspices of the *Holiday* programme and *Tomorrow's World* I had loved what I had seen and experienced. On one occasion, I was given a day off and spent it in the Royal Botanic Gardens in Sydney, a most beautiful location for any urban public garden. This was over ten years ago but I knew that I wanted to come back and that I wanted to find out more about it.

The vast majority of Australian homes are new. The vast majority have gardens, big ones by European standards. There is a healthy garden culture. But drive around or fly over the miles of suburbs and there is not much evidence of actual gardening. In other words it is not a vibrantly popular culture – yet.

You cannot just pitch up on a continent the size of Australia, give yourself a few weeks and hope to do anything more than scratch the surface unless you plan carefully, and ruthlessly restrict the scope of your enquiry. It meant not visiting the tropical north, not going to Tasmania and not, to my particular regret, going to Western Australia, although the wild flowers along the west coast are supposed to be ravishing. We just did not have time to cover the huge distances so I had to have a brief and stick to it.

I make no claim that these gardens represent the whole of Australia. But they do answer some of the questions that I had set out to explore and raise other queries that I had not considered before I went.

I wanted to see how the colonisation of the continent manifested itself in gardens and how that had evolved into modern, twenty-first century Australia. The British often think of Australia as a cousin, or even a younger brother, who regularly thrashes us at any sporting event and who has helped to bail us out of two World Wars. In many ways we are close. But, as any visitor knows, in many other ways Australia is very different to Britain and is becoming more different all the time. Was this evident in their gardens? How had their gardens changed over the past 200 years? Was there an indigenous style of garden? Did local plants feature much? So I departed on a memorably wet and dismal day in midwinter to see what I could find out.

Royal Botanic Gardens

Sydney, New South Wales

THE ROYAL BOTANIC GARDENS in Sydney are set in one of the most spectacularly beautiful urban positions in the world. Right slap in the middle of Australia's best known (but not capital) city, on one side it runs down to the waters of Sydney Harbour – surely the most beautiful entrance to any city – with the Opera House facing one of its main entrances, and on the other side it is fringed with dramatic skyscrapers. This is no botanical reserve. It is used, gratefully and greedily, by Sydney's citizens. In the middle of the day the joggers pound or plod around its circuit with a desperate intensity and at any time, circles of school children, mothers or businessmen can be found sitting under the shade of its enormous and especially lovely trees. It has always been at the heart of Sydney's life and the regal appendage to the name hints at its history and totemic status in colonial Australia.

Despite the fact that it had been occupied for at least 20,000 years by an indigenous population, to the British Australia came into existence on April 29th, 1770, when Captain Cook landed at Botany Bay. On a grey and blustery day I went to the site of this landing, which is marked by a stone column on the sandy beach and faces out over an industrial scene of tankers and aircraft landing and taking off. It somehow lacks much import. Cook did not stay long, but on his return to Britain in July 1771, the territory was duly claimed. The loss of the American colonies meant there was no current suitable ditching place for penal settlements and so in 1787 the first boatload of convicts set off for Australia. They landed at Botany Bay in January 1788 but discovered that the soil was desperately poor and there was no obvious water supply, so sailed further north and into an inland harbour at Port Jackson, noted by Cook in passing. This was the modern Sydney Harbour. On 26th January, 1788, they landed at Port Jackson and quickly set aside 9 acres of ground for corn at Farm Cove. That piece of ground is now part of the site of the Royal Botanic Gardens and has been under cultivation ever since.

It was a desperately harsh beginning. The ground was completely covered by the bush, composed of eucalypts, banksias and wattles, and most of the convicts were ill and pathetically weak. Their tools blunted as they cleared the scrub and sowed their corn in amongst the tree stumps. The ground was poor and thin and they all nearly starved to death.

The first Governor, Captain Arthur Philip, created a Governor's Demesne of some 320 acres and in *c.* 1808 this was enclosed by a ditch by Governor William Bligh – whose crew mutinied on his ship *The Bounty*. In 1809, Major-General Macquarie was appointed governor and he enclosed the outer boundary with a stone wall and developed a garden on the site of the original farm. Macquarie's architect, Francis Greenway, wrote 'the government domain was to be planted in the manner of the celebrated Brown, the landscape gardener'. However Macquairie only kept these new landscaped grounds to himself for seven

Previous page The Sitta Garden in the Sydney suburb of Mosman is an urban garden that draws upon the colours and plants of outback Australia.

THE REGAL APPENDAGE TO THE NAME HINTS AT ITS HISTORY AND TOTEMIC STATUS IN COLONIAL AUSTRALIA.

years. In June 1816 the Royal Botanic Gardens were officially founded, making them the oldest scientific institution in Australia. This, combined with their location on the ground first cultivated by the initial settlers, makes it a deeply symbolic garden.

The twenty-first century garden, now a series of graceful lawns dominated by vast trees, has gradually evolved from the initial scrub that the settlers hacked into in order to survive. The dominant tree was the Port Jackson fig, *Ficus rubiginosa*, and when the convicts arrived they gathered the fruits and ate them with relish. The outcome was spectacular, if a bit undignified. Ross, our guide, told me that the fruit proved too much for their delicate digestive systems. 'Made them really crook,' he said laconically. 'Shat for days.'

On the day of my visit, a large flock of fruit bats was hanging from the very top branches of half a dozen trees, squabbling and vibrating in the midday heat. They are fiercely exotic to the newly arrived European visitor, and devoid of the anarchic flutter- iness of their smaller cousins, instead fixed somewhere between fox and dinosaur. They cause great damage in the garden, stripping the branches of foliage as they land, swoop- ing in and hooking onto a branch exactly like a jet arriving on an aircraft carrier. At dusk they head off for their dinner, flying miles along the coast for the fruit of the season.

The white lorikeets are much prettier, although a lot noisier. They are extraordinary birds, sidling up to the visitor with a waddle like a librarian setting off for lunch. But they too can be destructive. 'You want to watch them, mate,' Ross told me, as I fed a group digestive biscuits. 'They've got a hell of a beak on them. Occasionally they take a chunk of ear off a visitor. Bleed like stuck pigs.'

*With the iconic silhou- ette of the Opera House and Sydney Harbour Bridge behind it, the Royal Botanic Gardens in Sydney have an idyllic situation. The abundant red-flowering plant is the Indian shot plant (*Canna indica*).*

Kennerton Green

Mittagong, New South Wales

AFTER THE INITIAL WAVE of settlement around Sydney, from about 1825 the colonisers from Britain began to move inland, to cooler, hillier areas where summers were not quite so harsh. For the first thirty years or so they lived in modest shacks or a 'humpy', where the garden was at best a few scraps of plants. There were no luxuries. But slowly these settlements became more established and homes and gardens emerged that borrowed from Indian architecture, making bungalows at first from wood and then from brick. These more solid, permanent houses also had gardens around them.

But the native vegetation was still seen as the enemy, to be cleared or conquered. What they really wanted from their new gardens were memories of home. Despite the climate, many did their utmost to mimic an English country garden. Primroses and snowdrops were imported and planted and even blackbirds and thrushes were shipped out to provide the 'right' birdsong. Lawns, clipped hedges and flower beds did their best to recreate a home country that would almost certainly never be revisited and increasingly, as the century progressed, that they had never seen.

At Kennerton Green there is a survival and recreation of just such a garden and we travelled to Bong Bong Road in Mittagong, a couple of hours south of Sydney, to visit it. The names ring sonorously out. Mittagong, with its cooler, wetter climate is traditionally the dairy area that supplies Sydney with its milk. It is an attractive, lush, well-heeled area.

Kennerton Green began in 1860 as a settler's humpy, then was enlarged and a small garden added by Sir Jock Pagan, the Agent General for Australia. In the 1940s it was bought by the Sangster family who were wealthy racehorse owners and the garden was developed further. In 1980 the present owner, Marylyn Abbot, bought it and has continued to enlarge and develop the garden, deliberately nurturing its Englishness. She also owns, lives and gardens in a large English house and garden, West Green, in Hampshire.

The first thing that struck me as we arrived down the curving drive was the extraordinary greenness. It caught the radiant fullness of an English June, despite the fact that this was almost the antipodean midsummer, and one of the driest on record. In front of the modest but elegant white clapperboard house was a box parterre infilled with the same gravel as the drive – a good ruse this, making the box seem to grow out of the driveway and effectively minimising the intrusion of cars into the garden. A bed of silvery-blue foliage faced the house. Just white flowers. Some apple trees, 'Granny Smith' and 'Jonathan' (Granny Smith originated in Australia).

Kennerton Green is, as might be guessed, subdivided into a series of garden 'rooms'. This is the British way, especially the wealthy, country way. I walk round, drifting from room to room. When I am filming a garden I always try and spend an hour or so just taking it in. I move slowly round, not talking, not thinking very much, trying to let the garden come to me. I jot some notes as I go, take some pictures. Then the rest of the day is spent recording the results of those first impressions, combined with any research or interviews. It is all a painfully slow process. But the vast majority of the material comes from those first impressions as I walk round.

Round the back of the house there is a lawn and a swimming pool, through a gate set in a low wall beneath a lovely, huge red oak. The trees in the garden are all huge and

The rose garden at Kennerton Green is contained within cypress hedging and centred around a koi carp-filled rill. The standard roses are underplanted with white alyssum.

lovely, not least because they have been skilfully pruned to clear the lower branches and expose their shape as well as to allow more light to reach the underplanting. Beneath the oak is an area containing more clipped box, in-filled with foxgloves, campanulas, hydrangeas and hellebores. The shade was distinctly cool and I was glad for my fleece. I suspect that on a warm day I would be equally glad for the shade.

I went through a narrow entrance into the rose garden, which is walled in with a cypress hedge and centred around a long rill with standard roses on either side underplanted with white alyssum. My grandmother always had white alyssum bedded out in front of her house in Hampshire. The connections were popping up like flaps in a fairground shooting alley. The roses were remarkably gnarled and old, the pruned joints like arthritic knuckles. Koi carp flashed orange in the green water.

Walking through an aviary mesh tunnel – the cages all empty – you go through into the Bay Tree Garden. All the garden rooms have names which makes it a bit like walking round a grand hotel. But rightly is it called the Bay Tree Garden. There are lots of them, eighty-one all together, all clipped into lollipops with a little ruff of clipped box around their trunk. It is entirely green. I am told the rectangular box-edged beds hold white flowers at other times – tulips, daisies, aquilegias, penstemons and lilies, I read from my notes. Perhaps it is a spring display and all over now. The rhythms of the bay are pleasing but there is something that is not quite working for me – I think it is the contrast between the clipped bay and the very rough grass and shaggy surrounding trees. The essence of the garden is slipping between tightly-clipped formality and a shaggy looseness. Both can be good but it is hard to make them work together.

Through a pair of huge metal gates is the best bit of the garden, planted by Marylyn when she came here. It is a wood of hundreds of white birch trees set in grass. For the first time my pulse quickens. This is beautiful and genuinely inspired. Apparently it is carpeted with bluebells in October – Australian spring. But it is lovely, the simplicity of the white trunks contrasting with the backdrop of grass and blue sky above. This is the edge of the garden and I look over the fence to a landscape of yellow-brown grass and scrub with a lovely humpy made of rusty corrugated iron in the mid-distance. It brings home the artifice needed to keep this English garden blooming in an entirely alien countryside.

There is also a lake, swagged around with roses, but this seemed unnecessary after the birch wood – like being offered another pudding after finishing a perfectly satisfying meal.

So too did the kitchen garden, or as it is called in best Australian Franglais, 'The Jardin Potager'. This is a perfectly nice vegetable garden with really nice things in it, like the bright red supports underplanted with poppies of the same colour and the charming mix of marigolds, roses, poppies, lavender and onions, beetroot and parsley all within, you guessed it, tightly clipped box hedges. But there is only so much nostalgic good taste that can be swallowed at one sitting and the birch wood had spoiled it for me. Its inspired simplicity had revealed the rest of the garden for what it openly is – a recreation of another land on the other side of the world. I have visited hundreds of such gardens at home. I have made one or two.

As we headed back to the centre of Sydney, I tried to sort out my reactions to Kennerton (it has since been sold and the new owners will no doubt have their own plans for the garden). It is all done well and does not claim to be anything other than an English garden. It was fascinating to see how powerfully the details of home life can be displayed and recreated but I felt this had nothing to do with modern Australia. I felt I had paid my dues. Now I wanted to see a twenty-first century, truly Australian garden.

My favourite part of Kennerton Green is the recently planted white birch (Betula papyrifera) wood which is carpeted with bluebells in spring.

The Sitta Garden

Mosman, New South Wales

Above *Surrounded by a border and drifts of succulents, a ponytail palm,* Beaucarnea recurvata, *dominates the tiny but vibrant Sitta garden.*
Opposite *To capture 'the burning red heart of the country', 33 tons of rock were quarried in Alice Springs and moved to the garden.*

TO SEE A MODERN URBAN GARDEN I went next to Mosman, a highly fashionable area of Sydney, and a small but very modern house with an extremely small but equally modern garden. Truly contemporary 'designed' gardens are rare anywhere and always something of a shock. It is garden as art gallery and the risk is that all domesticity is submerged in the preciousness of fine art. They can be like Chelsea Show gardens – lovely to look at but strictly not for messing.

There is no risk of this at the Sitta. It is too small, for a start. You climb steep steps from the street up to the house and the garden is mostly in the right angle of the building. Large sliding glass doors make up the walls facing on to it so that the garden is an important part of the living space.

It is certainly dramatic and challenging. Hewn blocks of bright orange-red sandstone make walls, with sharp corners rising up out of the ground like beached stone ships. The stone veers out of the ground with tectonic energy. It is damn clever. In this tiny space, this extends the garden down into the ground, completing the walls as they disappear and somehow making the garden seem bigger. This is a clever illusion because in fact the edge of the visible garden is constrained by a hidden wall over the steep drop to the street below.

Part of the commission had been to house the owner's collection of succulents, hitherto always in pots, but now planted in drifts within small beds or planting pockets. Gravelled areas seem to zigzag off from them, the angles jagging against each other. A grid of grey-blue *Festuca glauca* planted in the gravel nods towards a lawn.

The boundary is planted to provide a visual and weather screen using *Agave attenuata*, *Euphorbia*, *Echeveria*, *Aeonium* 'Zwartkop' and a large ponytail palm, *Beaucarnea recurvata*, whose water-storing roots hang from the three stems like solid tassels. Although there is a lot crammed into this small space and there is certainly not much room to kick a ball or have a barbie in, it does not feel crowded. On its own terms it feels right.

Round the other side of the house in a slim strip is a 6.5 ft wide infinity pool, lapping underneath the step into a bedroom, with a view out over Sydney Harbour. It is all very glamorous, yet it looks onto streets with gardens occupied by grass, basketball hoops, barbecues or a third car, parked out of the way. It seems to be an exception, even in this part of Sydney.

I met the designer Vladimir Sitta, a Czech who moved to Australia in 1981 but who still speaks in a thick eastern European accent and looks at Australia with the wry bemusement of the immigrant. He has designed a number of small gardens here in Sydney as well as large, ambitious projects like the 'Garden of Australian Dreams' in the National Museum of Australia in Canberra. I knew that this last project had been much misunderstood, if not roundly abused.

I asked him first about the indigenous gardening culture. 'There isn't one,' he said. 'The Australian culture does not lend itself to gardens. Too suburban and risk-adverse. They want grass, barbecues, swimming pools and no work. It is a play and leisure culture rather than a creative one.'

I pointed out that there was plenty of room for gardens. It was a pretty big country.

'It is all a matter of deciding what to do with the available space,' he said. 'There is plenty of room for roads and parking but none for gardens. All Australians are crammed around a thin edge, packed in without room,' he smiled. 'Yet it is the perfect climate, perfect idyll but there is no edge for creativity.'

Was this an urban thing I asked? Much of Australian life seemed to me to be suburban by choice.

'Cities are creative because they involve risk and uncertainty. Rural Australia is too harsh, too dominant to make a garden. But I wanted some of that energy in this garden.'

So for this garden he took a piece of red rock and went to Alice Springs to quarry more especially for the garden. 'I wanted to capture the burning red heart of the country.' There were 33 tons of it in total, all sawn to fit exactly. I dread to think what it must have cost.

'I admit I was scared,' Vladimir said, 'and so were the contractors. It was just a vast heap of raw, red stone in this tiny space, which was itself a raw building site. Everything was bedded on a structure of concrete. It took four months. And the workers went home every night coated in red dust. Like medieval stone masons.' He smiles his wry intelligent smile again. He obviously loved it all. The challenge. The confusion. And then the precision slowly forming out of it all.

I asked him if he gardened himself. He said that he hates gardening. Hates plants. Hates gardeners. He smiled again. We both sipped our coffees in silence for a moment. I was growing to like his eastern European gloom. I could see him drinking despairingly till dawn, smiling his smile, having a great time.

'The only problem with making gardens,' he went on, 'are plants and gardeners. It should be just like a work of art or building. To make a good garden in Australia you do not need a client, you need a patron.'

Koi carp provide a calming counterpoint to the energy of this urban garden.

I could see his point. There did not seem to be a thriving Australian sense of self when it came to the gardens in Sydney. There were not many people who would commission work based upon a shared horticultural vernacular. A patron on the other hand would pass the reins over to the designer, just as they had here in Mosman, and let them do whatever they thought fit. That might make spectacular and interesting gardens for those that could afford it, but it was not really gardening.

It was time to leave Sydney and its colonial influences and look for something more purely Australian. The best place seemed to be 'the burning red heart of the country', so I caught a flight to Alice Springs.

Alice Springs Desert Park
Northern Territory

BEFORE WE LEFT SYDNEY for Alice Springs we were all invited to dinner by our director Mark's cousin. It was a nice idea but we were all very tired. We had to be up very early to go to Alice Springs. A big party with lots of new faces would be too much. It will just be us and perhaps one or two others, Mark said. She's boiled a ham. That swung it and we turned up to a pretty house with a picture postcard view overlooking the harbour. The door opened and at least fifty people were visible. As many more were inside. The ham appeared at about midnight but by then we had all drunk too much of the delicious Australian wine to notice.

Everyone knows that Australia is vast, but whenever I have flown around it, I have been astonished every time by the huge emptiness of it. Within minutes of a plane taking off, it leaves the cities and conurbations and crosses what seems to be uninhabited land. Going to Alice Springs this soon became desert. Bright orange emptiness.

I recalled what Vladimir Sitta had said – 'Rural Australia is too harsh, too dominant to make a garden' – and wondered if this excursion to Alice Springs was not perhaps a waste of time. The idea was to get as far away from the large towns and cities as possible. Alice Springs is pretty much the centre of the Australian continent and is as distant from the coastal fringe as you can get. It is also surrounded by desert and I knew that the Aboriginal culture had a strong base there. Apart from reading Bruce Chatwin's *The Songlines*, I confess I knew very little else about it. But what I did know did not square with any conception of a garden – even though on my journeys round the world I was taking that idea as far as it could possibly go from time to time.

The air at Alice Springs was like a blast of oven heat. Suddenly we were in, to quote Sitta again, 'the burning heart of the country'. It was hot. 'Oh you should have been here last week,' our driver told us cheerily. 'Now *that* was hot.'

Alice is a fairly small town. Everyone wears shorts and a hat. The hats are fine but Australians put the short into shorts. On some men, especially those clearly fond of a beer or two, they have to be seen to be believed. It is a miracle that they can sit down without corrective surgery.

That afternoon we drove out of town to film in the desert, or 'Sand Country' as it is properly called. It is a staggeringly harsh, grand, bright orange landscape. Just outside the town the roads become packed sand. The vegetation is thin and scrubby, with spinifex, wattles and the occasional desert oak. Outcrops of pink rock break the skyline. Kennerton Green feels as far away as Hampshire (which is actually a tribute to Kennerton). We waited to film the sunset, which never quite happened. In the dark, 20 miles or so from Alice Springs, we had a puncture. There was no jack in the hire car. A frisson of outback fear jokily rippled through us. Luckily the other vehicle had one and by the light of a mobile phone we changed the wheel under a moon as orange as the sands.

The next morning at dawn, we went to the Alice Springs Desert Park and met Gary Dinham, the curator of botany there. He is stocky, direct and bright and turns out to be the best of companions. The park was busy at 6 am with staff getting as much hard physical work as they could done before the sun became too hot. Although the core area is 123 acres, the whole site is 3,200 acres, lying just outside the town in the lee of

The robust Australian grass tree, Xanthorrhoea thorntonii, *is a true desert species. It is drought resistant and will regrow after a bush fire. A mature specimen will reach 16 feet in height and live for several hundred years. They are slow growers – a young ten-year old tree may have substantial foliage but not have developed an above-ground trunk.*

an escarpment. It appears completely natural. I confess that my initial thought was, with a sinking heart, that it was no more a 'garden' than last night's landscape or a patch of seashore. I could not have been more wrong but luckily I was not alone in that first impression.

'It is the best compliment that we can get,' Gary said with a smile, 'when people say that it's amazing that this patch is here, so close to town. Everything is planted, land-scaped and man-made. If we make it look completely natural than we have done the job well.'

Gary told me that the park aims to combine all the aspects of the desert. 'It's where we have brought the plants, the animals and the culture together in one place.' This is a big idea. In Europe we take for granted the long line of human and plant history that every garden carries, but in Australia not only is that history much thinner and less accessible, it is also, in many ways, much older and more vibrant. The local Arrente people hold the landscape here as very significant and it includes parts of the Wild Dog and Caterpillar dreaming stories. These cannot be changed or altered without ripping away tens of thousands of years of cultural history. Nothing, but nothing in the out-back is without significance for them. Dreamtime exists inside the landscape. It is part of it. To alter it in anyway is to alter the dream stories and akin to announcing to the British that Queen Victoria will from henceforth be known as Barbara XII. Therefore you must tread lightly when dealing with it – the Desert Park, if set up with a theme-park heavy handedness, could have been a disaster.

Gary told me that they avoid this by including Aboriginal advisers in every detail. They monitor the park carefully and give guidance on every development. It is their land and they have as much of an impact on the park as the non-native creators and managers.

As we go round it is a treat. Despite the attention to every detail, clear labelling and subtle plant groupings and associations it feels entirely spontaneous. There is that sense you have in all good outdoor spaces that it would be worse if it was any different. The intention is clearly educational but is done with a light hand and is completely fascinating. The truth is that very few people understand how complex and subtle the outback is and how sophisticated the Aboriginal management and use of it. Seeing it as just hostile desert to be subdued is blunt and ignorant.

The park has flora and a lot of fauna in beautifully designed and integrated buildings along the route, from all the different recognised outback environments: Range, Gorge, the low scrub of Mulga Woodland, Desert Woodland, Desert Rivers and Sand Country. The salt lakes and clay pans showing only the ghost of water are as carefully made as any garden pond – and use almost identical techniques. Woods of large gums stand bare-barked and peeling, shimmering in the growing heat. 'Phew! It's hot already,' I said to Gary. 'You should have been here last week,' Gary said. 'That was pretty hot.'

Plants are carefully encouraged to behave as they do when untended. So there are dead and fallen trees and some that have been blasted by lightening to make charred sculptures as beautiful as a David Nash.

Spinifex dominates the Sand Country. This grassy plant has twelve or so different species, but all can live on virtually phosphorus and nitrogen-free soils, and have deep roots that survive extreme drought. The leaves look soft and grassy but are actually curled up spikes. In amongst them are curiously prehistoric trees, looking like over-grown mare's tails, which turn out to be desert oaks, *Allocasuarina decaisneana*. There is a thin meadow of white and yellow flowers, the poached egg daisy, *Polycalymma*

stuartii, that flowers in the desert after the rains. And everywhere the burnt orange soil sets each leaf and twig in stark display.

The following day Gary took me out for a four-hour drive to the south-west of Alice Springs with a local guide, Doug Taylor. It was even hotter and a gusty wind burnt the air. I shook hands with Doug. 'Sorry about the cricket mate,' he said by way of greeting. England were being humiliated in the Ashes. It was making the whole population of Australia very happy indeed. I touched the car and burnt myself. 'It's going to be really hot today,' I said, trying to change the subject and reverting instinctively to the weather. 'You should've been here last week mate,' Doug said. 'Now that was hot.'

The dirt road ran straight, for mile upon red mile. The first stop was to see a group of plants that looked like squat palms with a grassy head. These were *Xanthorrhoea australis*, or black boys. They grow infinitesimally slowly, making about 3 ft per hundred years and living for up to 500 years. That made this clump young plants when Shakespeare was writing *Hamlet*. The site is highly honoured by its traditional owners and we were privileged to be given permission to film there.

Gary showed me the mulga tree that, despite being scrawny and sparse in branches, would supply Aborigines with wood for nearly all their tools – the roots are ideal for spears and boomerangs. The seeds would be ground to make a damper bread which was very nutritious. Every plant has some use.

We visited a dried-up creek, bounded by huge lemon gums and a stony river bed as dry as a road. The heat was merciless, but not, of course, anything compared to last week...

We went on to a wood of desert oaks. Each tree was spaced well apart, so it looked more like a surreal park. The wind made the thin leaves whisper and hiss. Some of the bark was charcoal black having survived a bush fire. The desert oak is a tall lamp post of a tree for the first hundred years or more of its life. It grows slowly and the roots grow as deep as the tree grows tall and are hugely widespread. Then, at a point when the roots have sufficiently established, it becomes a broad-branched, mature tree. This two-stage development is a throwback to the Megafauna era when dinosaurs roamed Australia so the tree evolved to grow above grazing level before developing tasty, broader leaves. The huge root system was made before the tree needed it, so it could withstand extreme periods of drought.

Doug explained to me that in Aboriginal traditions, the land and the people are one. The stories and memories of the land are the stories and memory of the people. Every living thing belongs to the land. And there is no break in tradition. So the stories, laws and practical information that he learnt as a small child are exactly the same as those passed on 10,000 years ago. The chain is completely unbroken. To wrench it apart in any way is cultural vandalism of the worst kind. The so-called 'walkabout' was in fact a careful kind of land management. A family group would move around a set, well-defined area, staying ahead of extreme drought, harvesting 'bush tucker' like roots and seeds as they were available, using fire to regenerate the land and working entirely within the capabilities of the land. In this way they could exist within a seemingly wholly inhospitable environment where white people die if they get a puncture a few miles from the edge of town.

The next day we travelled down to Melbourne. I felt hugely enriched and reluctant to leave. The red, sandy wastes seen from the air now seemed pregnant with a rich and delicate web of human and natural stories. And I was sure that, as far as gardens went, the future of Australia was being told out there, in the burning heart of the country, as much as in the cities.

Cruden Farm

Melbourne

FROM THE RAW LANDSCAPE and ancient civilisation of Alice Springs I arrived in a Melbourne circled by the worst bush fires in living memory. Usually, it is an attractive and seductive place, less self-consciously frantic and business-orientated than Sydney. It feels like a good place to live.

Dame Elisabeth Murdoch was born in the city in 1909 and was also educated there. In 1928 she married Keith Murdoch, who was also born in Melbourne although educated in England, and they had six children, one of whom is Rupert Murdoch. She told me that she has twenty grandchildren and forty-seven great grandchildren, with the first great, great grandchild due. She became a Lady when her husband was knighted and was made a Dame in her own right after his death.

As a wedding present, Sir Keith bought his wife Cruden Farm, then in the countryside east of the city but now part of the suburbs, and they used it as a weekend and holiday home. It was then a small cottage with a little garden around it. Although Dame Elisabeth loved it from the first, she was only nineteen and her husband called in Edna Walling, then one of the leading Australian garden designers of the time, who made a pair of walled gardens. They still exist but have been dwarfed by the rest of the garden, the creation and management of which is entirely down to Dame Elisabeth. There can be few people on this planet that have gardened continuously in the same place for eighty years.

Even given that long stretch of time, the achievements at Cruden beggar belief. It is a garden of huge mature trees and all of them bar one have been planted by her. If I had been told that they were hundreds of years old it would not have been a surprise. But trees grow twice as fast in the Victorian climate as they do in Britain. There are huge mature elms, last seen by me thirty years ago before Dutch Elm disease killed them all at home. You approach the house and garden down a curving avenue of lemon-scented gums, *Eucalyptus citriodora*, with a mottled mauve bloom to their trunks and olive-coloured leaves rattling in the hot breeze. It is a bush plant but here becomes a statement of Australian identity and a glorious, deliciously fragrant one. The house, imposing but not grand, is surrounded by the garden, itself encircled by these giant trees. It is clear from the first glance that everything is highly maintained and watered although set amongst a wholly arid, burnt up landscape. I later quiz Dame Elisabeth about this and she made clear that the water was all from their own dam. 'The locals love it,' she said. 'It gives them a splash of vicarious green.'

I had about half an hour to spare before my appointed chat with Dame Elisabeth, so took a walk around. Hostas, thalictrums and hydrangeas – all plants of damp, cool places – thrive here. The fruit looks healthy. I especially like an espalier of cherry ringed round a cherry tree. An easy playfulness always improves a garden.

Everything is done well. I make the assumption that this is a direct result of having the wealth available to do it but later find out that there is just one gardener, Michael, a lean, shy man in his sixties. He works hard and well but Dame Elisabeth did most of the work until her seventies and kept working daily into her eighties. Look closer and you see that it is a garden that has the feel of being used and engaged with. She still oversees absolutely everything in the garden from her electric buggy and takes what she

Lemon-scented gums, Eucalyptus citriodora, *line the driveway to Cruden Farm. Dame Elisabeth Murdoch's impressive garden, now eighty years mature, combines an independent Australian spirit with a British influence.*

calls her 'daily trundle', charging round the place. I know because she took me, roaring down slopes, dipping under branches, noticing everything. If aging, with all its indignities, is inevitable, then this, for sure, is the way to do it.

I go into the walled garden designed by Edna Walling. I can see why Dame Elisabeth was frustrated by it. It is a surprisingly intimate space, set amongst giant trees and sweeping expanses of grass. In fact, it is too small, too narrow and the walls too low, but the borders it contains are lovely, dominated by the blue and purple spires of delphiniums. However, the lack of size appears as modesty rather than a design flaw. The other walled garden now contains a swimming pool, again very modest, where Dame Elisabeth was having her daily swim, alone, as we arrived. Just take that in. She is ninety-eight.

Finally I meet Dame Elisabeth who immediately enchants us all. She is probably the most charming woman I have ever met. Running a close second – and this is alarming but perfectly true – was Margaret Thatcher.

We go on our trundle, scooting round the back of the house where she created a large lake. She explained that she wanted water but did not want to impose it unnaturally on the garden. They made a dam to preserve water for the house and farm and she realised that it would overflow into a natural depression that could be deepened. There is a sizeable island in the lake, with yet more trees and the parrot-like orange of kniphofias reflected in the water. It is Brownian in scale and scope, balanced by the maturity of the trees set back from the water. Beyond is another wave of oaks, perhaps 30 ft tall, planted from the acorns of the majestic specimens that Dame Elisabeth also planted, fifty years earlier.

I ask her about these trees. 'Well they grow so well here. It is a long growing season, from early spring to late autumn [twice as long as the British one where trees stop most growth by early June]. We have 35 inches of rain and a plentiful water supply which all helps.' Later I spoke to the gardener, Michael, who stressed that Dame Elisabeth insisted on meticulous preparation whenever a tree was planted and all the necessary care for the first few years. This meant that the trees always got off to a good start. He also said that she is ruthless. If things aren't working she gets rid of them.

Directly behind the house is a rose and vegetable garden. Trees clustered with lemons stand against the white clapperboard of the house. The roses rise up out of poppies, nepeta, alstroemerias, more delphiniums and foxgloves – a soft and lovely mix of flowers that could be found in a thousand English borders and very unlike the bush plants of the outback. But as she takes me round it is apparent that every rose has a story and meaning to her. They are old friends.

The rose and vegetable garden is a formal garden, with neatly clipped hedges but bean sticks are reused and a pig-netting frame is stretched across what looks suspiciously like an old bedstead to support sweet peas. In short, it is not all just for show but a proper working garden designed to please those that garden and live in it as well as to impress the visitor. These visitors are important as Dame Elisabeth opens the garden regularly to the public and thousands come. She is apparently always there to greet them.

This is a garden of a matriarch, still vibrantly engaged with the modern world but belonging firmly to the middle years of the last century. It reflects an independent Australian identity but is expressed in very British ways. What makes it so remarkable is the character and persona of the woman that literally created it over her very long life.

Before I left Australia I wanted to visit a garden not so far away that I had been told took this sense of Australian identity a step further, that brought some of the austere beauty of the outback and bush into the garden and harnessed it horticulturally.

Next to the house is the more formal walled garden designed by Edna Walling, its green lawn and beds full of delphiniums and foxgloves looking distinctly British.

The Garden Vineyard

The Mornington Peninsula, Victoria

Above *Breakfast on the verandah wih Di Johnson and her daughter Jenny.* Opposite *The garden was started in an English style and gradually embraced native Australian plants. Behind this stone basin is a pair of huge mixed borders.*

MY LAST DAY IN MELBOURNE was apocalyptic. By 7 am the temperature was already in the high thirties and was to climb to become the hottest December day for fifty years. Bush fires ringed the city and we heard on the radio that the airport was closed due to poor visibility. The ashy tang of burnt brush and homes filtered through the air and the sun remained hidden all day, smouldering behind the searing smog.

I was to spend the entire day at The Garden Vineyard on the Mornington Peninsula, in the south-eastern suburbs of Melbourne, and had been invited for Di Johnson's birthday breakfast. The Garden Vineyard, or The Fusion Garden as it is also and more descriptively known, is a journey through the assimilation of Australia by an Englishwoman, committed to a life there, working as a GP and bringing up her very Australian children but homesick for England and especially for its countryside. It takes all the elements of an English upbringing and combines them with a fusion of a lifetime of care, expertise and love of plants, and a dedication to native Australian species. The result is idiosyncratically Australian and the expression of a native Australian horticulture that reflects the country's colonial journey. It is also very beautiful.

My first impression of Di's garden is that it is a parody of the most English of English gardens. Clipped box balls and a peachy brick wall, immaculate grass and nepeta, roses, tobacco plants and phlomis sing a song written in the home counties on the other side of the world. It is as unreal as bananas, palms and bromeliads in the Lake District. It is a show garden – brilliant and lovely – but under this smudged, broiling sky, it felt distinctly odd. As she showed me round, Di, brisk, slim and fiercely intelligent, explained. 'I was homesick so I made this section of the garden inspired directly from a photograph of an English garden. Yes it is a parody – shamelessly so. But it fulfilled a need at that time.'

The garden then takes you into an open square of exceptional cool beauty dominated by a semi-circular stone basin holding a small square basin of water planted with water lilies. This assurance of taste runs right through the garden and shifts my perception. Something more than supremely efficient parody is afoot here. A really good eye is at work. The gravel is raked with Zen-like care. The hedges are immaculate. This apparently is Doug's role – keeping up appearances. It has the air of a garden that is looked at. It is beautiful and it knows it. There is a vibe. So far it is all good taste and huge care but there is that tingle I get when I visit an excitingly good garden.

Turn left, through apricot-coloured stone gates, and a grass path curves between a pair of absolutely huge borders. They are made up from 17,650 cubic feet of soil bought in by Di, sight unseen. It was almost pure clay as opposed to the sandy natural soil. This is all on a scale

IT IS A MAJOR GARDEN. BUT THE WAY THAT IT CROSSES CULTURES IS BY FAR THE MOST INTERESTING THING ABOUT IT.

that I have never seen before in an amateur, private garden. The planting is still, by Di's account, strongly influenced by Beth Chatto and has a very English style, with great drifts of penstemons, kniphofia, salvias, dahlias, *Alchemilla mollis*, cardoons, opium poppies and a dozen more plants from a standard English plant list. But the tightly clipped columns that add structure to the border turn out to be lilly-pilly (*Acmena smithii* var. *minor*), which is native to Australia. Di says that they take the heat and dryness completely in their stride. However, the lushness of the mown grass is down to heavy watering despite the smoke hazing the air from the not-so distant bush fires.

Follow the path round the tight corner and everything changes. The halfway garden between England and Australia is left behind, with a garden area composed of perfectly clipped balls and mounds of lilly-pilly, glabra, *Rhagodia spinescens*, grey *Westringia fruticosa* (a rosemary like shrub with twenty-five species native to Australia) and lavender, all planted around white-trunked lemon-scented eucalypts. Paddock grass grows in the open spaces. The tight sculptural clipping of the naturally scraggy native plants transforms them. Surely this is the definition of gardening?

The garden then moves into a large, very European, formal area of garden made of lilly-pilly lollypops flanking broad formal paths. The lilly-pilly is underplanted with bedding of white agapanthus and heliotropes, and has a coppery tinge that doesn't quite seem to work with the heliotrope but when you look down the equally formal terracing and steps from the house with the tiers of cypress hedges, you can only see the white agapanthus and it looks superb. But it all comes as rather a formal shock after the restrained coolness and stylishness of the clipped mounds and gums.

We go down the steps to the 'Australian' garden. This is the work of Jenny, Di's daughter, a practising landscape designer. There is a dramatic change. Jenny developed this at weekends and holidays, allowed to do so by Di on condition that it never had to be watered. Di had enough to do without that. The grass is a parched brown. It seems impossible that it might survive. It will. All bare soil is thickly mulched with shredded bark. Newly planted areas are mere dots of new plants in a large sea of mulch. Nothing has been crammed or rushed here. Everything is measured and planned on a big scale.

'But we do a lot of plonking,' says Di. 'And I learned as I went along,' added Jenny. 'You have to be patient with Australian gardens,' Di said. 'They are very slow.' 'It has helped that I haven't been here all the time,' Jenny said. 'Every time I come there are changes that I notice.'

Many of the shrubs are clipped, as they are elsewhere in the garden, and many grow in their natural shape. The colours are muted – greys, ochres (including all the grass) and largely glaucous shades of green. Sculpture abounds, with beautifully carved inscriptions in stone. One, on a tall slim piece of grey stone in this part of the garden, reads 'And we shall walk and talk in gardens all misty and wet with rain and we shall never, never grow so old again'. I do not know this but, in this parched land with the fires burning all around, so very far from the damp, dark green of home, it is powerfully moving. Later I look it up and discover that it is by Van Morrison from a song on *Astral Weeks* called 'Sweet Thing'. The song is ravishingly beautiful. I then remember that I don't like Van Morrison. And another wall of prejudice comes tumbling thankfully down.

There is more to this garden – I have not mentioned the vineyard that rolls down the hill from the lawn at the back of the house producing, I can attest, a wonderful red wine – all of it is beautifully done. It is a major garden. But the way that it crosses cultures is by far the most interesting thing about it.

Jenny is taking her mother's skill, experience and love of gardening, rooted back in her British upbringing, and taking it into a modern Australia, using an Australian idiom and native Australian plants. The result is something genuinely new and creative and, I think, very beautiful.

But as Di became accustomed to Australia so her garden changed and this area uses native plants, such as Rhagodia spinescens with small artemisias in between, to create something startlingly original.

New Zealand

After the searing heat, dust and smoke of Australia, New Zealand was reassuringly familiar. It smelt like the countryside in Britain in May – fresh and very green. The grass had daisies and bents, skylarks sang overhead and the temperature was sunny and fresh – about 20ºC lower then it had been in Melbourne. Travelling through the North Island was like driving round Devon or the lowlands of Scotland on your summer hols in 1960 in a Morris Minor (and I did that then). It is charming, peaceful, beautiful, honest, decent and not always terribly sexy.

But however familiar first impressions might be, New Zealand is very different from the UK. The Pohutukawa tree blooms with bright red flowers. Some of these trees are over 1,000 years old and can, usefully in a country with a high density of volcanoes, colonise bare lava. Cordylines and phormiums grow freely. Parrots chase from tree to tree. Tree ferns – surely the most singularly magical of all plants – dominate any uncleared forest, never failing to impress or surprise. It is also unlike anywhere else in the world. Before Western colonisers came, New Zealand was close to an earthly paradise, with a very distinctive flora and fauna. It was dominated by its birds, many flightless, which had no natural predators. There were no snakes and no mammals. The temperate rainforest that covered over 80 per cent of the land was – and where it still exists, still is – a lush, green, safe place.

I had only a week there before returning home and we decided just to stay in the North Island. It seemed cruel not to go to the South Island, which is meant to be completely, exhilaratingly beautiful, but there you go. We also decided not to go to the tropical country north of Auckland but to concentrate on travelling down from Auckland through King Country to New Plymouth in Taranaki. On the way we stopped and met Maori weavers making their beautiful and highly valued cloaks from flax, *Phormium tenax*, spent a hugely memorable day in the rainforest collecting food which we then cooked in a *hangi* fire pit, and spent a few nights in small-town New Zealand. And everywhere I was still following the same thread of thought as in Australia, trying to see how colonisation had influenced gardens and how they were evolving into a distinctive New Zealand style of horticulture.

I also managed to lose another notebook. It tells you something about the country that within hours I received a phone call from the police, telling me that it had been handed in after I must have dropped it on the street in Taumarunui. They then posted it to me and I got it back at home three months later. My notebooks are gradually seeing more of the world than I have.

Ayrlies

Auckland

Above The unique and startling Puya alpestris. *Opposite* Ayrlies *is a huge garden with a series of ponds and streams entirely created from farmland. Lotus leaves lie flat on the water of the pond, which is edged by taro and Lousiana irises, with* Strelitzia nicolai *on the right. In the background, golden elms, liquid ambers, eucalypti and* Cryptomeria japonica *trees fill the skyline. Previous page* Familiar, but different, New Zealand is horticulturally unlike anywhere else in the world.*

AYRLIES IS JUST FORTY YEARS OLD but astonishingly mature. It is hard to believe that in 1964 the land was just a series of empty grass paddocks for dairy cattle. The trees are huge and the whole garden feels timelessly established. This is a large garden – 12 acres of dense planting and another 30 acres of woodland – but it seems much bigger than that because of the scale and sheer intensity of its planting. There are scores of different islands of plant groups more or less interlinked via paths, ponds, gushing streams, steep steps and lawns, but it is clear that design is secondary to the plants. There are no straight lines and few obvious directional routes. You wander or, more accurately, dive in. This is a garden that submerses the visitor in plants, dunks and wallows you in their colour, texture, shape and scent. The planting is ecstatic.

You wander around and find scene after scene, some that delight, some that intrigue and some that are perhaps not quite your thing. No matter. There will be more round the corner. It is like attending a carnival.

I have never been anywhere else where plants grow with such intensity. Everything is packed intensely together, everything growing more vigorously than their British counterparts do, although many of the plants would be familiar to British gardeners. I had not expected this of New Zealand. The temperature is pleasant but the light is glaringly bright. After Australia we are all hatless and relaxed and every one of us gets sunburnt. The truth is that there is more light here for more hours, and the light itself is more intense than in the northern hemisphere. Things just grow faster for longer. They have the four seasons, just as we do, but the garden never closes down as the British garden does for three or four months a year. Here there are 365 growing days a year. There are nearly 50 inches of rain a year, and the weather is never too cold, never too hot. Interestingly this means that there are hardly any herbaceous plants as they need a dormant period and the climate is too benign.

Ayrlies was made, and is still lived in and run by, Beverley McConnell who is the doyenne of New Zealand gardening. She married an engineer, lived in Auckland with a small garden, had five children and then wanted country life so in 1964 they moved to Ayrlies Farm, an hour south of the city. In England this is often a kind of upgrading – buying a large house in the country with some land attached. But the house at Ayrlies is a relatively modest bungalow. The farm was hilly pasture – like most of the southern part of North Island – and a working dairy farm. There was no garden at all.

I asked Bev if she came wanting to make a garden. 'Yes I did. I had the first three acres on paper.'

Three acres!

'It wasn't much. Not really. I married a man who thought big. In those days a lot of farmers would say to their wives if they

AYRLIES IS SPECIAL. IT TRANSCENDS THE GOOD TASTE AND HORTICULTURAL CONFIDENCE THAT IS TYPICAL OF SO MANY OF BRITAIN'S GRAND GARDENS.

wanted to make a garden, "What do you want to do that for?" But my husband would always say "Why not?" Gardens eat money but he wrote the cheques. I was lucky. I planted trees around 3 acres to protect it. We planted every single tree here. The farmer we bought this from hated it. For him, it was the destruction of a good dairy farm by a mad woman planting trees. That first three acres stayed the same for about ten years. Then we went to England to look for a gardener and found a wonderful man called Oliver Briers and his wife and family. Oliver has retired three times but he is still working here. It is his garden as much as mine. And on that trip to England my husband saw water gardens for the first time and wanted them here. We came back and there was a local man that needed work so my husband got him to dig four ponds. So the garden automatically increased to about ten or twelve acres.'

The way Bev tells it, it was a completely normal, modest extension, just as one might add a new bed or two where previously there had been grass. But nothing is usual about this garden. Clearly both she and her husband have huge amounts of ambition, energy and confidence.

'I have good genes,' she smiled. 'I am fortunate because I am really strong.' It is an unexpected thing to say but absolutely spot on. People tend to underestimate just

The Rockery at Ayrlies surrounds the pool. Subtropical plants like the Queen palms (Syagrus romanzoffiana) and the dragon trees (Dracaena draco) at the back were introduced to complement the temperate dwarf conifers.

how useful physical strength and tough-
ness is in making a garden. It is something that I have always had to spare and
taken for granted, but now that I am
getting older and am beginning to creak
a little I realise how important it is –
especially when gardening on such a vast
scale as this.

'It wasn't easy,' Bev says. 'The soil is clay
and we might not have frosts but we do
have drought, really strong winds and
rainstorms that crush everything.'

How does she think her garden relates
to New Zealand horticulture in general?
'I learned a lot from England and never
self-consciously followed any style. Most
of what we have done here has been dictated by a passion for plants and the lie of

the land. But perhaps some of it comes from farmers' wives who were dying to do
much the same and push out their fences – but weren't allowed to.'

I asked her what advice she would give to anyone setting out to make a large garden?
'Plant your trees and give them ten years to establish. Then get your water established.
Then infill it with plants. Create your own nursery to raise plants and above all, pre-
pare the ground well.'

Beverley's husband had a lot of spare rock from a job so she decided to make a rockery to house all the smaller plants she had accumulated in her previous garden. This
snakes around a swimming pool and flows into the Lurid Border, becoming good and
lurid itself as it goes. Oranges, reds and yellows flare hotly. It is like a flaming coral reef.
This kind of gaudiness is powerful but quite hard to do. It can be a one shot trick. But
Beverley combines her colours with truly brilliant sensitivity and touch. It came about
by accident. Beverley says that when she put the gleditsia 'Sunburst' up there, 'I said,
"My goodness!" Yellow is such a tough colour in our light that you've either got to go
with it and make a statement of it or get rid of it. So we brought the hot colours all the
way down the middle of the garden and they cool off.' Layer upon layer of oranges is
built up for the eye, not just including two plants sitting next to each other but also
those in the background. This applies everywhere in the garden and I think it is real
genius.

You see beauty throughout the entire 12 acres whether in the collection of clipped
hebes, the lush temperate rainforest ferns and woodland, the irises reflected in a pond,
or the shifting greys, greens and blues of the grasses and the jade flowers on a puya next
to a cactus. Every corner has a delight and surprise.

Ayrlies is special. It transcends the good taste and horticultural confidence that is
typical of so many of Britain's grand gardens. In fact, it is quite unlike anywhere else
that I have been to. It makes you look anew. I have never seen such a wide mixture of
plants in one garden and I have never seen colour and plant association handled
better. I left elated by the scale and vision and dream-like intensity of colour and size.
And rather sunburnt.

*The Lurid Border:
oranges, reds and
yellows are notoriously
difficult to place
successfully in a garden.
Beverley has managed
it by layering the
colours and confining
them to the centre of
the garden. On the left,
red pelargoniums are
edged by the yellow
Sedum adolphi, whilst
on the right, Kangaroo
Paw, Anigozanthus
pulcherrimus 'Bush
Noon' is backed by
Thuya occidentalis
'Rheingold'.*

Te Kainga Marire

New Plymouth

WE DROVE SLOWLY DOWN from Auckland to New Plymouth. The roads are all small and practically free of traffic and you pass through mile upon mile of agricultural land punctuated by small towns and villages. The volcanic landscape constantly and erratically undulates, creating sharp creases and ridges that the grass and the ubiquitous fences relentlessly carpets. This was all rainforest until it was cleared by settlers – by hand, in a feat of almost unimaginably laborious vandalism. The grass – 'bushburn' – was a mix of rye and clover introduced from the UK which meant changing the soil structure and soil nutrients so that it would grow well, changing the entire flora. But it is not bleak. The roadside verges are smothered with flowers, and the meadows positively shine beneath a clarity of light that is never found in the northern hemisphere.

Travelling through the Ruapehu district we stopped in one of the few remaining patches of rainforest in the country and went for a walk. It is heavenly. A green, cool, song filled heaven. You can sit by a splashing river looking up at the fan vaults of tree fern foliage with even huger podocarps covered with epiphytic ferns and listen to the bird choir. The bird calls are incredible. Dense forest meant that birds evolved with rather dull plumage – no point in being flashy if no one can see you – but with fabulous song that rings out unseen. The tree ferns dominate of course, growing toweringly huge at every level, and their trunks – which are actually a mass of packed roots – playing host to a range of epiphytic plants and mosses. The light is green. You breathe green air. The bird calls sing green. Unlike the tropical rainforest there is nothing creeping or crawling in the undergrowth to harm you. This is what the first settlers found and what they systematically removed and replaced with imported grass seed and pine plantations. It makes you weep.

We finally arrived at New Plymouth to visit my last garden on this trip, Te Kainga Marire, which is Maori for 'A Peaceful Encampment'. It belongs to Valda Poletti and Dave Clarkson who have been making the garden there since 1972. Ayrlies is spectacular and stands with any other garden on earth but it is huge, grand and exceptional. It has a range of plants from all over the world. Hardly anyone could hope to emulate it. Te Kainga Marire, however, is small, homely and famed for its wide use of indigenous plants. It is, in every sense, a New Zealand Garden.

Not least in its New Zealand identity is the fact that Dave is a Yorkshireman from Scarborough, who emigrated with his family in 1952 when he was fifteen. Valda's family were Italians who came to New Zealand in the 1840s. They bought the half-acre plot before they built the house and started to prepare the garden straight away.

'It had been *Ficus orientalis* swamp that had been dumped with clay.' Dave said. 'It doesn't look good but it breaks down to make good soil and whilst it's hard clay, it is free-draining. We have 70-odd inches of rainfall a year here and we can have hard rain in the morning and be digging by the afternoon. We do get frosts half a dozen days a year but the growing season is twelve months. It never gets too hot and the rain is spread evenly so

Below It might be tiny, but this gnarly Leonohebe ciliolate *is twenty years old. Every visitor to the garden is equipped with a spyglass to get close to the extraordinary plants.* Opposite *This view highlights some of New Zealand's shade-loving plants, including the* King fern, Marattia salicina, *originally cultivated by the Maori who used the starchy base as a flour. In the foreground is one of the four native fuchsia species, the climbing/scrambling* Fuchsia perscandens. *The native grass in the foreground is bush rice grass,* Microlaena avenacea.

there is no dry season. Visitors can't believe how fast everything grows here.'

Valda went on. 'We got a contractor to cultivate the whole half acre and then I spent that first Easter hand raking the whole area. I got some blisters! Then we sowed bush burn and mowed the grass regularly, pegged out the house and planted the perimeter trees and the orchard. We kept mowing and composting and built the house, laid the drive and sorted out the builders' mess, then we could start making the garden.'

The garden is on a whole range of levels created by walls, paths and steps. They have done everything themselves. You only have to be with them for a short time to realise that they are incredibly resourceful. 'It's the Yorkshire background,' says Dave. 'Building

One of the loveliest views at Te Kainga Marire looks from the alpine garden towards the fernery. It has taken over thirty-five years to create a mature alpine meadow, a wetland and a moist, cool fernery from a barren, volcanic clay wasteland.

stone walls is in my blood!' They were both working full time – which Dave still is, as a gardener now and in a health food shop before. 'We worked a seven-day week for years and used to come up here and work by lights at night.'

'We found our inspiration for the garden from wild New Zealand,' Valda says. 'No one had really tried to landscape a garden naturally using mostly native plants. We try and group plants together that grow together in the wild.'

Dave nods in agreement. 'People come and visit our garden and look at native plants with different eyes. Definitely. Especially if you send them out with a lens. It just blows their socks off.'

A lens?

'We give people a magnifying glass to have a really close look at these plants.'

Valda says that younger people are much more open to native plants. The older people still see gardens as a flower garden. There is a greater appreciation and awareness of local flora. It is a coming of age for the New Zealand gardening industry. The bush is now being valued and to an extent replanted. Both have an instinctive feel for plants and know a great deal about them but Valda is officially head plantsperson. 'She has the ability to remember their Latin names,' Dave acknowledges. 'I just recognise them and know how they grow.' However they divvy up the duties, they make a great team.

Valda took me round the garden. It is a series of areas that flow into each other seamlessly. Familiar vegetables like chard, beetroot and peas share space with oranges. Raspberries grow through espalier apples. It is a neat idea. There are half a dozen different types of potato. Valda picks one out of the ground. It is long and knobbly. 'This Maori one is called "Tutaikuri".' What does that mean? 'Dog poo.' Oh.

We move to the scree garden with its mix of alpine and coastal plants. Valda hands me a lens and I lie flat on the ground next to her to inspect the tiny flowers. This is the first time I have lain in a border with the owner of a garden I am visiting, and the experience is revelatory. An extraordinary hidden world of texture, depth and colour within each plant opens out like snorkelling over a rich coral reef. I remain there for half an hour, arse in the air, nose to a magnifying glass pressed against tiny plants.

A round lawn is fringed with tree ferns, shrubs and grasses. A path goes round behind this seeming boundary so you can walk in their shade, underplanted with ground ferns, and look through the fringes – with gleaming ebony stems – to the garden. This is suburbia. It is effectively a housing estate. But it feels just like the rainforest. It is some transformation.

We dipped down into a birthing channel filled with shade-loving ferns. Birthing passage? I go with it and come out the other side reborn into the light.

Valda and Dave have made an inspirational garden. I have come literally to the other side of the world to see what I know and have that knowledge celebrated in a way absolutely particular to New Zealand. Te Kainga Marire is a celebration. It shows that it can be done – not just the making of a beautiful garden good enough to open to the public and to be filmed by the BBC – but also a life well lived with all its share of problems and tragedies, through the making of a garden.

So I return from New Plymouth to Auckland and then make the long journey back across the world from the brightest of antipodean midsummers to a cold, grey British midwinter. Outside my garden is sodden and lumpen, hunkering down against the year's end. It has been an extraordinary trip and for days I am in a daze – not so much from jet lag as garden-lag.

Following pages
The garden at Jim Thompson's House in Bangkok is just as Jim himself would have wanted it to be – the jungle plants pressing right up against the neighbouring buildings.

Painters like Gauguin and 'Le Douanier', Henri Rousseau, and writers like Robert
Louis Stevenson and Somerset Maugham, all feed this sense of a richer, freer life
to be had against a backdrop of palms, bananas and lush jungle green.

7 Looking for Paradise

South East Asia

South East Asia

A trend that has developed in Britain in line with cheaper, more accessible travel is the making of so-called tropical or exotic gardens. Palms, bananas, cannas, gingers, bougainvillea and bamboos can transform a dull back garden bowed under northern light into a lush tropical paradise. Or at least that is the intention. I have never been convinced that this is a good idea or ever very successful but clearly a lot of people disagree with me and love it.

There is nothing particularly new about this either. Ever since heat and glass became relatively cheap in the first quarter of the nineteenth century through the combination of the development of plate glass (so there could be larger, cheaper panes), cast iron (so those panes could be held in large structures), and canals and railways (so that fuel could be easily distributed to keep those large plate glass structures artificially warm), people have built greenhouses to grow and display exotic plants. The glasshouses in botanic gardens, many of them the original ones built over a hundred years ago, are still hugely popular.

So why do we hanker after exotic and tropical plants? Is it because the 'other' is always desirable? That that which we cannot have always seems so much more tempting than all the things readily available around us? Or is there an instinctive response to lush, tropical planting that fulfils a special set of needs?

It is not just the shape and size of the plants. One reason that people have always loved the hothouses in botanic gardens is the wall of wet heat that hits you as you enter, the fecund smell of hot air and soil and the sense of life-and-death – all happening at a more intense rate than the chilly northern life cycle. The plants, although beautiful in their own right, represent all the richness of tropical life and suggest a freer, less inhibited world. It has become part of our artistic and fanciful culture that the East holds slightly wicked and yet delightfully innocent pleasures. Painters like Gauguin and 'Le Douanier', Henri Rousseau, and writers like Robert Louis Stevenson and Somerset Maugham, all feed this sense of a richer, freer life to be had against a backdrop of palms, bananas and lush jungle green.

So this trip to South East Asia was a simple exploration. Was there such a thing as an exotic garden that was a template for all the struggling plants striving to survive in a chilly British back garden? Is there a model that we can learn from and copy or is the concept of 'the exotic' always cultural and relative, a longing for that which we cannot have? So, packing my coolest clothes, sunglasses and sun hat, I set off towards the end of a dark and cold winter to Thailand, Malaysia, Singapore and Bali.

The Jim Thompson House

Bangkok, Thailand

Above Bright *Heliconia bracts hang over the paths, looking almost otherworldly.*
Previous page While *exotic palms look magnificent in this garden by the sea in Bali, I always find them awkward and ill at ease in cold, northern gardens.*

I ARRIVED IN BANGKOK at 6 am, went to the hotel in the middle of the city and had some breakfast with the film crew and then set straight off for a day of filming. The sense of dazed, up-all-night mental fuzziness that this regime induced was exactly the right tone. Bangkok is such a noisy, teeming city, the traffic so bad, and Thai people are so industrious and charming, and the food being cooked on the side of the road and on the pavement smells (and invariably tastes) so delicious, and the heat is so hot that, coming from the middle of a British winter and a fourteen hour flight that includes a six hour time difference you are bound to be fuddled. In fact I lie. It was not exceptionally hot. Bangkok was going through an unseasonably mild spell, which was delicious – hot, bright and sunny but not oppressively so.

I visited Chatuchak Market, selling a strange and eclectic mix of plants. The nursery trade is a big business in Thailand because of the climate. I met a stallholder, Nok, whose family nursery grows frangipani that get sold to America and Australia because she can get them to begin flowering in six months whereas in those countries it takes two years. Nok told me that Thai people love fashion and will avidly collect the latest plant craze and that cacti are the hottest thing at the moment. To them they are exotic.

From the market I went across Bangkok in a tuk-tuk – the ubiquitous three-wheel motorbike taxi that roars round the city. Travelling in one is a cross between sitting on the back of a bike and being pushed in a motorised wheelbarrow. My destination was The Jim Thompson House. This was the home of the eponymous American entrepreneur who founded the Jim Thompson Thai Silk Company and built a house on one of the klongs – canals – that run through Bangkok, right in the heart of the silk district. The house, which is set back from the street and surrounded by its garden, is an exquisite traditional wooden building, painted red, with steep tiled roofs. Inside, the wooden floors and walls are a burnished brown and the whole building is filled with paintings, prints, sculptures, porcelain, books and beautiful furniture. It is clearly the home of a wealthy aesthete and apparently still as he left it, meaning to return a few days later.

The garden weaves around and even under the house, rising on various levels and with large trees screening out the city on three sides. In fact, in its wholly unregulated way, there is an office block literally inches away from the garden, imposing itself like someone squeezing between two people on a bus.

There are two further buildings in the garden, single-room servants' quarters, built in the same style as the main building. All is small and tightly enclosed.

Jim Thompson finished building the house in 1959 and disappeared after going for a walk in the jungle whilst on holiday in Malaya in 1967. The house and garden are open to the public and there is a restaurant and a shop selling the lovely silks that the company still makes. This little garden, lived in for only eight years by a foreigner, attracts as many visitors as Sissinghurst. I had arranged to meet a friend of Jim's, Bill Warren, who was also one of those that worked on the design of the garden, to show me around.

Bill is now an elderly man, American, who has lived in Bali for forty-seven years. He is white haired, erudite and impeccably mannered with a dry and ironical turn of

The undergrowth is spectacular, so dense that it creates the impression that the garden is much larger than it actually is. The dominant plant here is Raphis excelsa.

Plants crowd in upon the tiled pond, as they do everywhere else. Lily pads provide extra shade for the giant goldfish that swim underneath them.

humour. He explained to me that the house was made from six or seven pre-existing buildings and took a year to assemble and join. It is all based upon wooden columns and hung with wooden panels – and all pegged without a single nail or screw in the building. Despite the sense of complete authenticity Bill told me that in a 'real' Thai house each building/room would have been separate and arranged around a central platform. Jim Thompson liked them as one large building which was awkward for the roofs. Jim would entertain in the house every single night and Bill came to many parties here and often stayed as a guest.

The location, situated right on the klong that divided him from the village of Muslim silk weavers that he employed to make his silks, was carefully chosen. Every day he would cross the klong and visit them all, buying and ordering new material. It reminded me of a northern mill owner with his big house above the mill and the workers' homes in sight – impressive. Officially the klong entrance was the front of the house although the back was always used in his time – the gravel yard there is now a car park.

Bill said that Jim knew nothing about plants – he just knew what he liked and the effect he wanted. He wanted the jungle to press right up against the building, but after his death no one did anything to the garden for twenty-five years and, as jungles and Bangkok buildings will, it grew enormous and unregulated and became impenetrable. Bill was called in to help and advise and he let sunlight in. Some large trees were taken out and others planted so that you could see the roof line from the garden. Paths were added, lots was cut back and down – and the feel of the garden as Bill remembered it in Jim's day was restored although not the exact layout. At the back of the house, by the gateway to the klong, is a huge rain tree, *Samanea saman*, which is beautifully elegant and sports a mass of epiphytes in its branches. The rain tree seems to encourage epiphytes more than any other tree and is often grown simply for this adornment.

The garden is quite extraordinarily fulsome and lush and you cannot see through the undergrowth, which makes it seem much bigger than it actually is. Jungle recreation with its intense, almost claustrophobic growth, suits small gardens much better than big ones. The *Alpinia purpurata*, or red ginger, with its 5 ft stems topped by coral flowers looks very fine but Bill told me that it was introduced to Thailand after Jim's death so would not have been in the garden in his day, but that he would certainly have liked it and wanted it there. Bill also put dracaenas in the front of the house, clearing out shrubs to make room for them. They look good.Hanging down by a path in long and absurdly unreal looking festoons are the plastic flower bracts of *Heliconia*. It has banana-like leaves on tall stems and when the flowers open, like parading cockatoos, it becomes even more unreal. I struggle with the truly exotic. To see plants that you have some familiarity with at home in their true setting is always exciting and enlarges your knowledge of them. But coming across something startlingly alien always fills me with a degree of suspicion. What is it looking like that for? What is it up to? Not noble sentiments I know – I am too parochial by far – but that's the way it is.

But Bill pointed out that this is not a traditional Thai garden. Thai people wanted to clear the jungle and keep it away from the buildings, not least to try and reduce mosquitoes. Jim, the American in love with this exotic country, was creating his own notion of Thailand from an assembly of buildings and an idea of a safe and domesticated jungle.

The Klongs

Bangkok, Thailand

A KLONG IS THE NAME given to any of the waterways that vein through Bangkok, some of which are tributaries of the main Chao Phraya river and others canals made to link these natural waters. The name is a good start. Who could not love a thing called a klong?

I am cheating a little here because what I really like about the Bangkok klongs are the gardens that are displayed all the way along them, from the poorest shack to the groovy apartments. I did stop at one and spend an hour there but it was not particularly remarkable. In fact I stopped precisely because it was so typical, and we also had an introduction. It is the massed effect of them that I think is special and that I liked so much and that contrasted so strongly with Jim Thompson's house and garden. The key feature of the klongs is that they are the street and frontage of the buildings. The gardens are designed to be seen and admired from the water (whereas Jim Thompson's was walled and mostly hidden from the klong).

I was taken on my boat ride by Patravadee, an actress who runs a theatre in Bangkok but was bought up living on the klongs. We met at the boat quay, away from the metropolitan culture of the centre of town with its department stores, traffic and tower blocks. This was a mass of food stalls with fresh shellfish, fruit, soups, dumplings, chickens, rice,

Despite everything having to be planted in containers, the houses along the klongs are always packed with plants.

During our boat ride, my guide Patra explained to me a lot about Thai behaviour and customs.

THAIS ENJOY GROWING
PLANTS THAT HAVE
FRAGRANCE, FLAVOUR
AND SYMBOLISM,
AND THAT ARE PART
OF A RITUAL.

cakes, vegetables – all being cooked from early morning till late at night. They say that the Thais live to eat but they have every reason to. It is as good as any food in the world, completely fresh, made while you watch and wait and as unprocessed as food can be, and the very best of it is to be had on the street from any number of these tiny stalls. Thai people seem to eat all day long and yet I did not see a single one that was not slim.

Our boat, like all the klong taxis, is very long with a prow that rises up high like the arched roof of a pagoda, and a truly enormous engine at the back steered by a long pole. The drivers live on the boats and are expert at steering them round the back ways of the klongs – which is just as well, as they tear along with a monstrous roar and a rolling wake, slipping between gaps which would be a crash had they but another coat of varnish.

As we went down the huge river before turning off on to the klongs themselves, Patra explained to me the Thai ethos of saving face. She pointed out that people are far more likely to lie to you than disappoint your expectations. Also it is very rare for anyone to say that they are sorry because if you do something wrong no one would ever point it out to you because of the shame that this would cause. She said that all Asian culture is essentially shame-based whereas in the West it is based upon guilt. In Thailand losing face is the worst thing that can happen. If you do wrong then you must rectify it – not apologise. None of this in any way diminishes the charm, politeness and sheer good nature of the Thai people.

Turning into the klongs we started to pass right by a succession of houses whose verandas, hanging over the water, were filled with plants in pots. The colours of the flowers mingled and blended with the brightly coloured washing on the lines. Flags and furniture juggled for available space. Some of the buildings were hardly more than shanties, others more modern flats and houses. All had wonderful terracotta pots for their plants as well as the empty oil cans and plastic containers that you see all round the world. Of course, everything had to be in a container of some kind and quite large trees grew out of quite small pots. Mangoes are considered good luck and there were plenty of those, whereas the absence of papaya was, Patra explained, because they are considered bad luck. Most of the plants were for some direct culinary or medicinal purpose although the money plant, whose leaves are tipped with gold, featured prominently. The Thais love work and money more than gardens but where the two can combine, even symbolically, they relish them. Patra said that although they have no desire to garden as such, they enjoy growing plants that have fragrance, flavour, symbolism and that are part of a ritual. Thais are immensely practical. They rarely garden for the aesthetics of it – although that pleasure is there, it is bound up with the practical use of each plant. Buddhism dictates that every plant has some use. Trees provide shade, fruit nourishment, flowers are offerings, fragrance cleanses and even pure abstract beauty improves the soul.

Small boats piled with stores, groceries, drinks and fruit paddled from house to house and approached us as we stopped to look. It was a watery street. Patra told me that until thirty years ago the houses were all on dry land with boardwalks down to the klong, but now the waterways have been made wider and the buildings are in and above the water.

We pulled up outside a small wooden house on stilts with a veranda curtained with plants. The owner and his wife, both now retired, were happy – if a trifle bemused – to let us come in and admire their veranda and its garden. Inside pictures of the Thai Royal family were everywhere. Packaging of all kinds was on display plus a collection of clocks, all of which told a different time and none of which was working. It was all impeccably neat and clean.

From the inside you look out on the veranda and the curtain of plants. There were peppers, lemons and chillies for the kitchen, pomegranate for treating diarrhoea and dragon's tongue for asthma. Euphorbia helps constipation and cat's whiskers is good for the kidney. Lemon grass not only tastes good but also wards off mosquitoes. All was practical. I asked how they used the white hybrid tea rose that was looking very healthy. Patra explained that it was a sign of sophistication and Westernisation. Rich people grow them.

All the plants are grown in soil collected from the land and watered every day. They barely change around the year although there are few flowers in the rainy season. Was this not a little monotonous? I asked. No. Everything grows very fast and changes from day to day. I felt doltish for bringing my Western rhythms barging into the speed and subtlety of these little river gardens.

We said thank you and left. The plants were cared for and looked marvellous but there was no culture at all of what we would recognise as gardening. They served a purpose, part of which was to make the people feel happier and purer. But the concept of creating an outdoor space to delight in was not there. Interestingly, Bangkok has less open public space per capita than any other city in the world. There must be an element of choice in that. The truth is that Thais prefer to eat rather than garden and most of the gardens they have serve that purpose. So we scooted back down the crowded klong with its lovely, useful gardens, hit the big river and went and found a market stall for lunch. It was fresh, very spicy and completely delicious.

The Grand Palace

Bangkok, Thailand

I was incredibly privileged to be given special permission to go into the concubines' private garden, a part of the palace that is not usually accessible to the general public.

I ASKED OUR WELL-EDUCATED, intelligent guide what she would say to the king if she had the opportunity and she replied that not only would she be unable to speak but she would also be unable to look at him. Yet she felt sure that the rumours of the king being driven round the city at night so that he could keep his eye on things – including her – were true. Who knows but it seems that her attitude was not unusual. The Thai royal family are regarded by the Thai people with genuine reverence. The image of the king is everywhere and any kind of disrespect towards it is regarded as sacrilege and a very serious criminal offence. The royal palaces, then, are places of huge significance to Thai people and it seemed to me that I should visit one to see its gardens on the basis that they must have a profound influence on the Thai people and their own gardening.

Before going, I made a trip to Chitlada Palace, which is run as a kind of model farm to educate and inform the Thai people. It reminded me of a university or corporate research station. There was no aesthetic consideration at all – everything was considered in terms of its practical use – but it was all treated as though it were especially lovely. Part of this is to do with the Buddhist idea of everything having a use and internal beauty and partly to do with the Thai hagiography of anything royal. For example my guide told me that the king 'can make the rain. He makes big, full clouds that bring rain and he makes the rain go away if it is too much.' No wonder they revere him so much.

The best known Royal Palace is the Grand Palace – a major tourist attraction. It was built by King Rama I in 1782 when he established the new capital of Bangkok on the other side of the Chai Phraya from the old city, and occupies 60 acres in the heart of the modern city. Its golden spires can be seen rising across the river and from the streets from a long way away. Although the Palace is open to tourists, a high level of respect is expected and enforced. It is a curious mixture of sightseeing and solemnity.

The gardens are intended to create a calm atmosphere and a reflective state of mind. Religion (in this case Buddhism), the state and the tangible world of buildings and plants all merge together in a fashion that the Thais accept without thought and yet which is unusual and even uncomfortable for the Western visitor.

The outer palace has large topiary specimens with much yellow on display. Every day in Thailand has an allocated colour and yellow belongs to Monday which is especially lucky because it is the day that the king was born on and is therefore his personal colour.

A broad avenue of clipped cones leads to the gates of the middle garden, which has a surprising and eclectic mixture of tightly-clipped cloud topiary (strongly influenced by Chinese gardens), Thai temples and the Chakri Mahaprasad Hall, looking rather like nineteenth-century French empire architecture. The orange, blue, yellow and green tiled roofs of the temple make the cluster of trees clipped into full-size versions of bonsaied trees seem even more surreal than they are. Strange. Monks with bright orange costume and shaven heads pose for pictures for the tourists. Further on into the palace, tucked into a more intimate courtyard against a building of extreme cream and gold opulence, is a *Khao mor* or 'mountain of pebbles'. This is a large rockery, set with plants and statues of animals, and topped with a small shrine. It is rather beautiful in a wacky way and much revered because it represents the centre of Buddhist cosmology.

The royal family use it for the cutting the top knot ceremony where Thai children have their hair cut to symbolise the progress into adulthood when girls are eleven and boys fourteen. A hand painted sign said 'Please do Not Climb. Fine 300 baht.'

Whilst we were there filming we found that we would be allowed to go into the inner garden where the concubines lived. This was a huge honour as visitors are seldom allowed in there at all – especially if they are men. I went expecting to find a rare and wonderful pleasure ground suitable for a harem. The reality was interesting but curiously unfocussed and underwhelming. There were many huge ceramic pots containing bonsaied trees remarkably similar to the full-size versions in the outer courtyard, and an elaborate rock garden lushly planted and with a water display, turned on especially for us, that ran a waterfall into a pond for the cooling delight of the concubines.

What was really interesting about the Grand Palace was not the aesthetics of the gardens, but the lack of them. All the elements were there – manicured topiary, plants in pots, rock gardens, shrines, flowers – but there was no sense of the garden having its own coherent space. On the klongs the practicality of the gardens had a busy informality that gave them life and a real, vital beauty. Add the mix of reverence and the self-consciousness of the public gaze and that charm was swamped and lost.

Outside in the street, fish were grilling above charcoal bowls, vegetables were stacked high in beautiful baskets and panniers, and soups were lovingly stirred as the tuk-tuks and traffic piled by. I suspect that each of these little stalls, and the verandas on stilts over the noisy, polluted waters of the klongs is much closer to the Thai ideal of a garden.

Anyway, I had to move on. From the polite chaos of Bangkok it was time to go to another city and although I had only changed planes there a few times in the past, I knew that it would be very different. I was off to Singapore.

The round, cloud-pruned topiary creates a surprisingly surreal picture against the brightly-coloured temple roof in the Grand Palace grounds.

The Garden City

Singapore

I TOOK THE ORIENT EXPRESS to Singapore. It is a special trip and a glorious way to travel, albeit your fellow passengers are hardly rich in local colour. But certainly rich. As we went through Malaysia we passed mile upon mile of plantations of oil palms, the rainforest cleared to make space for this particularly blanketing monoculture. I was intrigued to learn that in the nineteenth century it was much valued as a lubricant for the machinery that powered the industrial revolution and also for making Palmolive soap. Now, of course, it is used mainly as a cooking oil and, ironically, as biodiesel – although the removal of the rainforest causes a huge increase of carbon into the atmosphere as well as being a major ecological disaster. It was introduced into Malaya in 1917 and the plantations were run by English landlords until the 1960s, when the government gave new settlers 10 acres of land each to plant with palm oil or rubber. But we, in our swish train, served with delicious food and drink, did not mind. We were rich, comfortable and heading, suitably, for Singapore.

Singapore is a strange place. We were there because it proclaims itself to be the archetypal 'Garden City' or 'City in A Garden'. The capitals are significant. It is a brand we are considering, instigated in 1967 by the first Prime Minister Lee Kuan Yew, whose son is now at the helm. Gerry, the cameraman who filmed six of our ten trips and a man I admire, like and respect without reservation, spent some months working in Singapore and said that it was a great place to live. You can immediately see why. It is clean, comfortable, law-abiding and a paradigm of the modern, aspirational urban life. But from the moment that we arrived at the station I disliked almost everything about it.

We stayed at the Shangri-la Hotel, chosen because it has a garden made in 1971 as one of the first attempts to follow the government directive of making Singapore self-consciously gardeny. It is a big, international hotel so it is unfair to condemn it for lack of intimacy or quirky charm, but I shan't let that fetter me. There are some dramatic and inventive parts to it. I really like the idea of the lush, soaring green in the well of a balconied atrium, the sky a small scrap of blue through the green fronds. But although it is pleasing, it is floral muzak laid out by the yard. And the concrete faux rustic pole rails and steps are truly horrid. They would be inappropriate and bad if they were real but in concrete they are almost the worst possible thing that they could have done when combined with the rectilinear architecture (quite good) and soaring green. Just a very bad call.

Gardeners work hard to keep the parks weed, and character, free.

We set off through the streets to Bishan Park and there is no question that some of the roads, lined with fabulous mahogany trees (*Swietenia macrophylla*) and rain trees, just as in Jim Thompson's Garden in Bangkok, smothered in epiphytes, are lush, green and extremely beautiful. This is Road Glamour.

Bishan Park is held up as a fine example of Singapore's creation of open spaces for their citizens to relax, take exercise and be stimulated in. It is a small island so such spaces are at a premium. They must earn their keep so the park has to pay and hives off space to a spa, which at the same time must fit the corporate brief and be green and pleasant land so it was designed to fold into a 'garden'.

There are moments and spots of aesthetic pleasure but it is actually rather depressing and irritating. It feels like walking about a plan. You expect to see a design number etched into the grass or tree trunk. The public-convenience side intrudes at every turn: street lamps, electricity boxes and tarmac spoil each potentially rewarding eyeful. In the context of Singapore it illustrates very well the way that the best intentions cannot work without humanity. Gardens simply cannot ever be good and corporate. They must have soul and passion and quirkiness and above all, individual humanity riven through them.

There was one lovely image in the park that made it worth the journey – an elderly man taking his parrot for a walk on a lead. Both waddled along side by side, old friends.

I met Dr Lawrence Leong Chee Chiew, Head of Parks in Singapore. He was thoughtful, articulate, pleasant but unable to conceive of a garden as separate from amenities and purpose. His favourite garden in Singapore is one where he can go and jog. Throughout our chat the same buzz words keep being repeated: Urban Jungle, City Garden, City in a Garden, Greening of the City. It was like talking to a New Labour politician and equally depressing. He never once referred to the irony of increasing the city directly at the expense of the rainforest or the fact that the original rainforest was cleared in order to make the city. If the line had been one of repairing the damage then there might have been some logic – but all was spoken of as if this – modern Singapore – was created from swamp and is mankind's gift to nature. I tell myself that I ought be interested in the plants, most new to me, but I can't fake it. In a boring setting all plants are dull.

Even the wide variety of tropical plants in Bishan Park failed to provide the level of interest that can only exist when a garden has soul and character.

A walkway takes you right over the top of the jungle – all that remains of Singapore's rainforest – and provides you with a fascinating bird's eye view of the upper canopy.

In fact there is a scrap of rainforest left uncleared and I went and visited it. One man's scrap is another's cast off and the Singaporean rainforest is in fact 2,225 acres although it is all secondary rainforest (no older than a hundred years) and so not exactly virgin. There are signs everywhere, tarmacked roads and access is encouraged as long as you do exactly what you are told. There is absolutely no sense of wilderness but it is Singapore's conscience. Tracks blaze through like railway cuttings to provide access for water pipelines. But it does have a wonderful suspension footbridge (sponsored, you will be glad to know, by a bank and opened, significantly, by the Minister of State for Finance and Transport), which is educative, exhilarating and beautiful in that you can walk along it and look down on the canopy. But look through your binoculars at the horizon and you focus on the manicured green of a fairway and bunker…

It is significant that there is only one orchid that flowers wild in the so-called rainforest in Singapore, the vanilla orchid, *Vanilla griffithii*, which flowers for just one day in March and April. The Botanic Gardens, on the other hand, are full of orchids. Thousands of them, all in pots and sunk into beds to make them appear 'natural', and with names like 'Margaret Thatcher' and, obviously, 'Princess Diana'. This is orchids as operatic bedding. Park Orchids. A large bed of them is like eating nine puddings in a row. An orchid looks best hanging in solitary splendour from its host branch or trunk and there were a stray few like that, allowing you to see them for the exquisite beauties that they are. As we left, we spotted one magnificent epiphytic orchid growing from a tree, with no others in sight. Really lovely. If it were all like that it would be tremendous.

Whereas in Bangkok aesthetics are always secondary to practicality, in Singapore you have a feeling that aesthetics are always second to wealth and most fools know that money cannot make true beauty. However, not everything was negative. I did find one high spot in Singapore when I paid a visit to Wilson Wong.

Wilson Wong's Garden
Singapore

WILSON WONG LIVES on the tenth floor of a High Density Building with his parents. He is twenty-eight, writing his PhD on Chinese medicinal herbs and has what he calls his 'light garden' in his room – shelving with lights and various bromeliads and other low-light jungle plants growing in what almost amounts to Petri dishes. There are plants sprawling on the stairs but like everyone else he is only allowed two pots on the communal balcony outside his flat – and then only if they make no mess. This is Singapore. Balcony glamour.

However, nearby, he has another garden. Throughout Singapore, tower blocks form squares around small, open green spaces. His is not entirely open. In the centre is a small, hedged garden about the size of an allotment. It contains impressive raised brick beds, full of vegetables and herbs. In itself this is not exceptional and there are tens of thousands of gardens of this ilk all over the world. But not in Singapore. In Singapore, Wilson's garden is a beacon of individuality, courage and bloody-mindedness.

At first meeting, Wilson hardly seems to fit any of this description. He is small, charming and nervously polite, desperately eager to show me his garden. He says that he started to be fascinated by plants when he had to grow mung beans as a five year old

Although unexceptional at first glance, Wilson Wong's garden is quite remarkable for the sheer fact of its existence, and also has real charm.

Wilson Wong himself is an unassuming young man, but his dedication, enthusiasm and perseverance are impressive and an inspiration.

schoolchild. 'I thought, "Where did the growth come from?" I had to know more. I always dreamt of a garden but it was impossible.' So this small, ordered, patch of garden is the impossible dream made flesh.

He created a gardening website to meet like-minded people and talk about plants. Wilson told me that they all tend to be fanatical about one genera of plants – with carnivorous plants the most popular. I suspect that this is because these are non-garden plants that can be grown in pots in the HDBs.

Wilson was persistent. He nurtured his dream, got the funds from the local council and the garden was opened on November 5th, 2006. I was there just a few months later but it looked as though it had been there for at least two years – everything growing astonishingly fast. There is a sign – Singapore loves its signs – saying that it was opened by the same Minister as the rainforest suspension bridge as part of 'Clean and Green Week 2006'. I like the order of the words. Cleanliness is very much a Singapore virtue – you get the feeling that all dirt is kept firmly underneath the carpet.

But the garden is driven entirely by Wilson. He designed it, set it up, organises the running of it, everything really, although he has a battery of young, smiling but earnest helpers – and one marvellous old man, garrulous, gap-toothed and slightly batty.

It is a simple rectangle with hedges of what looked like photinia but almost certainly wasn't. Like everything else, the hedges are ridiculously advanced for their planting age. The ghost of the cleared rainforest reappears in the speed and virility of the plants that are permitted to grow. The first third of the garden is laid out as a European herb garden based around a central bed. Practically all the herbs are unrecognisable to me and are mostly medicinal rather than culinary – although there are things like coriander (not ours but shrubby and thick-leaved) and much else used in cooking. People still collect herbs for use, even on the housing estates.

The vegetables are all grown in raised beds – practically every variation of Chinese cabbage, all sown thickly. The greens are then hand-thinned for use in soup, leaving space for the larger ones to mature. This is the traditional style and I had noticed it from the train as we went from Kuala Lumpur to Singapore.

The soil is poor and heavy clay – and all brought in. There is no compost and no manure in Singapore – so Wilson uses the grass mowings from the square and fallen leaves to make compost. In the thick heat and humidity this will turn to useable compost in weeks. They can grow six or seven crops a year, taking as little as twenty-eight days from sowing to final harvest when the weather is good. Good weather means not too hot and no torrential rain which bashes the seedlings. There were no weeds visible but then there are currently about six people to weed each raised bed.

Wilson Wong's community garden was undoubtedly the best thing I saw in Singapore, even though in itself it is wholly unremarkable. It was filled with the passion and enthusiasm of one individual bucking the corporate blandness that engulfs the rest of the city.

I left, rather depressed, and seemingly further away from any kind of exotic jungle paradise garden than ever. But things were looking up because my next stop was Bali.

Pura Taman Ayun

Ubud, Bali

BALI, A SMALL ISLAND in Indonesia, is famous for being an idyllic holiday spot. So famous that it is hugely crowded and has apparently the densest population of any island state. The towns and villages merge, buildings lining the roads. But all are well built and dominated by the traditional style of family and temple compound, where the layout of the buildings, their relationship to each other and the role of the gardens is tightly proscribed. Spirituality of gardens and homes is essential.

Before the Dutch arrived in the early seventeenth century only kings had gardens in Bali and these were very similar to the temple gardens (the majority of Bali practises its own version of Hinduism). To understand the modern domestic Balinese garden I was advised to go to a temple garden and the most famous of these is Pura Taman Ayun, built in 1634. *Pura* means palace, *taman* garden and *ayun* beautiful, and Beautiful Palace Garden is not a bad description. When we arrived at 8 am, the heat was burning and it got steadily hotter all day. The temple is surrounded by a palm-fringed wide moat, crossed via a bridge flanked with carvings of evil spirits and the idiosyncratic gate shape that one sees all over Bali of the 'Splitting Mountain' – a curved peak sliced so that the two gate piers would form the peak if they met. The mountain is essential in all Balinese gardens and temples because that is where the gods reside. Ideally Balinese people would worship at the mountain but a temple is a practical substitution for that.

The temple is divided into three sections, outer, middle and inner. The outer is a public space with a large meeting house for village gatherings. There are wide expanses of grass, a square pond and pots either side of a central path. It feels like a public park.

A wall divides the outer from the middle section, where the temple goes from the profane to the sacred. The central court is used for preparation for ceremonies and offerings and is where dances are performed and holy food prepared. Not everyone is

The temple garden in Bali must be amonst the most exotic in the world.

The tiered, black-thatched roofs of the shrines stand out against the sky like beautiful, spiritual sculptures.

always welcome. There is a sign saying 'During menstruation ladies are strickly (sic) not allowed to enter the temple. Thank you.' In the corner is a bell tower to call people to ceremonies and in the centre a thatched shrine. To one side is a music hall which must be positioned there so that it does not block the entrance. These positions are essential, and cannot be arbitrary. They are reflected in all Balinese compounds from the grand to the humble.

The plants in this section are chosen for their practical use in ceremonies. A frangipani tree, *Plumeria rubra*, is in bloom. The flowers are a main part of offerings and it is the predominate fragrance of Bali, although it is in fact a native of Jamaica and Mexico. The ancak tree is a relative of the banyan, and provides good leaves to place offerings in as well as shade. Yellow bamboo is also planted as this too is used in ceremonies. There are gardenias, mangoes, bougainvillea, hibiscus and mangosteen (*Garcinia mangostana*), with purplish-chocolate fruits that enclose a delicious white flesh.

A huge terracotta brick and stone gateway covered in carvings of gods and demons forms the entrance to the inner part. These doors are only opened for ceremonies that take place every twenty-one days and every full and new moon. The visitor cannot go into this inner sanctum but there is a path around it and a low wall with a moat in front of it. I looked over this to a series of shrines with tiered thatched roofs. They made a staggeringly beautiful succession of outlines against the sky, the thatch black and lined like the underside of a field mushroom. The size of the shrines indicates their status, with the tiers all odd numbered and eleven the most important of them all. It is an enclosure of astounding sculptural beauty, unlike anything I had seen before and I stayed there fully two or three hours in the blasting heat, transfixed by them. Some are hundreds of years old and are repaired every generation or so using exactly the same materials and techniques of the original construction. The black roofs are made from palm fibres, last for twenty-five years and are only used for mountain shrines. The grass roofs of the smaller, hut-like shrines only last for ten years and are used for prayer and music and to make offerings.

Lotus and water lilies flowered in the moat. All the shrines are made of sandstone, wood and reeds. Nothing is painted or embellished although the carvings and outlines are fabulously ornate. The essence of these Balinese temples is to preserve a natural simplicity with tranquillity and serenity provided through choice of materials. The carvings on all the shrines are done after they are built, carving into the building itself rather than assembling it. What they aspire to is authenticity rather than sincerity.

The temple is cared for by the whole community because this is a way to obtain the best karma. In Balinese culture, the key elements are God and the temple, the high priest, humans, the environment and your ancestors. All must be respected and cared for. All these elements still function in Balinese society as they always have done, through temples, homesteads, ritual, dance and music. All are indistinguishable from one another.

Everything, from the mundane to the spiritual seemed to be integrated. But what I, a hot, weary Westerner, trying to make sense out of hugely contrasting types of Asian culture, remember are the astonishing stacked roofs of the mountain shrines. It is a garden and they are human edifices of great beauty. That makes it an extraordinary, wonderful garden, albeit more complex than the lush cliché of the exotic tropical paradise.

A Traditional Home Compound

Ubud, Bali

THERE WAS A LOT to take in. On the one hand there was the overarching scale and monumentalism of the mountain shrines, and on the other the access and integration of all aspects of Balinese life. The temple gardens were clearly defined spaces yet their role and the role of the garden and shrines in general seemed fused. So my next port of call was a household compound.

I met up with Braggie, who had spent his working life as a gardener, although now he was retired and spent his days fishing. He had been to London in 1975 where he visited Kew a number of times. He came back to Bali strongly influenced by the tropical gardens there and worked on creating a modern tropical garden idiom in Bali. He spoke good English and was able to explain the role and meaning of the compound layout and how the plants and outdoor spaces worked in the traditional Balinese family compound. All Balinese people live in these compounds, with their very precise layout, and he took me to a traditional one whose buildings had changed little over the previous hundred years.

As we approached, the sun streamed through smoke, creating lovely hazy shadows between the thatched buildings and the stone entrances. Nothing could have been more romantic and yet the compounds are completely practical places. Nothing is placed, planted or created for aesthetic effect. The ground was bare beaten earth. The buildings are thatched with rice straw with deep eaves to provide shade and protection from the occasional rainstorm but all are open-sided save for the building for the newly-weds to preserve their connubial privacy.

In the centre of the compound was the building used for ceremonies, where a woman and her daughters sat making up little leaf baskets of flowers to be used as

In the shade of the central open-sided building of the compound, the family go through the daily ritual of making flower offerings for their shrine. Surely this is a form of gardening?

offerings. Chickens scratched around. A cat eyed the kitchen building, to the right of the entrance where an old woman, bent almost double and wearing only a cloth around her waist and a purple turban, added wood to a fire and prepared food. In one corner an older man carved animals and evil spirits from wood, sitting with the carvings held between his feet. After a while he took up a bamboo flute and played. It is a thin, reedy sound. I complimented him. He laughed and offered it to me to have a go.

In the far left hand corner of the compound, behind a low brick and stone wall, was the family temple, with its own cobbled yard. There were half a dozen thatched shrines, each with a white cloth attached like a napkin. The floral offerings were then placed at these shrines. I asked Braggie how many gods there were. 'Only one God but many names,' he said. 'Like us.'

Braggie explained that people regarded trees as more important than buildings and until recently it would have been unthinkable to have cut one down to make space for a building. The building would always go round or beside it. Destroying a living thing unnecessarily was bad karma. Even in this old, very simple compound all the buildings and shrines were stone and there were beautifully carved figures, gates and plinths.

At the back of the compound was a wooded area with tall coconut palms, bamboos and flowering trees and shrubs which we might separate as the garden, although Braggie told me that the whole compound was one. The back part was simply a different kind of use. Everything had a distinct role, just as it did at the Temple. The coconut leaf was used to make the little baskets for the offerings and banana branches used to make funeral pyres. Bamboo was used for every kind of construction and every compound had to have these three plants. Flowers such as frangipani were used every day for offerings. 'Normally,' said Braggie, 'there would be pigs and chickens. Perhaps a cow.' The point was to be as self-sufficient in all things as possible. Nothing was especially planted. They just grew. Nothing trained or pruned or tended.

But the daily ritual of gathering the leaves and flowers for the offerings and carefully making them into beautiful little posies of pink, orange, pale blue and white flowers appeared to me as much gardening as our horticultural primping and preening. We in the West seem to be locked into a very restricted view of what a garden could or should be. To really make a garden that captures the true flavour of the tropics perhaps we should not slavishly plant a fanciful mixture of 'exotics' but carefully gather our own

The space at the back of the compound is home to a range of plants, all of which have a practical use in community life.

flowers and make offerings to our own deities. But then, like Singapore, perhaps these would be the gods of Shopping and all things Clean.

When Braggie came back to Bali after his visit to the UK, he bought with him a realisation of organising plants and choosing them for the way that they looked as much as for their usefulness. He found himself working with new garden designers, making a distinct Balinese garden idiom. One of these was an Australian called Michael White, who came to Bali in 1973, learnt about gardening from Braggie and went on to become one of the most successful garden designers in Asia and an authority on South East Asian architecture and gardens. Along the way he changed his name to Made Wijaya. I had heard from others that he was a character and that I should go and see him. So I did.

Villa Bebek, Made Wijaya's Garden

Sanur, Bali

MADE WIJAYA is a remarkable man. Flamboyant, erudite, complicated, articulate, outrageous and completely dedicated to Bali and Balinese culture. Did I say flamboyant? I had a wonderfully enjoyable morning with him at his house and garden (which is also his office), at Villa Bebek in Sanur on the southern coast. He came as Michael White to Bali from Australia in 1973 as an intended short break in his architectural studies but never went back. Instead, he met Braggie, who taught him about gardening. This, combined with his architectural background and his fascination for Balinese culture, inspired him to design gardens, to date over 600 in total in Singapore, India, Mexico, Hawaii and Morocco. He is a dominant figure who has taken the Balinese garden and made a modern idiom from it – and a thriving business. He employs ninety people at his home at Villa Bebek where he strides round from group to group dressed in shirt, turban, dark glasses and long wrap-around, shouting, cajoling, flirting, roaring with laughter and working on twelve different projects at once.

It is always much more interesting to visit a garden designer in their own garden rather than in one that they have made for a client. His is a series of interlocking areas with lily pond, swimming pool and seating areas all interspersed with shrines, statues, buildings and lush plants. The Balinese compound is there but exuberantly, dramatically planted. Unlike Jim Thompson's in Bangkok, where the intention was to mimic the jungle pressing in on the house, this does not ape any kind of natural planting. It is a performance, and a very self-conscious, self-confident one where every detail works towards the desired effect. These details accumulate relentlessly and are invariably loaded with wit, charm and a sense of playfulness. It was the first garden that I had come across in this journey that made me smile. It was ornate, crowded, intense, loaded with textures, fragrance, shapes, colour – although inevitably green dominates – and objects and yet it felt of a piece with the lushness and intensity of light and heat, as if the underlying jungle was just waiting to return and engulf everything. Made Wijaya's brilliance is to understand that growth, to ally it to the culture and traditions of the Balinese temple and compound gardens and to create something modern and original from it.

I sat with him in the centre of his garden with the scores of people working in the various pavilions scarcely heard or seen, and asked him how his garden was conceived. 'I was very influenced by the wild colours, the fecundity and the peopling of the gardens with these wild shrines and things. So I have tried to edit out the Dutch colonial influence of gentrification and use the natural garden style without making it too kitschy or Disneyfied. You have to retain that spiritual element. This is a testing ground for ideas. I wanted it to be a little mini-history of all Bali trends. So I have water features I had seen in palaces of east Bali, I have a sand garden, I have tried to collect ornamental courtyard trees and shrubs, so it is a sort of museum of Balinese garden traditions and compounds. There are twelve pavilions and forty-eight different courtyards.'

Forty-eight courtyards! The garden, as far as I could see was not particularly large but by any standards that is a lot of different garden areas. 'A small garden just requires a big idea. It's no easier to do a small courtyard. If you have pavilions in a compound you end up with lots of different spaces. The big part of Balinese traditional gardens are the gates

Made Wijaya might be Australian by birth, but his enthusiasm and passion for all things Balinese sings out in his garden.

and walls and shrines. But in the villages it's just baked earth and a couple of frangipani trees. But there will be water buffaloes grazing. The idea of plants as part of a decorative garden is fairly new to the Balinese.

'Any garden is temporary because if the elder son is to be married everything gets pulled out. This garden we are sitting in was built for a book launch. Things come and go. That's why things are often in pots because they have lots of ceremony and they have to move things round. Any good tropical architecture allows itself to be thrown over for a big garden party! Everything is temporary. It grows and comes up quickly but disappears quickly too. It is a lot of maintenance.'

How does this square with the long tradition of the temples? 'The Balinese keep their finest work for the temples but they live in a temple environment in a way. Every house has its temple. In palaces and houses it tends to blur. Flowers for the offerings are from the main courtyard. The priests who look after the temples are really priest-gardeners. They sweep them, gather and pick the flowers for the offerings.'

So do you take the temple garden and provide a version of it for new gardens? 'You don't gift a shrine to a garden that will not respect it. But you can use dancers or warrior figures. The man-made and the natural can combine. The artful garden. You can create a well-balanced garden that is still Balinese with its passageways for food to be carried across for life lived outside in a series of pavilions – like the Islamic and Persian gardens.'

I asked, given the huge increase in tourism and building, where the future of the Balinese garden lay. 'Bali survived colonisation, survived islamisation, it has pretty much survived mass tourism – but will it survive the real estate boom? They don't want to give room to the gardens. It is a dynamic culture but they are easily bored. They will resist the trend for minimal gardens because they are gardeners. Bali is more on the edge of the Chinese civilisation and is a sponge for all Asian trends from Buddhism and the Mughals from India to Hinduism and colonial influences. Thailand had no garden culture and would cut back the jungle. But they came to Bali and saw that they could make gardens.'

I asked Made what he thought of the exotic, 'tropical' gardens that you can now find all around the world, not least in Britain. 'Tropical gardens are getting bad reputations. Sticking in crotons and a few palms doesn't make a tropical garden. You need to have cultural and geographical reference.' I agree. Gardens must have meaning at every level be it the geographical, personal, practical or spiritual. Preferably all at once. I later visited a couple of smart holiday homes nearby with acclaimed gardens. Pleasant but I could have been anywhere where the sun shone and the sea was warm and blue. They were anonymous and meaningless and after the busy richness of Made's garden they felt static and dull.

So my journey came to an end on a high note. I had not found the perfect, natural tropical paradise but I had found a truly creative garden entrenched in a local idiom and making something new from it. I had seen fascinating things along the way. Bangkok is a crazy, busy and rather wonderful city with no real interest in gardening but the klongs hint at a culture that is practical, modest, busy and adores its food. I found Singapore's obsession with money and consumption vulgar and rather depressing. The tree lined roads were lovely but the idea of a City Garden is marketing claptrap. There was no poetry, no soul. Bali is shockingly crowded with people and new buildings. But it is exhilaratingly beautiful and every stick, stone and leaf sings. The temples are spiritual gardens of an order I had never experienced before.

I returned home on February 15th, my wife's birthday and the day when we usually begin to sow the summer seed for our own northern, very untropical garden.

Opposite *At Villa Bebek, I felt for the first time that I had found the truly exotic tropical garden that I had imagined would feature throughout my trip to South East Asia.* Following pages *Pickers are dotted amongst the crazed paths of the tea plantations up in the hills near Munnar in Kerala, India.*

The colours, scents, sounds, food and sheer physicality
of every waking moment in India range from an assault
to a balm, but you simply cannot avoid or escape them.

8 Drowning in Sensation

India

India

This was my first trip to India. I confess that I was rather scared of the place and I had avoided it in the past, thinking of it as a rather frightening mix of poverty, diarrhoea, heat and unimaginable numbers of people. I certainly found all those things – on a level beyond my wildest imaginings – but India is also the most vibrant, colourful, life-enhancing place that I have ever been to. I now deeply regret waiting so long to go there.

Nowhere on this planet is more sensuous than India. The colours, scents, sounds, food and sheer physicality of every waking moment range from an assault to a balm but you simply cannot avoid or escape them. The Western world tries to create a series of bubbles and cocoons to escape humanity and in the process desensitises itself. In India that is impossible. Life – in every imaginable guise – moves in and through you in every possible way.

Now this is exhilarating but could also be exhausting and overwhelming. However, having gardens at the core of my first visit to the sub-continent gave it a level of focus and context in which to place the turmoil. Not that it meant being away from people. In India you are never alone. We could be filming in a wide open plain and before we had set up the camera there would be a group of fascinated onlookers. I invariably found Indians to be more polite, more friendly and much better mannered than Europeans but the concept of private, personal space, especially in public, is not one that they share with us. But that is India and you can only accept and respect it for what it is.

And it is so much! It is such an old, wise civilisation and such a varied, beautiful country and there are such changes going on and so many people and it was so, so hot! I was there in April in Delhi and Rajasthan and it was rarely below 40ºC in the day, rising up to 45ºC. If you have not experienced it, this is unimaginable, and it was due to get hotter and more oppressive before the June monsoons arrived.

But my journey began in the cooler more humid south at Kochin in Kerala. I then went north to Delhi, visited Agra, drove down to Jaipur in Rajasthan, back to Delhi and took a train north to the foothills of the Himalayas at Chandigarh before heading home. It was a few weeks of incredible intensity with every day bringing new experiences and sensations. But starting in Kerala was a gentle introduction to India because it is the lushest, best-educated, least harsh part of the country. All food in India is superb but some of the meals in Kerala were the best I have ever had – although I might be influenced by the fact that I had yet to come across the full phenomenon of Delhi Belly.

Mr Abraham's Spice Garden

Thekkady, Kerala

Above Giant jackfruit *hang from the trees, looking just like large prickly pears.*
Previous page The Monsoon Pavilion at Deeg Gardens in Rajasthan *was designed to provide relief from the summer heat. Two vast tanks of water would have filled the canals and fountains, cooling the surrounding air for the Maharajah and his court.*

MR ABRAHAM'S GARDEN is up in the hills at Thekkady, about three hours from Kochin, but I spent a day in the town first to acclimatise myself. Kochin has been the centre of the Indian spice trade for millennia. The Romans and pre-Islamic Arabs came there as well as the Chinese, all after the supremely valuable spices, so sought after because they transformed an otherwise plain diet. Medieval Europe in particular grew to love what was, by modern standards, highly spiced food. It was a sign of all that was exotic, wealthy and special. Ginger, cinnamon, turmeric, cloves, nutmeg, mace and saffron were all imported from unimaginably remote lands, and had instant cachet and glamour that the wealthy were prepared to pay huge sums for. There was also a practical reason for going to huge lengths to get black pepper, the most highly valued of all the spices. In autumn, all but essential stock and animals providing milk were slaughtered and preserved by salting, so the only meat for most people in the winter months was salted. Pepper makes highly salted food palatable – which is why we always serve salt and pepper together – but there was never enough of it, hence why it was so valuable. And the best quality pepper in the world, the most valuable of all, grows in Kerala.

Kochin was the main port for the trade, and the hills above and around it provided many of the spices. Vasco de Gama arrived in 1498 (and died there in 1513), making it a Portuguese colony. Then the Dutch took over in the seventeenth century and ran the town until the British took over at the end of the eighteenth century.

Wandering through the old port of Kochin you can see these different cultures in the architecture, especially the beautiful old Dutch quarter. I visited some of the few remaining spice warehouses, although in this age of the internet spice traders do not need to be anywhere in particular so the concept of a physical trading district is dying out into cyber anonymity. (O Brave New World!) There was an intoxicating balm of fragrances, of the spices themselves, of course, but also the hessian of sacks and bundles bound with coarse twines, of rush baskets and the slightly feral tang of the street. But each open sack spilled with bright yellow nuggets of turmeric root, different grades of pepper ranging from dark chocolate through shades of green to white, vanilla pods and the flat green cardamom seeds that are so highly prized.

Down by the sea, the famous Kochin fishing nets, bamboo frames lashed together, gracefully arched in and out of the water scooping a meagre catch at each pass, each net hauled by a team of sweating, laughing, shouting men. A bus passed behind them, filled with more people than could possibly fit. It was a *Guinness Book of Records* bus. I was to see buses, cars, lorries, taxis, every and any vehicle, crammed fuller than this every day.

So I took to the hills, a six-hour drive up through small, winding mountain roads, where beautiful women in turquoise, saffron, tangerine, magenta and shocking lipstick-pink saris stood waiting for a bus, and lorries

WHILST IT MIGHT LOOK RAW AND WILD, IT TAKES A GREAT DEAL OF SOPHISTICATED CARE TO MAKE IT WORK.

crawled, tooting at every bend. Nowhere is as colourful as India. We passed through towns dressed like carnivals. The shops parade colour. Every truck is brightly painted (and impossibly overloaded). As we drove through the forests, pepper vines climbed the trees and cardamom, with foliage such as lush strap-leaved ferns or small cycads growing as an understorey. The coffee trees were all in bloom and the fragrance from their flowers was clear on the warm, humid air.

We finally got to Thekkady, and stayed just outside the Periyar Tiger Reserve, which is supposed to be superb for seeing elephants and tigers, although hugely crowded with tourists. That night, as we were staying at a hotel with an Ayurvedic centre, I had an Ayurvedic massage (in the name of research, of course). Ayurveda is based upon developing an individual's immune system to such a degree that it can fight off infection before disease can take hold. My massage was, as they say in my part of Herefordshire when confronted with something wholly alien if not frankly hostile, 'something different', and involved donning a paper jock strap, lying on a carved wooden table and being very vigorously rubbed all over with hot oils before being showered and meticulously dried, all by a rather serious young man for 500 rupees (about six quid).

Next morning we went down the road to Mr Abraham's Spice Garden. Mr Abraham greeted us. He is a fit, handsome man in his late fifties, with a moustache and splendid tufts of grey hair protruding from each ear. His family have been spice growers for generations and he was brought up on the family farm nearby. His grandfather started the farm in 1952 and planted the first trees on this plot and Mr Abraham built the house in 1980. Every bit of it himself. It is entirely organic. He still does everything needed for his spices, climbing high into the trees to harvest them. His father is eighty-six and still fit and strong, and his grandfather died at ninety-three after six hours of illness – the first and only one of his long life. Needless to say they all practise Ayurvedic medicine.

This garden up in the hills near Thekkady is amazingly colourful.

India is unbelievably colourful. Even the horns of the Brahman cows in a roadside cattle market were painted brilliant reds, blues and yellows.

The display area is 2 acres and not in the least primped or even, perhaps, conforming to the conventional notion of a garden. The lines between domestic garden, forest and smallholding are blurred to my constrained English eye. I put it in a 'forest garden/permaculture' pigeon hole and then take it out again. It is what it is. Mr Abraham's garden.

It is, of course, full of spices. He grows cardamom, cinnamon, pepper, cloves, vanilla, ginger, turmeric, old spice, galangal and gonglu. He also grows coffee and bananas. Twenty-three different varieties of bananas. We went on a tour, starting with a group of cardamom plants. The flowers and seed are at the base of the plant on stems shaded by the foliage. It will only grow in shade with plenty of water and only grows well above 1,950 ft. It flowers all year round, leaving little green berries along the stem and Mr Abraham picks it every thirty to forty days for the best quality. It seems hugely labour-intensive but cardamom is enormously popular as a flavouring in tea, coffee and cakes and to improve blood circulation, and people are very sensitive about the quality, paying a lot more for the best.

Pepper vines grow twined about trees with the berries hanging in long bunches like tiny elongated grapes. The vine – which is indigenous to Kerala – is pollinated by rain running down the flowers so the dry season means no berries. It hybridises indiscriminately and produces varying leaves, sizes of berry and yields but the taste is essentially the same. The pepper is red when ripe and each red skin is rubbed off by hand to reveal the glistening white peppercorn. Green pepper is harvested in October and November and remains green when it is dried. The red pepper is sun-dried on the roof of Mr Abraham's house and turns black in twenty-four hours. Before pepper was mainly sold by auction in Kochin, the strings that the berries are attached to were removed by foot, gathered up and piled in the road so that the visiting European pepper merchants would know that there was a harvest to come and buy.

The plum-coloured fruit of a red banana hang in fingers from the flowering stem whilst the huge leaves – the biggest of all the banana family – arch up and out. I am struck, as I increasingly am in these travels, of how much better plants like bananas look in their natural setting than in an English back garden. Plants that want to grow in a particular setting are not only healthier and happier but invariably look better too. Cloves, the flower that each was the centre of now fallen, grow on stems like green pearls in a claw setting. To collect each one and fill sackfuls seems an epic task. No wonder spices were so costly. And now we are so careless of these things! The jackfruit hang like giant knobbly pears. Mr Abraham says that they make very good mulch for the cardamom.

Everywhere the leaves and litter are left on the ground and raked around the base of the plants. It soon rots down and feeds and protects the plants. It works. This is forest gardening or permaculture in practice, growing a range of crops within the indigenous setting, using a mixture of permanent trees and shrubs with temporary crops in their shade and in clearings. Whilst it may look raw and wild, it takes a great deal of sophisticated care to make it work and is a triumph of mixing production with aesthetics and learning. Gardens are like people. The more at ease they are with themselves, the more that they know what they are trying to do, the better and happier they are.

We go up onto the large flat roof and look across to a high, pointed hill. Mr Abraham and his wife, good Catholics both, walk to the top as a pilgrimage every Good Friday. When they reach the top they look back and see their little patch. He smiles broadly.

The Railway Garden

Munnar, Kerala

FROM THEKKADY there was another long drive, going even higher up the mountains to Munnar. The next day, after breakfast we went half a mile to the Railway Garden. Dew was on the ground and there was a nip in the air. Compared to the tropical heat at Kochin and Thekkady it evolved into a pleasant day. The garden is in the grounds of the headquarters of KDHP (Kanan Devan Hills Plantations), the largest tea company in South India. The headquarters building used to be a railway station – hence the name of the garden – but a flood in 1918 damaged both the old headquarters and the track, so in 1924 the railway line was scrapped and the station became the headquarters. It sits in a bend of the river with a road running above it on two sides so that you look down on the steeply embanked garden however you pass.

The garden was only made in 1980 and was originally designed by a manager's wife and latterly run by a group of 'ladies' with a head gardener and five staff. This is an enormous workforce for a garden of only around an acre.

All this work is done so that the garden can look at its best in February for the annual flower show. It obviously pays off because it has won every year. That seems to be its main function other than an adornment to the headquarters. No one is allowed in either from the public or employees working at the headquarters. No photography is permitted. Yet there is no privacy. The traffic is constant and every inch is overlooked.

It is a curious place, gaudy by European standards – like a seaside bedding scheme, all immaculately kept but with the air of a garden that is passed by and admired rather than contemplated. Viewed from the road it is as bright and instantly visible as a group of women waiting for a bus in their saris, or the painted lorries waiting for the lights to change on the old railway bridge above the garden.

There is a lovely greenhouse that feels as though it has been there since the 1930s but has perspex roof and is, rather oddly, painted silver. There is more silver paint on the gate and the rather municipal lamp post. I realise everything that can be painted has been done so from the same job lot.

Sweet williams, fuchsias, red salvias, alstroemerias, white alyssum, blue hydrangeas, carnations, cuphea are all used as bedding. More hydrangeas and alstroemeria, together with agapanthus and achillea are all lined out in a comfy, bulky row, like elderly women sitting in deck chairs facing the sea, all dressed up for a proper day out.

Epidendrum radicans, orange crucifix orchid, is an intense, fiery, sari tangerine and a new plant to me. The almost identically coloured lantana growing nearby is more familiar. Thankfully Mark, our director, to whom no orchid is a stranger, explains the connection. Apparently the crucifix orchid mimics the lantana to get butterflies to pollinate it for free, in that it does not give any nectar back to the butterfly for its fertilising pains. Across the river a truck exactly the same colour as both lantana and orchid rumbles by. I half expect a cloud of butterflies in its trail.

Hybrid tea roses are marshalled in dead straight ranks in exact squares of soil cut into the mown grass. This aesthetic precision sits oddly with the wonkiness in all the other functioning aspects of the garden. There is immaculate hand maintenance – weeds are wholly absent, the grass beautifully knapped and not a single gap exists in the

Pots of prayer plants (Maranta leuconeura 'Kerchoveana') wait in the greenhouse to be planted out, next to an old, but well-cared for lawnmower.

planting, but there is no real evidence of skill or perhaps love. No single hand. There is a strong presence of corporate life: satellite dishes, hawsers, pipes and The Monsoon Machine – a rusty old pump that sprays water at high pressure – with no attempt to hide or disguise it all. Pipes and wires go directly across paths and need stepping over or round. But there is also a curious lack of functionality – steps, slopes and paths all feel temporary and badly made. This is all consistent with the garden having no real purpose other than to appear colourful and win the annual flower show.

However it does have profound significance. Although an Indian garden, it feels like a time warp, a relict from colonial days, although the Raj was a distant memory when it was created. In fact, Munnar was a favoured summer spot during the colonial days and the garden, consciously or not, mimics an English garden as perceived from gardens left over from the Raj by people who never knew that time. In other words it is the manifestation of a kind of folk memory. And it is, in all its glorious eccentricity, rather marvellous.

We left to drive to the High Range Club for lunch, established in 1909 as a planter's club soon after the tea estates were started in Munnar. It has tried not to change since then. There are trophies on the wall, the bar is entirely brown leather and brown wood and a 'No Women' sign is proudly displayed. Solar topees are hung up – a sign of thirty years of occupation as a planter, similar to winning your colours at public school. Like the garden, it celebrates and maintains a world that passed forever in 1947.

But the tea plantations themselves are thriving. They are wildly, overwhelmingly beautiful, making lovely crazed patterns across entire hillsides and valleys. Some of the plants – all *Camellia sinensis* – are still from the original planting and have taken on a bonzaied air of impressive age. Walking through the pickers' paths between the waist-high bushes – all cut to exactly the same height across thousands of rolling acres – is like wading through a bristly green sculpture, and seems as thrillingly modern as the Railway Garden seems quaintly dated.

The bushes are now all grown from cuttings and left for five years after planting out and then cut with a trimmer and collecting bag every fifteen days. Every five years they are coppiced back and then hand-picked every week for sixteen months. The older plants, pre-1960, were grown from seed and are still picked by hand, the pickers plucking just the bud and top three leaves. This constant pruning means that they never flower. To make 2 lb of tea requires 10 lb of leaves and each person plucks 130 lb every day. This growing and picking process is identical whether you are drinking the coarsest builders' tea or the finest Earl Grey.

We then went to the factory where the tea is processed, the whole drying, rolling, milling and fermenting process taking as little as two to three hours from picking to being ready for a brew. There are two types of tea: leaf and CTC, which stands for Crush, Tear and Curl and is a granular tea used in most tea bags. It is less well flavoured but much stronger than leaf tea. Local people traditionally prefer CTC, made boiled up with milk and sugar because it is more restorative and refreshing when they are at work. High-quality tea is always made from leaves. But whatever your cup of tea, think of those hillsides covered with camellia bushes pruned by plucking fingers into tyre-tread patterns that are as beautiful as any garden.

Below and opposite *The Railway Garden is like stepping into a handprinted postcard of a 1930s British garden, but although it looks like a time warp it was created as recently as 1980.*

Akbar's Tomb

Sikandra, Uttar Pradesh

I RETURNED TO KOCHIN, winding six hours in a bus, mostly downhill, before going on to Delhi, stopping in Mumbai just long enough to see the corrugated roofs of the slums and the streets looking as close and narrow as the paths in the tea plantations. Delhi was another cultural shock and awe. Does anyone ever get used to a line of three-year olds sleeping on the road? Yet for all its unbearable poverty, India is an enormously wealthy country and becoming more so by the hour. That money, much of it new, is as evident in Delhi as is the depths of its poverty.

From Delhi we took the road east to Agra in Uttar Pradesh. Driving through India is like watching a huge fascinating film. Cattle wander in the central reservation along with onion sellers. A wedding party dances in the street. A camel with comically vast packs, full of chaff, made from patched sacks trudges down the same road as a bus with six, seven, no, eight people clinging to the back. A Mercedes with blacked-out windows impatiently hoots behind a cart pulled by oxen. As the road leaves Delhi further behind, the cars thin out and the land is biblical in its simplicity. Camels, donkeys and wheat fields busy with families gathering the harvest. Home-made tractors built from Diesel pumps.

I am heading to the great Mughal capital of Agra to see the Mughal gardens there. Then on to Sikandra, just half an hour west of Agra, where Akbar is buried. Jalaluddin Muhammad Akbar was the grandson of the great Babur, the first Mughal emperor who ruled from 1508–1530, invading India in 1518 from his capital in Kabul and bringing with him the Persian garden of the Chahar-bagh. Babur loved gardens and created a series of them along the banks of the river Yamuna in Agra, his new capital. He also

The raised walkways of the Chahar-bagh would have butted onto a rich tapestry of trees and flowers. Today there are few large trees in an open expanse of grass grazed by the animals.

founded the vast dynasty that stretched from Kabul to Assam, dominating northern India until the last emperor and the Indian Mutiny of 1857.

Akbar was Babur's grandson and ruled from 1556–1605. The greatest of the Mughals, he built the Red Fort at Agra and, like his grandfather, was a great garden builder. He also embodied the extreme tolerance of the Islamic rulers, marrying Rajput wives and employing local Rajput craftsmen, enabling a fusion of Indo-Islamic art.

His tomb is centred in the middle of a vast garden that is completely enclosed within high stone walls. The whole thing is at least twice the size of the much more celebrated Taj Mahal. Like all Persian gardens it is divided into four equal squares, two of which are likewise quartered again.

This fourfold garden, or Chahar-bagh, reflected the importance of the four sacred elements and the division of the world into four equal segments, with a spring of life at its centre. This style of garden dates back to 2000 BC and all subsequent Islamic gardens have been square or rectangular enclosures divided into four. The divisions were not marked by paths, as in Western courtyard gardens, but by water channels that met at a central pool or fountain. They are always in a courtyard, enclosed from the outside world and a self-contained entity.

Water is an essential component, both as a physical presence and to represent the most essential element of vitality. One of the features of paradise in an arid climate is that it should overflow with water, which is why all containers, pools and canals in Persian gardens are carefully kept topped full to the brim. Aquatic plants are never used as they break the visual purity of the surface. The gentle sound of overflowing water, be it from pool, tap or fountain, is precisely exploited to create a further air of harmony.

The gardens would invariably contain fruit (and it is not hard to make a cultural leap to the Garden of Eden and its tree of knowledge of Good and Evil) and animals. This is where Akbar's tomb is really exceptional because there is still a menagerie of blackbuck antelopes, peacocks and monkeys within the garden walls. Parakeets fly from tree to tree and roost on the crenellations of the tomb.

The British cut down much of the trees in the garden to try and make it look like a Capability Brown landscaped park, which is mostly as it remains but the structure is untouched and as a park, grazed by deer and running with macaques and langur monkeys, it is very impressive. In one corner there is a baobab, or upside-down tree. These were brought to India from the east coast of Africa by sailors.

The four quarters of the Chahar-bagh are divided by huge raised walkways 75 ft wide and with a channel running down the centre of each, meaning that you look down onto the gardens. The walkways also act as containing walls, enclosing the animals.

It is a place of great grandeur and solemnity. The gatehouse is a vast building of red sandstone inlaid with ornate white marble designs and the tomb itself is a palace in a similar style. When I was there, the water channels were dry which felt both a pity and a travesty although given the drought I could see that there were other, more vital calls upon available water supplies. But I wish I had seen it with its water running true. However we did get a sudden and incredibly ferocious sandstorm that bent the trees and sent the saris – and my hat – flying. One quarter has been replanted a little and another has not been cleared to parkland, so you have to guess at the glory of the original garden. But the animals are a treat and the whole place is a good introduction to the Mughal monuments and gardens of India, preparing you for what is surely the most famous monument of them all – the Taj Mahal.

The grassy parkland was created by the British to resemble a Capability Brown landscape, and some trees and small shrubs still remain from the Mughal gardens.

The Taj Mahal

Agra, Uttah Pradesh

No matter how many times you have seen it on television or in photographs, you can never be prepared for your first experience of visiting the Taj Mahal.

WE ARE A SECOND-HAND SOCIETY. There is no corner of the planet, no rare creature and no obscure experience that cannot be seen on television or in print. Even when we do visit rare and beautiful places, most people only seem to want to photograph or video it, with themselves posing in the foreground. Things are only real if there is a picture to prove it. So when faced with an icon as well known as the Taj Mahal there are problems, both of your own reaction (after all you have already seen it a thousand times via magazines, books, television, calendars and the backs of matchboxes) and of adding to that endless portrayal of it. But as with everything, you really do have to experience it first-hand to know it for yourself. Also, the story behind its creation is a good one.

The Taj Mahal was built between 1631 and 1654 by Shah Jahan as a tomb for his beloved wife Mumtaz Mahal, 'the Light of the World'. She died in 1631, aged thirty-nine, giving birth to their fourteenth child, of which four sons and three daughters survived. They had been childhood sweethearts and married for nineteen years although she was only queen for three years. Shah Jahan survived her for another thirty-five years but never ceased to mourn her. Under him the Mughal Empire experienced its period of greatest prosperity and stability and his rule is seen as the golden age of the Mughal Dynasty. It was a time of liberal Islam and of unity with Hinduism and it produced astonishing works of architecture, poetry, art and, importantly, gardens. There are stories of Venetian craftsmen being called into work on the Taj Mahal but there is absolutely no evidence for this. It was made by local Rajput craftsmen, exhibiting extraordinary skills, plus 22,000 labourers working for twenty-three years.

The garden was of central significance in the Mughal world and it would have been unthinkable for the Taj Mahal not to have been set in its own its Chahar-bagh. Remember that Mughal gardens were paradise gardens and Shah Jahan intended the Taj Mahal to be an earthly replica of the house and garden that Mumtaz was now inhabiting in paradise.

There was much precedence for this. Agra was a city of gardens, all fronting both sides of the river Yamuna, one of the great holy rivers of India, with the intention being to move by boat from garden to garden. By the time Shah Jahan came to the throne in 1628 it was considered one of the great cities of the world. The Taj Mahal was, on one level, another river-front garden in a well-established and distinguished tradition. The river has been dammed and extracted for irrigation since the Mughal period and is now much diminished and polluted. It must be imagined running pure and much wider than the present-day version with its wide and ugly mud banks.

The Taj Mahal was intended from the outset to be the supreme monument of the supreme moment of a great empire. It was quite deliberately built for posterity to preserve the memory of Mumtaz Mahal for as long as possible. Shah Jahan took the established river-front garden and made from it the exception.

I woke early and we got to the garden by six in the morning. It was already hot and beggars were sleeping in the shade of doorways. Even at this time, queues had started to form outside the gates. My wife went to the Taj Mahal in 1977, getting there at dawn, as I did, and had the place to herself. Those days are long gone. You now must expect to share your experience of it with a crowd.

We entered the large, arcaded outer courtyard, built at right angles to the gatehouse, which is very like the one at Akbar's tomb, made of red sandstone inlaid with marble. In itself it is a magnificent building. The arched entrance beneath it is small and in deep shade and frames the most famous building on this planet. Lit by the rising sun, this is a moment of heart-stopping beauty. More than that, it is one of profound emotion and I found that I could not speak and my eyes were filled with tears at the intensity of the experience. It is the moment of *samvega*, that untranslatable Buddhist word, where (I think) you experience an aesthetic shock loaded with a sense of deep sorrow at the suffering of life together with an awareness of absolute purity and simplicity. It is the moment when you see the face of your newborn child or the two-year-old beggar on the street. Rembrandt's portrait of *Hendrickje Bathing* in London's National Gallery. Thrush song on a high branch in an April dusk. It wears a thousand faces but we all recognise it when we meet it.

The tomb is built of white marble, tinted a pale pink by the morning sun. It is obviously beautiful but its genius lies in the four minarets set back at each corner that create volume and form out of the space between them and the main building. It is this that gives the Taj Mahal its exceptional sense of lightness and elegance. There is also the sense of wonder that a man might a love a woman this much. The garden is huge. The buildings inconceivably magnificent. Every inch of it is a testament of love and sorrow.

Instead of being at the centre of the garden, the mausoleum is at the end of a long courtyard that is divided into the traditional four quarters, with a large water basin at the centre axial point. Each of the four quarters is divided again into four and each of these subdivisions makes a large square garden. The scale and imagination of every aspect of the Taj Mahal is effortlessly epic.

Behind the monument is the river. The elements of the garden are predictable and similar in essence to Akbar's tomb, minus the animals or the touch of Capability Brown. Raised walkways contain the central canal, or rill, leading from the gatehouse to the

The Moonlight Garden, the Mahtab-bagh, part of the Taj Mahal's garden on the other side of the river, is full of fruit trees. Grassy and peaceful, it is as much a part of the Taj Mahal as the main courtyard and no trip there is really complete without visiting it.

tomb and look down on ornate parterres. Each quarter is divided by a canal although the two lateral ones were empty and dry at the time of my visit. Undoubtedly the quadrants would have been planted with fruits and flowers although now only two parts of one of the quarters have trees in them. But the details of the planting are subsumed beneath the scale and power of the monument and the setting. The garden is a vital part of the Taj Mahal but without the building it would have a fraction of its impact.

However there is one other element of the garden that has only come to light in recent years and that is the Mahtab-bagh or Moonlight Garden. I said that the tomb was placed at the end of the garden on the river but on the other side of the river an extension of the Taj Mahal was excavated in the 1990s. Looked at from the air this places the building exactly in the centre of the garden, with the river running through the middle of it.

It took over an hour to drive round to the other side of the river, by which time the sun was truly fierce, but it was worth it. For a start there was no one there. A large octagonal tank, colonnaded and with its own pavilion, was placed directly opposite the tomb so that its reflection could be enjoyed in the moonlight. The view of the building is superb. This is as much part of the Chahar-bagh and Taj Mahal as the courtyard in front of the building that all the tourists flock to.

The garden behind this tank is laid out in the Chahar-bagh with four expected quarters and has been planted as an original paradise garden with fruit trees as a series of orchards. It is grassy, still something of an archaeological site, and has none of the hard-edged stone structure of the finished gardens but it is entirely necessary to visit it to see and understand the Taj Mahal. It completes it.

Finally I went to the Red Fort, built by Akbar, where Shah Jahan was imprisoned by his son in the Glass Palace for the last eight years of his life. It is luxurious and beautiful but a prison nevertheless. But it does have a view of the Taj Mahal and the Shah would sit and look out at the testament to his true love. When he died in 1666 he was taken by river to be buried next to Mumtaz, together again on earth and in paradise for ever.

The Monsoon Pavilion

Deeg Gardens, Rajasthan

EARLY THE NEXT MORNING we drove south-east from Agra to Deeg, about 10 miles west of Govardhan and 25 miles north of Bharatpur. Deeg was the capital of the Jat rulers in the eighteenth century before they moved to Bharatpur and it remained their summer palace until the 1970s. In 1730 Maharajah Suraj Mai built a massive fort in the middle of Deeg, with a deep moat as protection against raiders. Across the moat he created a palace complex with a range of gardens. It was designed almost entirely as a relief from the unbearable summer heat of Rajasthan. Two huge water tanks, Gopal Sagar and Rup Sagar, one on each side also helped to bring down the temperature considerably, and provided water for the complex hydro engineering.

The Jat rulers were influenced by the magnificence of the Mughal courts of Agra and Delhi and the design of the gardens, although entirely Hindu, has been inspired by the Mughal Chahar-bagh. There are hundreds of fountains scattered all over the gardens, which spew out coloured water during the festive season.

But not when I was there. It was neither watery nor festive. The pools and canals were all dry and the fountains still. It was a day of intense, crushing heat and Delhi Belly had found me. Not the most pleasant day of my life and yet this did not lessen the fascination of Deeg Gardens.

The garden is entirely based upon the control of water, but, whereas the Mughals used water symbolically and where they did have fountains they were invariably modest and tinkling, Deeg is a liquid firework display. It is a watery, riotous carnival when in full flow. The Mughal gardens were based upon order, restraint and harmony, but

Though there was no water filling the canals and fountains when I was there, the trees were still green.

Hundreds of jets and scores of small fountains fill the canal leading to the pavilion. When the water was running and brightly coloured, it must have been an outrageous performance.

Deeg, made a hundred years after the Taj Mahal and at a time when the Jat armies were triumphant against Mughal forces, is extrovert, slightly kitsch and technically ingenious.

The waterworks are all based upon a gravitational feed from a huge tank on the roof of one of the palace buildings that holds 6 million gallons of water, all drawn up in a large leather bucket from Gopal Sagar, the rope pulled by oxen trudging up and down an incline for weeks. Grooves are cut deep into the stone where it has hoisted innumerable buckets.

These are spilled onto a stony slope and into the tank and gradually, very slowly, it fills up. Along the stone walls of the tank are holes, each numbered, which lead to specific fountains and jets in the garden below. These holes are plugged with powdered flower petals packed into muslin bags and then stopped with wooden bungs. When required, the bungs are removed, the water saturates the compacted petals and works through, taking the dye with it to emerge somewhere in the gardens below as a coloured jet.

The most extraordinary waterworks in the garden – perhaps in any garden – is the Monsoon Pavilion, or Kesav Bhawan. This is a single-storeyed arcaded and colonnaded building at the end of the garden facing out over the huge square tank Rup Sagar with the massive walls of the fort beyond. When I was there scores of women were washing clothes in this water, laying the cleaned garments – white, bright pinks, blue, orange – upon the stepped retaining banks to dry. It was a glimpse of colourful life from an empty, baking garden that needed water to come alive.

But when the waterworks are put into play they must be something very special indeed because an arcade runs around the interior of the pavilion, over a canal that has fountains set down the centre. The walls of the canal are pierced with hundreds of minute jets that would arch coloured water. Water would also fall in a curtain from the roof into the canal and metal balls in the columns would rumble and roll together producing a thunderous accompaniment to the water. The Maharajah and his retinue would sit inside this, surrounded by all the force and cool dampness of the monsoon in the hottest, driest time of the year. Their hour or so of watery pleasure over, it would require weeks of preparation to bring more water up to the holding tank for the next performance.

Nowadays the water is only put on display twice a year and the rest of the time the coolness must come from the large trees where the fruit bats slowly fan their leathery wings. The canals and ornate fountains of the Chahar-bagh, all in a delicate pink stone, hold only hot air.

Below the huge reservoir, and to one side of the tiny tiger cage set high into a wall, is a building that was transported lock, stock and barrel in 1756 from the Red Fort at Agra. In Agra it was used as a school, but here in Deeg it was turned into lodgings for royal female guests, with the women's purdah garden beyond. It is by far the most attractive building in the palace complex. The white marble rooms are charmingly small, cool and intimate after the potential bluster and railway-station architecture of the rest of the palace. A fine marble swing was also brought here as a war trophy from the Mughal court and stands, hanging from huge marble pillars with an arch between them, overlooking the gardens.

Jal Mahal

Jaipur, Rajasthan

JAIPUR IS THE CAPITAL of Rajasthan, always a fierce, wealthy and independent state. The Mughals were canny enough to try and subdue it but to choose Rajput maharajahs to be their ministers and generals, giving them wealth and power and letting them keep their religion. The men have wonderful moustaches and red turbans and the women, are exceptionally beautiful and wear brilliantly coloured saris, even when working in the fields. Peacocks roam the roadside fields. We stayed a night in a maharajah's palace with a uniformed and turbaned sentry with pikestaff at the entrance. It did not seem odd.

The city itself was laid out in 1735 and the centre remains largely untouched, the broad streets and plastered buildings painted a terracotta pink, with doors and windows framed with white. It was a city famed for the craftsmen it produced, especially stone carvers and jewellers, and there is still a thriving jewellery trade in the city.

Just outside the old city is an extraordinary garden in the process of complete restoration, financed by one of Jaipur's wealthiest jewellers. This is Jal Mahal, original-ly built as a pleasure garden in 1725 by the Maharajah of Jaipur, Jai Singh, who had his principal palace on the hillside above it. Although a garden, it is in fact a magical build-ing set in the middle of a vast lake. The garden is on the top floor of this building, which looks like a palace but which exists simply to support the weight of the soil and pavilions set around the outside. On three sides are hills with the honey-coloured stone of the maharajah's palatial pavilions across the water.

Except there was no water. When I was there the lake was dry and the building strand-ed in hundreds of acres of sand being grazed by cattle. But when the monsoon comes the lake rapidly fills. We walked across where, in the rainy season, we would have to row. The building had an armature of bamboo scaffolding bound with thick hessian twine. I have restored a few old buildings myself and know a little about the sensitivity needed and the

The Jal Mahal sits in the centre of a vast lake. The pleasure pavilion was actually built solely to support the garden on the roof. The Maharajah and his retinue would come and stay just for an evening, or even for a week or two.

Sari-clad women tend the young cinerarias, Senecio cineraria 'Silver Dust', waiting until the extensive renovations are complete, when they will be planted in the white stone beds.

specialisation of matching stone, mortars, plasters and paints, and I could see that this was all being done with extreme skill and care. The interior had been plastered and the openings for doors and windows created honeycombs of apricot light. Women in saris went to and fro with bowls of lime mortar on their head. The overhead sun attacked.

Up on the roof of the building is the garden, also a building site but with large trees and eight pavilions placed at each corner and centrally around the sides. In the centre is a fountain and raised walkway above the quartered format of a Chahar-bagh. Scores of people were at work, including a team of four stone carvers squatting under the sun and chipping delicately at blocks of white marble.

I had arranged to meet Mitch Crites, who is in charge of designing the garden. Mitch is an American who came to India forty years ago, converted to Islam and married an Iranian wife who was descended from the Shah that sacked Delhi in the eighteenth century and stole Shah Jahan's – he of the Taj Mahal – treasury and peacock throne.

He told me about the original role of the building. 'It was purely a pleasure pavilion based around the garden. There were living quarters and kitchens down below. Originally it was one storey and then the top floor was added later in the eighteenth century. The centre of the building is a solid earthen core. The arcades wrap around the two storeys and the lower rooms are cooler and come up to the garden at night where there is a nice breeze.'

I commented on the high level of skill clearly at work. He pointed out that the carvers are all direct descendants of those that worked on the Taj Mahal. The skills have been passed down through the generations and are just as good now as they were then.

Are they trying to restore the garden as it originally was? 'No. It has gone through so many stages that we do not know exactly how it was. We did not want to make a purely Mughal or Rajput garden but one which combined the elements of both as well as something modern. We will have the birth of a new garden from an ancient tradition. If we get it right it will be paradise.'

We talked in the shade of a pavilion and I remarked that it was a relief to be out of the sun. 'It is not hot yet,' said Mitch. 'Before the monsoon comes it will become hotter and hotter – 47, 48, 49 degrees. The sky will turn yellow and the sun lavender. It becomes more and more humid. You know that the rain is up there but it doesn't come down. You feel like clawing at the sky to make it come down because you know it is there. When it does at last fall, whatever you are doing, riding a car, eating, working, whatever, you go and stand in the rain. Finally it has come. It is a great, great relief. It is a time celebrated in poetry. The animals give birth. It is a very, very lyrical time, a time that everybody loves.'

Mitch went on. 'With God's blessing that will be in the second half of June. Then the lake will fill up. The plan is to filter city water to top it up so there is water the year round. And when it is finished there will be performances, weddings and tourists just wanting to see the garden. There will be a small restaurant and then we will make a museum on the second floor. Jaipur is a city of artists. The museum will show the best of Jaipur.'

When I was there the garden was a building site. As the women gracefully carried the bowls of mortar up and down the stairs and across the garden site, I watched ten men carefully place cinerarias in pots within the arabesque scrolling of white plastered stone. The plan is to have the garden predominately white. White jasmine, white poppies, white bougainvillea and white wisteria. By the time you read this, the garden will be made. The museum will follow. Go to Jaipur. Visit it. November and February are said to be the best months. But avoid the yellow skies and lavender sun of May and early June.

The Rock Garden
Chandigarh, Punjab

AFTER VISITING JAL MAHAL we drove back to New Delhi, the roads gradually changing from crazily potholed routes used by lorries, elephants, camels, oxen carts, bicycles and people walking with bundles of wood on their head to the absurdly busy traffic jam of a modern city, albeit with more people fitted into individual vehicles than any combination of mathematics, human ingenuity and flexibility would seem to permit.

I spent a day in New Delhi visiting Lutyens's government buildings and the Red Fort, built by Shah Jahan between 1638 and 1648 (exactly contemporary with the Taj Mahal), when he made Delhi the new Mughal capital. Despite crushing what I was taught at school was the Indian Mutiny, but what in India is referred to as The First War of Independence, and sacking the Red Fort in 1858, the relationship between Britain and India was always based upon trade, not colonisation. India was never a colony and the British kept the capital in Calcutta where the East India company had originally established its headquarters. In December 1911, George V, the new king of

All the walls and statues are made from material that Nek Chand rescued from the rubble of local villages that had been knocked down. The whole garden is sheer genius – surrealist sculpture on a par with that of Picasso, and even more remarkable when you consider that it was all created by one man, in secret.

England and Emperor of all India, from Afghanistan to Thailand, announced that the capital would be moved to the ancient capital of Delhi. A relatively young and unknown architect, Edwin Lutyens, was chosen to design and draw up plans for the new capital on a site south of Shah Jahan's city. Work finished in 1933, revealing huge vistas established with massive confidence in stone. It is a staggering architectural achievement and despite being created by an Englishman as a statement of imperial grandeur, it is an honourable and beautiful remainder of the Raj.

But that is old India. The next morning I rose early to catch a train to the north, to Chandigarh, a new town in the Punjab designed after the partition with Pakistan by the French architect Le Corbusier, under the aegis of India's first prime minister Pandit Jawaharlal Nehru. It is a clean, orderly place, with high degrees of literacy and well-above average income for the 900,000 odd inhabitants – three hours by train (punctual, clean and fun) but a million miles from the slums around the railway station in of New Delhi.

In 1947, as a result of partition, when he was twenty-two, Nek Chand fled from his home in a village near Lahore and came to the Indian side of the Punjab and the new town of Chandigarh where he found work as a road inspector. To make the new town, over twenty villages were cleared, with a huge amount of rubble and waste.

In 1953 Nek began to collect bits and pieces of this rubble, broken plates, light fittings, door handles, stones, tiles – anything at all – and take them on his bicycle to a small clearing that he had found in the jungle at the edge of the town. This was not his land. He did not know who, if anyone, owned it but no one found or disturbed him. Gradually he used the bits and pieces that he accumulated to build a small fantasy garden. It cost him nothing other than his time and skill. Only his wife knew that it was there. For eighteen years it was undiscovered, a totally secret fantasy that Nek created without any need to share it with anyone else.

In 1971, bulldozers began to clear the jungle to extend the town and they discovered Nek's work. They, like every subsequent visitor, were astounded. Nek had created acres of ground covered with hundreds of sculptures set in twisting paths, waterways and rock faces. It was all completely illegal and should have been destroyed but, to their eternal credit, the local authorities not only decided to keep it but gave Nek a salary to work on it full time, plus fifty labourers to assist him. In 1976 it was formally inaugurated as The Rock Garden of Chandigarh and the world began to take in the immensity of what had secretly and quietly been created. The garden now runs to 25 acres, is visited by nearly 2 million people a year and has been acclaimed as the greatest artistic achievement in India since the Taj Mahal.

I met Nek in his garden. He is seventy-eight years old now, with a face set in slightly bewildered resignation, a simple man that is attracting the attention of the world, and rightly so, for he is, I believe, having seen his garden, one of our greatest living artists, a true genius.

I asked him why he started it? 'As a hobby. Only as a hobby.' Why here? 'I knew that no building would be erected here. So I started working here after five o'clock. I used to bring things on a bicycle.' That must have been hard work? 'It was hard work. My job was hard work. Making the garden was hard work. Minimum four hours a day I was working here after five o'clock.'

I have done many interviews in my time, some have been fascinating discussions and others frustratingly obscure – especially when politicians are involved – but I am

glad that Nek did not intellectualise, explain or discuss his work. He just did it. It is there. It is completely, utterly unique and stands alone.

The garden is a series of tableaux or fantasies constructed entirely from found objects. Large birds made from broken plates perch on walls made from cobbles. Pieces of stone, worn into shapes that Nek liked, are set alongside others that he has constructed. There is no division between natural objects and wholly fanciful ones. No rules. No boundaries. Pipes made from concrete writhe out of a wall like a mass of beautiful tree roots. Above, a real tree grows directly out of the wall. What could be catacombs are cut into the rock and fronted with carved hieroglyphs. Water cascades down a green mossy bank within a gorge. Little houses perch on the rocks above. There is a simple wall of ceramic insulators topped with tiny terracotta pots threaded on wire like beads on an abacus. There is no question of taste or style or design or intention to please or win admiration. Nek did it like this so this is the way that it is.

Carry on round corners, down steps, squeezing through narrow stone passageways and you come to a series of spaces – rooms? – peopled by animals and people, hundreds and hundreds of them, each one modelled out of terracotta or concrete and embellished with broken pottery, pebbles or glass beads. They make an army whose massed effect is incredibly haunting and yet each one is different, a sculpture in its own right that rivals the work of Miro or Picasso although I suspect that Nek had barely heard of these two when he made them. All these figures seem to represent India as surely and accurately as the Taj Mahal, elephants painted for display, or the rivers. Music, temples and myriad other signifiers of this extraordinary country. Broken plates, clinker, stone and the waste from a new town are all made into works of art that are filled with humanity.

Is it a garden? Of course. Anything that is made up outside by humans for the pleasure of humans is a garden. There are plants aplenty, albeit playing second fiddle to the creations of Nek Chand. But it does elevate gardening to a work of art, especially as it is so unself-consciously not attempting to do so. It is also significant that Nek does not and never has owned any of it. He has never sold any part of it. Everything there is done for love and a curious compulsion to create against all odds. How can that not be a shining inspiration to any gardener, wherever they come from?

I left in a happy daze and caught a late train back to Delhi, packed, had three hours' sleep and got the plane back to England and my own familiar garden. But visit India and nothing will ever be the same again.

Left *A phalanx of women, each wearing a slightly different dress of brightly-coloured glass beads in the Rock Garden. There are thousands of people and creatures in Nek's fantasy garden world and every one of them is different.*
Right *Nek Chand is an unassuming man, bewildered by all the attention and the praise that has been heaped upon his garden.*
Following pages
The prairies of Kansas have a diversity of life second only to the Amazon rainforest.

Although it may seem an endlessly waving sea of grass, the prairie is second only to the Amazon in the richness of its ecodiversity ... and is perfectly suited to a subtle and rich horticultural interpretation.

9 The Restless Giant

North America

North America

There was a time when I went to America fairly regularly, but without planning it I realised that my last visit had been nine years ago, in the autumn of 1998. On that occasion I had gone to give a talk for the New York Botanical Garden. It was a charity lunch, the slide show was a disaster, no one wanted to listen to me or my story and it was, in short, humiliating. But directly out of the experience grew a garden, a book, a new friendship and the best pizza I have ever eaten (it's a long story). This pretty much sums up my relationship with America: scary but astonishingly positive.

Yet the world has clearly changed since 1998 and America is, whether it wants to or not, driving most of those changes. Most seem to be for the worse. The energetic land of opportunity that I knew in the 1980s and 90s appears to have become riven with doubt, anxiety and conflict. It is still the world's great dominating power but much of the rest of the world looks at it with a mixture of fear and loathing. America has a serious PR problem.

So what has any of that to do with gardening? As this book shows, gardens reveal how people view themselves. They tend to tell you more about the gardeners than the gardens. When I was last in America, the gardens of the east coast were still looking admiringly at Europe. The ladies at that lunch in New York were hankering for the kind of rural idyll that we had found slightly dull in the 1980s. There did not seem to be any kind of gardening culture. A beautiful garden was something that one aspired to as a result of success. The concept of making such a thing with one's own hands out of the resources and space to hand was, at best, elusive. As Anna, our TV fixer on the east side of the country, told me, 'gardens are synonymous with luxury'.

Anna also told me that Americans have no real concept of 'stewardship'. The world is there to be used, enjoyed and then remade as desired. Newness equates to success. This made me think about stewardship and gardens. Most of the world's old cultures – European, Chinese, Japanese, Indian – have stewardship at their heart, and this is expressed in gardens more than almost anything else, simply because to care for a garden over a long time means almost daily detailed care. To keep the thing that is valuable the same means a succession of continuous small changes.

Yet America is undoubtedly one of the most beautiful countries in the world. The people are a joy. I was slightly anxious that my own instinctively liberal, vaguely socialist, angry world view would get me into trouble but over the course of my all-too-brief whisk across the continent I met nothing but charm, hospitality, intelligence and a genuine desire to embrace the problems of the world that they see themselves as part of. I also saw some fascinating and beautiful gardens. I would not presume to say that I came anywhere near to being in a position to judge the general state of gardening – let alone the people – in that simply enormous country, but I certainly had my faith in their energy, optimism and resourcefulness restored.

My guess is that when Americans begin to really care about their gardens – or even consider them as a personal concept rather than just an all-grass yard butting up to the walls of their houses tended weekly by a 'maintenance man' – then the necessity of stewardship that will ensue will dramatically change the way that we care for this planet. It will not be a moment too soon. The world needs those American gardens and needs them now.

LongHouse Reserve

East Hampton, New York State

Above *The life-size bronze statue of an elephant by Miquel Barcelo is supported by its trunk in an impressive mix of art and engineering.* Previous page *Tall Washingtonian palms are everywhere in Los Angeles. Here at the Mia Lehrer garden in Brentwood, seven of them were put into position before the house was even built, and work carried out around them.*

WHEN I VISITED EACH OF THE GARDENS in this book, I took a camera and note-book and snapped and scribbled notes as I went. This is always an indiscriminate process of gathering in as much information as possible and then when I get back to my hotel room I try and transcribe the notes and edit the pictures. I have a basic rule of a maximum of 100 thumbnails on my screen for any garden and usually reduce it down to this without too much trouble. But it is telling that in Jack Larsen's garden at LongHouse Reserve, East Hampton, this was almost impossible and I ended up retain-ing over 120 images and still knowing that the garden was not properly represented.

Jack Larsen is a weaver and textile designer and has had a long and enormously successful career. LongHouse is set in 16 acres of gardens and was built partly as his home but also expressly as a place to display works of art of all kinds and is now run as a foundation. Work on the house began when Larsen bought 26 acres of farmland in the 1970s. He developed the first 10 acres around a building that he called the RoundHouse, where he also lived. While he was living there he began to plan the layout of the remaining 16 acres, planting the cryptomeria avenue and a hedge along 2,000 ft of farm fencing.

He then sold RoundHouse in order to finance the building of LongHouse, which is based upon a Shinto shrine at Ise in Japan. Work began fifteen years ago when Larsen was already sixty-five. It says something about the American spirit of optimism – as well, of course, as his own – that such a buoyant, long-term project was entered into at an age when most British men are contemplating their cruise holiday catalogues and an extra round of golf a week. It is open to the public, yet it is Jack's home. It is his garden, and yet self-consciously an art gallery with changing exhibitions.

This is one of the reasons that I visited the garden. I wanted an east coast garden that challenged the normal European idea of what a garden could be or do, albeit by virtue of being on the eastern seaboard and a reflection of many of the European influences and styles. It is also a self-confessed, eclectic mix of cultures and styles which, perhaps paradoxically, seems to me to be a good way in to finding some sense of American culture and style.

The mission of the LongHouse Foundation is 'Living with Art', and the garden and the sculptures within it are inextricably bound. What is rare for America is the lack of derivation. It sets out to be the summation of Larsen's life and work and therefore reflects eighty years of an artistic life rather than any kind of theme park, which, by definition, must be generalised and appeal to as many people as possible. There are, however, fifty people involved in the Foundation, although only two gardeners.

Enter through the lynchette gate of LongHouse and the well-planted, soft autumnal planting of the well-heeled Hamptons is left behind. This is immediate-ly something self-consciously 'other'. There

IT IS OPEN TO THE PUBLIC, YET IT IS JACK'S HOME. IT IS HIS GARDEN, AND YET SELF-CONSCIOUSLY AN ART GALLERY.

are berms created with sand excavated from under the house with sparse plantings of clipped azaleas, grasses, oaks. Acorns spread on the sand like spilt beads. I go over to read a label and it says, 'Yoko Ono wish tree for LongHouse Reserve, black tulepo gum (*Nyssa sylvatica*), collection LHR'. This is impressive and confusing – as I am sure it is meant to be. A tree as work of art in a sculpture garden. Good old Yoko! She always gets it. A spidery, creepy, sculptural prostrate pine – *Pinus densiflora* 'Pendula', (weeping Japanese red pine) – on the side of the sandy berms is truly wonderful. Living with living art.

The sculptures are generally more obviously imposing. Follow the route and you go past a succession of blue glass rods, vast metal rings, an even vaster golf ball (which turns out to be a fly eye – either way it didn't do it for me). Already a pattern was emerging. Where the sculpture dominated, the garden became a more or less satisfactory backdrop, albeit park-like. But where the boundary between garden and sculpture became blurred – beautifully pruned trees (as they all are), sculptures made from wood or ceramics that looked like tree trunks and of course Yoko's tree – then the whole place came alive in an idiosyncratic and much more interesting way. I really like how having

The aim of the LongHouse Foundation is to bring modern art and gardens together through a combination of sculptures and plants.

Sculptures are at every turn in the garden. This one is made of steel and stands at the edge of the amphitheatre.

a tree-like sculpture next to trees makes you look at the organic forms as sculpture and vice versa. The senses sharpen.

Conventional gardening butted in a little awkwardly now and then. So there is a grass garden, nice enough as these things go, with *Molinia caerulea* 'Heidebrant' (purple moor grass) really good and *Deschampsia cespitosa* and *Molinia caerulea* 'Karl Foerster' lovely in a familiar-enough way. But I am not sure that they were really *necessary*. The mark of good planting is that it should feel inevitable. Much of the LongHouse planting feels arbitrary. Not bad, but a bit random except – a much repeated and entirely glorious exception this – when the sculpture and plants combine and become more than the sum of their parts.

The garden is, as my large batch of photos attests, big, and the works of art many. There is more than one visit can possibly digest. But there are three places where it really sings. The first is round the corner from the grass garden, where you come to a small grass amphitheatre like a Celtic hill fort – slightly concave like a shallow grass bowl and a place of instant and complete beauty. It is a lovely green empty space. How I should love to have this in my garden! It seems that it was born of the practical need to dispose of the soil that was excavated to make the pond but it is none the less pleasing and the perfect synthesis of sculpture and horticulture.

The second thing is the much more self-conscious Red Garden, which comprises a path flanked by cloud-pruned azaleas, assuredly red in flower and, spaced along both hedges, eleven pairs of red uprights made from brightly painted sections of tree trunks, complete with all the knots and gnarls that make them tree-like rather than posts. These diminish in size and become closer together as they approach the end, which is marked by a sculpture by Toshiko Takaezen that looks like a pot or a stone but which is neither. It is just its ceramic self. The simplicity of all of this and the containment, the inevitability of it, makes it work both as garden and as art.

Finally, standing at the cross-roads of two paths, one leading from the house via a swimming pool down to another distant work and the other running across the garden, there is a wonderful sculpture by Miquel Barcelo called 'Elefandret' – a life-sized bronze elephant balancing on its trunk. I wanted to take this home too.

This is not to ignore the house and the dry garden around it, the pond and the perfectly pruned cherries and so much more. It glides past a score of other large, good, arresting works and a hundred well-tended, good, harmonious plants. Like my snaps it will not submit to editing neatly down.

But as an introduction to American gardens, overloaded, open, charming, energetic and full of the possibilities of what a garden could do beyond any safe convention of horticulture, it seemed the right way to be pitched forward. And pitched I truly was because the next stop, a couple of hours down the road, took me from the eminently comfortable Hamptons to the middle of Manhattan.

Liz Christy Garden

Manhattan, New York State

I FIRST VISITED MANHATTAN in August 1984 when we had our jewellery business. We had just enough money for air fares and a cheap hotel and had one telephone number of a buyer we had met once. We were there four days and that number led immediately to a stream of meetings, meals, sales and contacts. We visited the Frick and MOMA, walked everywhere, got hot, exhausted and scared and had a great time. I loved it instantly and returned at least once a year for many years. Since my last trip in 1998, Manhattan has become the epicentre of events that have changed the world. I am older and less enthusiastic about noise, hustle and bustle. Would the attraction still be there? I need not have worried. Manhattan smells good. There is something about the place that you have to inhale to understand. It has a special energy and vibe. Manhattan, more than any part of any other city I have been to, accepts you exactly as you are. No qualifications.

But Manhattan has changed. Part of this is inevitable. The energy and dynamic of the place feeds off constant change. But there is a new sense of conformity and commercialisation, especially in the downtown areas, that is at the expense of much of the bohemian charm that typified it with its mass of art galleries, lofts, one-off shops and bars. All the little individual galleries and freak shops have either been made into the inevitable luxury apartments or designer shops.

The luxury apartments are everywhere, but many are environmentally friendly – I visited Teardrop Park, looking out to the Statue of Liberty, and was shown the roof gardens, the solar panels and the recycling system, all of which saved up to 66 per cent of the building's energy consumption. But all was ordered for the enjoyment of the apartment owners. I wanted to find a public garden with private identity, that captured the quirkiness and independence of spirit of the Manhattan I had known and loved. I went to Gantry Park in Queens to talk to Thomas Balsley about his work, creating a public garden behind yet another bloody luxury apartment conversion. He has done more than sixty such schemes across New York and there is a genuine sense of neighbourhood involvement and identity in his work. But the one garden that really caught my imagination I stumbled upon down in the Bowery. This is the Liz Christy garden.

It is a strip of vegetation on the corner of Houston and Bowery. It is a hugely noisy site with constant traffic – not a garden that one could sit *quietly* in. Not good for luxury people wanting luxury privacy. But very good for people who want the connection and activity of caring for a space, plants and soil within the middle of a city.

Even though it is on the edge of one of the busiest roads in Manhattan, the Liz Christy garden is a refuge with a delightful collection of plants, from hornbeam and persimmon trees, to kiwis and ivy. Shrubs include Weigela, *while penstemon, phlox and hostas fill the herbaceous borders.*

I chatted with the delightfully eccentric L. Brandon Krall, artist, one of many volunteers who help look after the garden.

I confess that I knew nothing about Liz Christy, let alone this garden, before I saw it. But there is a website that told me that it was founded by the eponymous Liz Christy in 1973, making it the first community garden in Manhattan. Liz, along with other guerrilla gardeners, started out by planting 'seed bombs' on vacant lots, found this particular site and in 1974 got permission for it formally to become the 'Bowery Houston Community Farm and Garden' with a rent of $1 a month. Sixty raised beds were planted with vegetables, then trees and herbaceous borders added. Now there are autumn-flowering camellia, a large persimmon tree laden with flattened peach-like fruit, beds of native asters, roses, buddleja, cryptomeria, carefully shaped and pruned azaleas and box, bits and pieces of carved stone rescued from bulldozed buildings. There is a beehive and a wildflower habitat, an arbour covered with a grapevine, a tiny grove of weeping birch trees, fruit trees, a dawn redwood, vegetable garden, herbs and hundreds of varieties of flowering perennials. It is a garden that has had thirty-four years to mature. It has accumulated plants and ideas – and this is usually much more interesting than a mere display of these things put on for instant gratification. It is a work in progress – as all real gardens are.

There was one woman working in there when we visited and she introduced herself as L. Brandon Krall, artist. 'Everyone calls me Brandon.' She lives nearby in the rent-protected loft she has occupied for the past thirty years, shared with an uncaged flock of various birds and an increasingly apparent obsession with Quentin Crisp. On her little camera, she took a film of us filming her, to use as part of her 'artwork'. This was recognisably the Manhattan I had known and loved.

This is a tiny space. There is not much to it. Half of it is very much under construction and the other half just a piece of garden. But it works. It is alive. Although not without a struggle. Brandon showed me the end section that was railed off from the road on one side and backed by a large building on the other. A few pots of plants stood on the bare, baked earth. A pile of dead vegetation. Some timber. This was formerly 'Rock-on Row', lovingly created and tended by Bill, who lived in an apartment in the building. 'It was nice, had real character, you know, with roses, rocks and honeysuckle. Beautiful really.' When the next-door community centre, abutting the green buildings, became – you guessed it – luxury apartments, the Parks Department preserved the site and protected it from the corporate raiders wanting to build on it but then bulldozed Bill's garden – so that a garden could be made as part of the Liz Christy garden. 'None of us wanted this to happen. Bill's garden was great. But they just went and did it.' The absurdity of this encapsulates so much of America and Manhattan. There seems to be little sense of gardens as an integral place with personal identity. They are a commodity. Enjoy! Brandon seemed as bemused and deflated by this as she might be. But the department is not all bad. 'The city has recently been given $300 million for its parks. All the common gardens were invited to the discussion on how to spend this and ways of keeping it going for the future. So that is hopeful.'

Over a new fence pointlessly inserted between the garden and the new block of apartments – presumably to keep the riff-raff of the garden away from the tenants – I was able to peer at a garden made to go with the building. It was sleek, rather well done and devoid of anything approaching soul.

All gardens need personal and local identity to become alive. The point of the Liz Christy garden is that it was made without wealth or power. It was made and is tended by individuals like Brandon and Bill. Quirky, delightful people that have no desire to admire an environmentally sound eco-garden made for their luxurious delight and tended by a 'maintenance man'. It is small, noisy and completely, utterly delightful.

James van Sweden's Garden

Chesapeake Bay, Maryland

AFTER THREE DAYS IN MANHATTAN we drove south down the New Jersey Turnpike to Maryland and Chesapeake Bay. On the way down I chatted with Anna, our east coast fixer, wise, sassy, smart and possibly the worst driver it has ever been my misfortune to get into a car with. During a discussion about gardening in America, she made the following points, a couple of which I've already mentioned: 'Gardens are synonymous with luxury; Americans have no concept of stewardship; Americans want to possess and protect – with a gun.' All three remarks were to resonate throughout my journey and as we drove south houses started to appear with lawns right to the front door and no evidence of any concept of a garden attached to them. The only sign of stewardship was the mown grass.

Mowing grass was significant because we were on our way to visit the garden of James van Sweden. Van Sweden is one of America's leading landscape designers, based in Washington DC, and we were heading to see him at his weekend retreat by the sea in Chesapeake, an hour or so by car from the centre of the capital. He had attracted my attention because of his self-avowed 'new American' style based upon the prairie grasses. This uses mainly indigenous plants and a great deal of grasses and requires minimal maintenance. It is loose, easy and, from the photographs I had seen, very beautiful.

As soon as we arrived the beauty was self-evident although there was not a mown blade of grass in sight. Whilst coffee brewed I took a look around. Cut paths in the grass – crudely mown on quite rough ground – define the space in the landscape and, as it is all grasses, this then becomes a garden. There are no edges. It all merges out into the landscape. The bay is exquisite. Incredibly quiet. A sky full of hawks floating with menace.

There is a brilliantly confident merging of the house garden – that is, the area immediately surrounding the house – and the more natural garden and the water's edge. Other than the decking there is no obvious demarcation except through the planting – a tapestry fading out to its edges. It has great confidence in that it appears natural and effortless – which is always a sure sign of a master at work.

And despite the apparent naturalness, I realised that he has used a wide and extensive range of plants to create the artless effect. Flanking the path to the front door were great stands, perhaps hundreds strong, of rudbeckia, aster, *Eupatorium*, *Inula* and *Helenium* amongst others. It was as though he had taken the idea of a flower border, shaken it up and set it down with all the pretension and preciousness taken from it.

Amongst the grasses were little bluestem (*Schizachryium scoparium*), the most common prairie tallgrass, and another prairie grass, *Panicum virgatum*, reaching over my head. I recognised the garden grass *Calamagrostis* 'Karl Foester' and scirpus growing by the pond area in the front. As a mown path curved into tall stems I realised that it had exactly the same arch to it as the path in Jack Larsen's grass garden. But whereas his was a carefully constructed space between events (the sculptures), this seemed an end in itself or perhaps something without beginning. It flowed.

James van Sweden was an inspiring host. I learned more from him about native American plants than anyone else. His garden is very sophisticated and subtle.

We sat by the pool on the decking, which is bleached, salted pine. As a rule I loathe decking, especially in the slimy damp of a grey, northern European winter but here it is the same tone as the sand and the grasses and driftwood and looks absolutely right set against the blue of sky and sea. All the chairs and tables on the deck were made out of sun-bleached driftwood, as is the palisade-like gazebo down by the water's edge.

I asked him about the setting. 'I wanted the house to be floating in a meadow,' he told me, 'like the Michigan meadows I grew up with. So all the grasses used in the garden are native and the garden is based around grasses.' There is practically no maintenance and no watering at all, which is some claim given that this is a place of extreme summer heat and that they had had no rain for over two months when I visited.

Although the garden needs minimum maintenance, James had had 'maintenance men' come in before our visit to tidy up a little. In doing so they carefully cut off the dried flowering heads off all the *Rudbeckia* to 'tidy' them. James was furious and apologetic. 'Americans generally have no sense for the beauty of seeds or drying stems.' Then, his annoyance escalating, 'Americans just don't get gardening. Americans don't go outside. They are frightened of it. Frightened of bugs and wildlife. Frightened of the heat and the cold. They don't want the work of a garden. Maintenance companies come in and cut and fertilise the grass. That's it.'

James uses mass planting – 'up to 1,000 of each plant' – laying them out then cutting pathways through them. This is a novel and brilliantly simple way of establishing natural paths and defining planting areas with natural planting. Here, the tall Panicum virgatum *is planted behind the pinkish little bluestem* (Schizachyrium scoparium).

His gardens are clearly the exception. Coming from a culture where gardens and gardening saturates into almost every aspect of life, this was a breath of fresh air both in attitude and setting. By using indigenous plants and embracing the flowing natural grasses of the prairie, James van Sweden has touched the nerve of what American gardens could be, using indigenous species, without aping European ideas and being sustainable in a slowly cooking world.

Jack Larsen, community gardens in Manhattan and James's modern creation all pointed to the future. But I wanted to see where the American idea of gardens – or 'not-gardening' – had come from. I wanted to go south a little, and back in time a couple of hundred years to the very beginnings of the modern United States.

Monticello

Charlottesville, Virginia

MONTICELLO LIES A FEW MILES outside the small town of Charlottesville in Virginia. It was the home of Thomas Jefferson, the third president of the United States, the author of the Declaration of Independence and in many ways the true founding father of modern America. He had huge, restless energy and curiosity and, amongst many other things, was a gardener and an obsessive, compulsive note taker, letter writer and chronicler of his household accounts and activities, so we have a very accurate portrait of Jefferson's garden at Monticello. I went there to look at a kind of beginning – given that native Americans occupied and exercised a sophisticated civilisation for millennia before the white settlers arrived with their mixture of evangelism, colonialisation and genocide.

The pavilion looks out over the 1,000 ft vegetable garden, the orchard and a vineyard and was used by Jefferson as an escape from the bustle of everyday life. Destroyed by a storm in the 1820s, it was rebuilt in 1984 using archaeological evidence and some of Jefferson's own records.

Monticello is the nearest that America gets to a stately home. There are plenty of bigger and less modest modern villas nowadays but it was exceptionally grand for its day and its place there in Virginia, south of Washington. In Jefferson's time (1743–1826) it had 5,000 acres of farmland and there are now 2,400 acres with fifteen full-time staff. They get 460,000 visitors a year although this is a fall of 100,000 in the past ten years. According to the head gardener, Peter Hatch, this is a trend that the majority of gardens and museums are experiencing. People, Peter says, don't have the time, inclination or concentration. But the great and the good usually make the pilgrimage. Every president (except, at the time of writing, George W. Bush, another one short on time, inclination and concentration) has paid their respects to Jefferson's grave in the grounds. Bob Dylan came the week before I did – just queued up like everyone else and bought a ticket but then walked round with a black motorbike crash helmet on so nobody would know who he was. It was a very hot day so instead people stared at this person drawing attention to himself by wearing a crash helmet.

At the beginning of the nineteenth century, this was just about the edge of the West. The Blue Ridge Mountains are across the horizon and that was the edge of occupied land. Monticello looks down over a vast, endless plain of trees, like a seascape. The sense of scale is overwhelming.

Jefferson's father settled at Monticello in the 1730s, aided by a large grant of land. Thomas Jefferson began to build the house – designed in every quirky detail by himself – in 1770. He married in 1772 but his wife died ten years later, having given him six children but long before the house was anywhere near finished. In fact it was never finished – it was always a work in progress to the day he died, forty-four years after his wife. Jefferson never remarried and Monticello has the quirkiness of a bachelor pad. All the details are specific and suited him. He designed Monticello from scratch, including clocks, doors, dumb waiters in fireplaces, cellars – he was endlessly, rather madly inventive.

Jefferson's brain was more active than one man could deal with. His energy and curiosity was all consuming and everything at Monticello is a testament to this. Although he was an obsessive recorder of everything – meals, cellars, weather, expenditure, planting, income (every letter was copied by a pantograph) he never balanced his books, never saw that the record of what was coming in did not match the record of what was going out. He had no business sense at all. When he died he was in debt to the tune of $1 million and the estate had to be sold up to pay it off.

He never went upstairs so the staircases are tiny – only 2 ft wide – and tucked away to one side of the main entrance hall. He slept downstairs in a suite of library, greenhouse and study, with his bed set in an alcove open on both sides so he could literally get out of bed and work. Guests also slept downstairs and the families – his daughters and their twelve children who also lived there – occupied the upper two storeys. He had a clock in every room – recording the time – at an age when most Americans could not tell the time. I imagine it as a teeming, busy household dominated by this overwhelmingly dominant figure, half mad professor, half powerful politician. There is no modern equivalent.

Outside the garden grew from two impulses. The first was the need to grow fresh fruit and vegetables for the kitchen – the current vegetable garden was made into a flat terrace retained by a huge stone wall over the course of three years between 1806 and 1809 (whilst he was president) by seven slaves that he specifically rented from a nearby farmer, using a cart and mule. It is 1,000 ft long and represents a vast feat of manual labour. Below it are the fruit orchards. Being Jefferson, there was an astonishing range of vegetables and fruits for the time

When I was there, in autumn 2007, Virginia was in the grip of drought and they had not had a drop of rain for over two months. Peter Hatch apologised profusely for the absence of crops to cover the 2-acre terrace or indeed flowers in the borders up by the house. But this did not matter at all. Visiting Monticello is essentially an historic outing rather than an horticultural one. That the two combine and overlap sets American gardens into a modern historical context rather than, as James van Sweden or Jack Larsen's gardens had done, an aesthetic one.

The second influence on Jefferson's garden was his time spent as Minister to France, between 1785 and 1789, when he also went to England and systematically visited many English gardens. He loathed the British but greatly admired their gardens and brought back with him, amongst other garden concepts, the idea of the *ferme ornée*. The *ferme ornée* placed productivity side by side with beauty and for Jefferson the orchards, or 'fruitier' as he called it, contributed much to the beauty of the landscape. In 1979, the restoration of the vegetable garden began and today it is pretty much as Jefferson had it in the early decades of the nineteenth century, divided into twenty-four squares, each with its own crop, and is constantly productive. The soil is dusty and the colour of baked terracotta, although apparently heavy, and Peter Hatch told me that every inch is mulched each year with some kind of compost or manure. Jefferson responded to crop failure or so-called pests and disease with a holistic view of the garden. He wrote to his daughter Martha after she complained that the vegetables were plagued by insects, 'We will try this winter to cover our garden with a heavy coating of manure. When earth is rich it bids defiance to droughts, yields in abundance and of the best quality. I suspect that the insects which harassed you have been encouraged by the feebleness of your plants; and that has been produced by the lean state of the soil.' Would that modern politicians were so wise.

Yet the energy and remorseless quest for knowledge and control over nature is evident at every turn of the garden. When he returned to Monticello after completing his presidency his focus turned to planting. Jefferson planted over 330 varieties of vegetables, thirty-eight varieties of peach, fourteen cherry, twelve pear, twenty-seven plum and twenty-four varieties of grape, the latter now supported, as they were in his day, by the most beautiful riven oak rails. Most of the varieties failed to thrive and many died in the fierce Virginian climate but the sheer numbers tell us much about Jefferson if not about perfect fruit culture.

One element of eighteenth- and nineteenth-century southern life that is skirted around whenever one reads material about Jefferson is his use of slaves. He paid lip service to the evils of slavery but the facts are that he did nothing to abolish it and actually used many slaves to create and manage Monticello. At any one time he had at least a hundred slaves at Monticello and fifty odd at his other place further south, plus ten to twenty black servants. Most of the slaves lived in the fields in huts on the plantations, but some lived in huts on Mulberry Row, the avenue running above the vegetable garden that also housed the estate workshops. It seems likely that Jefferson treated his slaves well – but he never freed a single one. It is significant that the whole of the vegetable and orchard space was protected by high, close set paling fence – to keep out slaves as much as animals.

Brown's Mountain, known as 'Montalto' by Jefferson, rises behind the vast vegetable garden.

Jefferson brought ideas from Europe to his flower gardens too, and made a winding floral walk much in the style of Humphrey Repton, whose work he saw when he visited England. By modern standards this is unremarkable – a series of flower beds around a large lawn behind the house with a path running alongside them. These beds were divided into 10 ft sections, each for a different species and planted to provide year-round colour. Again this is neither fashionable nor remarkable but it was an extraordinary thing then – turning what had been a plantation carved out of virgin territory into a place of beauty and culture.

Jefferson did as much as any individual to make the America we see today. It is his ceaseless, restless energy, enthusiasm and curiosity that drove the expansion west and the taming of what was seen as wild, hostile country. His direct connection to the land, to the soil itself, was vital in creating the spirit of the early pioneers heading west. He personally created a huge amount at Monticello but it is fair to say that he preserved very little. He seemed to have no real concept of stewardship. Because Monticello was sold to pay off his debts, only chance and much private benefaction have preserved and restored it.

It is a fascinating place to visit and gave me a real insight into the mentality that made the country through the medium of a garden made by one of the truly great men of the nation at a seminal moment of history. Where else in the world can you say this?

Prairie Interlude

Cottonwood Falls, Kansas

THE FIRST SETTLERS FROM EUROPE had colonised and pretty much clung to the eastern seaboard. But from Jefferson's time – and with his direct encouragement and promotion – pioneers struck out west into vast unknown lands to conquer, chart and cultivate. Given the very limited time that I had, I now wanted to go in their direction and visit California for the first time in my life. But first I made a stop off at Kansas in the Midwest or more specifically in Cottonwood Falls, in the tall-grass prairies of the Flint Hills.

Although it may seem an endlessly waving sea of just grass, the prairie is second only to the Amazon in the richness of its ecodiversity. There are four signature grasses – big bluestem (*Andropogon gerardii*), little bluestem (*Schizachyrium scoparium*), Indian grass and switch grass – but forty other grasses too, as well as many other herbaceous flowers and herbs such as the familiar *Solidago* (golden rod), which the Americans call forbs. Smooth sumac grows along tracks and creeks and this was an autumnal brilliant

The Tallgrass Prairie National Reserve seems vast, but less than 4 per cent of the original 170-million acre prairies remain today.

red like poppies in field when I saw it. All this flora attracts and supports a huge range of invertebrate life and birds. This is also the flora that James van Sweden's garden in Chesapeake is based upon and which is perfectly suited to a subtle and rich horticultural interpretation.

These prairies are known as 'tallgrass' because the bluestem can reach heights of 9 ft on lowlands and 5 ft on uplands (about 1,500 ft) and the native Indians would describe grasses so tall that they could ride through them on horseback unseen. But most of the prairie is underground with a huge mass of roots bound incredibly densely into the soil.

This grass quickly creates a mass of clogged, dead material, blocking light and water to the ground beneath it unless cleared. However there is a pattern of natural fires roughly every seven years. By this time the grass biomass is enormous and the fires burn with furious intensity. The roots of the grasses are at least 5 ft (and often up to 30 ft) deep, however, and easily survive the fires – as well as drought or extreme cold. Once the fires have gone there is apparently an incredible greening of the prairie and within three weeks there is enough regrowth for grazing. The new growth of the tall grasses are particularly nutritious so that bison – or cattle – put on up to 4–5 lb of weight a day until August, when the plant starts to store its goodness in the roots ready for winter, cold nights trigger it to turn brown and it is no good for grazing. This growing cycle was the basis of the whole cowboy story.

From the 1850s cattle were herded from Texas to the tallgrass prairies to fatten before being sold. In 1868, Kansas state law decreed that settlers had to fence boundaries. Thus the prairies were possessed and eventually lost. The last buffalo were slaughtered by 1870 and by then cattle were mostly transported from Texas by train to the great ranching towns like Kansas or Dodge City and then herded to the prairies in early May and grazed for ninety days before being sold. This way huge gains were made in cattle weight for very little expense.

The scale of the place is wholly unimaginable to one brought up on the patchwork of an English countryside. It is a 'limitless and lonesome prairie', to quote Walt Whitman. But almost all the prairie has vanished under plough or pavement and what remains is a tiny fraction of the prairies that the first travellers west discovered or that the native Americans had lived harmoniously with for millennia. The Kansas Flint Hills is now the largest unbroken prairie with the Tallgrass Prairie National Preserve on what was the 10,894-acre Spring Hill/Z-bar ranch. Ten thousand acres was the average ranch size – divided into fields of about 1,000 acres.

The day I spent on the prairie was bitterly cold, with a wind that ripped through the huge sky and would have sliced through me had I not stopped and bought a cowboy jacket in Kansas (much to the subsequent derision and embarrassment of my children) but I loved it. It is a spectacularly beautiful place. And I felt that I had learned something important about America, something that the massed, busy, rich cultures of both coasts could not tell. It was beautiful and inspiring but also a sad story. James van Sweden's remark of a few days earlier was given an extra poignancy. 'America has so much beauty,' he said, 'that we waste it.'

THE SCALE OF THE PLACE IS WHOLLY UNIMAGINABLE TO ONE BROUGHT UP ON THE PATCHWORK OF AN ENGLISH COUNTRYSIDE.

Huntington Botanical Garden

San Marino, California

AFTER FLYING TO LOS ANGELES (sitting by a window and flying over the Grand Canyon, Death Valley, salt lakes, petrified forests, Las Vegas and raging Californian fires), I went out to San Marino to the Huntington Botanical Gardens.

Henry Huntington was a railway magnate. He was born in 1850, the year that California became part of the United States, when the West was still truly wild, and died in 1927 when California had become the centre for the burgeoning movie industry. America had changed unrecognisably in his lifetime and he was one of the key men responsible for that. He was the nephew of Collis Huntington, one of the big four responsible for the creation of the trans-continental railway and when Collis died in 1900 Henry inherited much of his fortune as well as, rather unusually, marrying his uncle's widow.

Henry Huntington founded the Pacific Electric Railway that opened out California but he was not in the same raw mould of the previous generation that had initially tamed the West. He was an avid and competitive collector and he used his wealth to finance collections of manuscripts, paintings and rare books that are today housed at the Huntington Library on his estate at San Marino, just outside Pasadena.

Huntington's botanical gardens cover 127 acres but I was visiting a small section of it, the Desert Garden, although this itself is 10 acres big and has one of the largest collections of cacti and succulents in the world, with over 5,000 different species of xerophytes. I was fascinated to see what kind of garden the great magnate made and how cacti, the symbol of barren desert and intractable land, were so key for Huntington.

It was an overcast morning when I arrived and the Desert Garden – let alone the whole botanical gardens – seemed enormous. Faced with 10 acres of succulents, my mind froze. It all feels inaccessible – like walking into a party where you do not know a soul and everyone seems locked in discussion in a language you do not speak. But in these situations I have learned to simply walk, look and let my reactions look after themselves. I scribble banal comments in my notebook. Slowly some kind of sense begins to intrude. Cacti, euphorbia, aloes, agaves and puya all combine to produce a recognisable botanic rhythm.

But as I wandered and wondered, the vistas through the deep beds were out of all experience. It was a surreal garden, a garden where plants looked like rocks or dry, bristling bones. These are plants as far from my own familiar botanical terms of reference as anything found outside a coral reef. In fact walking through is remarkably similar to snorkelling through a reef without the bother of coming up for air. And there are flowers too, flowers with familiar forms growing straight out of cacti as though pinned to them. The dull, overcast morning was working for us, keeping the night-blooming plants like the *Cereus dayami* blooming well into daytime. A sign told me that this particular one was over a hundred years old. Cacti live a long life and carry the reminder of every cut and knock to the end of their days, so they end up gnarled, scarred and weathered like blasted oaks, yet flowering like water lilies.

Luckily I was able to meet and chat to the present curator, Jim Folsom. He is only the third curator in the hundred-year history of the garden and a man of remarkable articulacy about both his charges and gardens in general.

Aloes, agaves and all shapes and sizes of cacti nestle together, from columnar Cereus *with their colourful fruits to squat, round Golden Barrels* (Echinocactus grusonii), *some of which are over eighty-five years old.*

I asked him how the Desert Garden began. 'William Hertrich, the first curator, was left with a piece of land that was an earthquake fault, exposed, terrible soil – cobble and granite mixed together – it wasn't suitable for making a good garden. So Hertrich said, "Let's make it a good place for cacti." Huntington had had unpleasant experiences with cacti as they made miles of clearing for the railways – a difficult and at times dangerous business – but he was persuaded to do this by Hertrich. But then when people started noticing it and saying what a wonderful garden, he took notice and the trains were sent out to southern Texas and Mexico to bring back big specimens because then it became a challenge and then he fell in love with it. It is not finished now but it came into being in the first fifteen years after it began in 1907.'

So he fell in love with the challenge rather than cacti? 'I think so. But then it ploughed directly into his collector's instincts. Then the scientists showed up and said it was important. Then it became beautiful. It went from being a challenge to being a dream.'

I asked Jim what curating a collection like this entails. 'In many ways they are distinct and are not like other plants to look after. Frost is our biggest problem. Some of the damage doesn't show for years. It may be two years before you know how serious the damage is. Drought is no problem. Just the challenges of rainfall in the winter because of our cacti prefer dry winter and summer rainfall. So we do water in summer. In winter we deal with the rainfall by making sure the beds are all raised up and drain well.

'There are incredible microclimates here. Last winter there were shrubs – myrtle – that were untouched in one place and frozen to the ground 100 yards away. All depend on movement of air. Aspect makes all the difference in the world. Being so close to being frost-free makes plants incredibly sensitive to the slightest frost.

'Another big challenge is the growing number of pests that will attack a plant – with cactus the same green is there for fifty years. If you damage it then that plant is marred and scarred for ever. It never rejuvenates or repairs itself.'

The tall, thin, gnarly Cereus is startlingly enormous, while the Golden Barrels in front of it are the size of watermelons.

What did Huntington expect to get out of this? 'We have lost the feeling that earlier generations had that plants were intrinsically important. Huntington believed that if you put enough plants together in southern California – where you could grow almost anything – then you could create an important economic climate. But it was not just economics. He also felt philosophical about plants. He felt that this was the new world. If you could grow anything here then you could be anybody. You could produce anything. He loved southern California and thought that plants were part of its culture. Huntington was a cultured – if not highly educated – man. He was well read. He paid a lot of attention to what he thought was good for society. He thought that southern California was where American society was moving. It was for him the core of America.

'Our role now as an organisation is to put a little bit of science in everything. To get people to understand how the world works and take a role in this. To do this through their garden is as good a way as any.'

It was all I could do not to stand back and applaud. What a culture! Sunshine (it finally broke through the grey), energy, money and philanthropy of the highest order expressed through gardens! I felt my liberal, Bush- and Blair-despising self being seduced by the Californian dream. The truth is that there is a streak of very high ideals in America that exist and persist strongly. Huntington's rather manic brilliance founded something altogether more sober and straightforward but at heart thoroughly decent.

All this in a field of cacti. I went into the Huntington Gardens a blancmange of thoughtlessness and came out fired and inspired by the American Dream.

Lotusland

Santa Barbara, California

THERE IS NO GOOD WEATHER quite like Californian good weather, especially if you come to it from a grey European autumn. It predisposes one to enjoy anything and everything outside, and if the brochure for Lotusland is anything to go by it is a garden best approached with a mixture of reverence and delight. The truth is that parts of Lotusland are very beautiful, parts are very interesting and most of it is completely bonkers. Its main feature is that it is an unedited stream of horticultural consciousness, a version of Edward James's Las Pozas in the Mexican jungle (without the jungle or the building or the same plants), a kind of self-published novel 2,000 pages long or a meal where meat, sweets, elaborate pies, vegetables, puddings and soups are all served indiscriminately and all day.

The garden is so huge, so fantastical, that I don't quite know where to look first. This huge Agave americana is just a taste of the vast extravagance to come.

This is not intended as criticism. The garden is beyond that. It is fascinating and all the more enjoyable for its oddness. Lotusland is a 37-acre garden in the foothills of Montecito to the east of the city of Santa Barbara, created by one Madame Ganna Walska, who owned the property from 1941 until her death in 1984.

Ganna Walska was born Hanna Puacz in 1887 in Brest-Litovsk, Poland, but took the stage name of Madame Ganna Walska. Over the next decades she sang in New York and Paris and toured America and Europe, married six times, obviously wisely if not successfully because she accumulated great wealth in the process. By the time she came to California, the culmination of her steady progress upwards and westward from Poland, her sixth husband was on the way out. According to her niece Hanjya he was a swami who married her for her money. 'Everyone knew it. No one liked him.' It was he who persuaded her to buy the estate, saying it would be an ideal place, with all its cottages and outbuildings, for a Tibetan monastery. In the end the monks never came and the smarmy swami went. Madame never married again but devoted the remaining forty-three years of her life to her garden.

To set the garden into context it is important to realise that, in her day, she was a star. A diva. Hollywood flocked to her parties and within her world she ruled imperiously. This meant that there were no checks or restraints on her. There is no question that she knew her stuff. Her cacti collection is surpassed, in private hands at least, only by Huntington. When she wished to create a new cactus garden towards the end of her life she sold $1 million worth of jewellery to pay for it. She was serious, a real player.

Making a 30-odd acre garden and running it for over forty years is no mean feat. Hanjya told me that she strictly controlled every detail. Each and every planting, every pruning cut had to have her permission.

But what is her huge, indulged, intense garden *like*? Much of it boils down to taste. It is a performance – carnival opera. I don't think that I like it but wonder that it exists. One of the very American elements of the garden is the way that there is little sense of quiet accumulation. Because there was so much space for her to play with she could spread out almost endlessly – all her ideas are big and brash. Hanjya told me that she never planted in ones or twos. 'If she wanted something she had to have 200.' It was a kind of imperial greed ruled with a rod of Polish iron.

Above *The shallow kidney-shaped pool in the middle of the Aloe Garden is overhung by large Chilean palms that look quite at home here, in the middle of California.*
Opposite *The cascading fountains of giant clam shells pour water into the pool, which in turn has a border of abalone shells. Behind the shells, the branches of large tree aloes entwine around each other.*

But there was – still is – real charm. Hanjya was brought up there and Madame made the new swimming pool for her, huge, deep blue and surrounded with an exotic garden, and the place where the potentially lonely only child had many swimming parties laid on by her aunt for her amusement. To one side of the pool is a sandy area with dozens of huge shells. More surrealism. As Hanjya was telling me this, I overheard a guide taking round a group of school children and saying, 'Madame wanted the little girl to have her own beach'. The 'little girl' was sitting next to me now, in her sixties, face suspiciously taut, coiffed, bejewelled, anything but a little girl but actually a nice, modest funny companion to be sharing a garden with on a beautiful day.

She obviously cut a dash in southern California. They liked her style. I think I do too. She was big and brash but, by Hollywood standards, old money. She had class and spread it about her garden for us all to admire.

There is so much to describe. Impossible. Walk round and you have a flood of random impressions. Blue grass and obsidian edging 'stones' – taken from the clinker of a nearby glass factory. Dragon trees (*Dracaena*) wonderfully grown so that the branches entwine to form a succulent, bloated canopy. Next to them the Californian black oak (*Quercus agrifolia*), with an astonishing sculptural sinuosity, for me the best thing in the garden. And next to this cacti, and then strelitzia, and then a smudge of smoky olive foliage against the blue sky. The Blue Garden is a conceit realised almost entirely without flowers. I was told that it was not at its best but it pleased me well enough with its interweave of glaucous foliage. Agaves, *Senecio mandraliscae*, chusan palm, *Festuca glauca*, blue atlas cedar, Chilean palm all mesh subtly.

Across the huge lawn – bright green in the middle of a drought and whilst much of southern California was suffering the worst fires in its history – where Hanjya remembers with the sadness of recalled simple childhood happiness 'sprinklers on the lawn that were such fun to run through when it was so hot' and where Madame assembled all the Hollywood rich and famous for her parties, is a formal section behind a vast Monterey cypress. Formal verging on the caricature. The rose garden leads you via a Mughal pool and rill down to a clock the size of a roundabout decorated with signs of the zodiac. It kept perfect time but looked as if it had been got up by a Parks department for a floral display. Around it were topiarised cartoon figures, all beautifully done. The last time I saw this kind of thing was at Disneyworld. No it wasn't. It was closer to home than that. It was at Het Loo in the Netherlands and at Villa d'Este in Italy. This kind of extreme wealth and unbridled power expresses itself like this in every age. We have a tendency to be snooty about it, casting a sheen of dignity over the kitschier excesses of baroque or Renaissance gardens but you only have to see Het Loo, restored as new to its 1700 glory to see what extreme kitsch looked like 300 years ago. The old bird was behaving no different to William of Orange or a Borgia.

The only part of the garden I thought unredeemably hideous was the shell pond. It was apparently intended to be completed with a flock of pink flamingos which would have made it a kind of horticultural Danny la Rue. Perhaps I was just tired by the time I got there. Ironically it houses a very comprehensive and serious collection of aloes. But it is like meeting someone who is telling you interesting and useful facts whilst revealing an astonishingly extreme face-lift. Distracting (and not unusual in California).

But it was a great day out and took me right into the Californian deep end. From Huntington's noble belief in plants as part of California's cultural future, I was now immersed in Hollywood's glorious, slightly seedy past. It was time to get up to date.

Roland Emmerich's Garden

Hollywood, California

Statues of various buddhas abound, tucked away against walls, or hidden amongst the green of the plants.

IN HOLLYWOOD ALL HOUSES AND GARDENS are fantasy. Money buys you whatever you want. Every house and piece of land are open to reinterpretation any time you like – and can afford. So new houses are knocked down and rebuilt differently. Gardens are ripped up and replanted every few years. It is a bit like a revolving Chelsea Flower Show – except it doesn't rain. I very much wanted to visit the home of someone from the film world who had set out to make a garden from scratch. There are plenty of those about but not many that are happy to have an unknown from the UK, clutching a notebook and a film crew, come and invade their space. Most doors remained very locked. I also had to face the slightly uncomfortable fact that gardening in America in general, and Hollywood in particular, is on a par with doing the laundry or valeting the car. It is something that you get people to do for you – usually Mexicans. *Gardeners' World* cuts no ice at all.

However Roland Emmerich, the director, amongst other films, of *Independence Day*, generously agreed to let us film his garden. It is in Hollywood, up on a hill overlooking the city. Emmerich chose it because it had plenty of land, but he wanted to screen the view both to hide the city from the garden and also to protect his privacy. The existing garden was – of course – to be scrubbed and the whole thing started anew. So he called in the landscape designer Susan McEowen to come up with a plan and put it in place.

I met Susan at the garden and immediately liked her. She had a no-nonsense dry humour and is a practical, down-to-earth mid-westerner. She told me that the brief that Roland Emmerich gave her was to make the garden like a glamorous old actress's garden – and block the view.

When you arrive, the first impression is one of astonishment. That is clearly the desired response. Ta da! You want a garden? How about *this*! In the middle of the parched Mediterranean-like chaparral is a lush, tropical paradise. It could be Bali.

To obscure the views both in and out Susan has filled the space with a mass of trees. Bananas, Washingtonian palms – the ubiquitous street palm of Los Angeles – and three fantastic date palms. There were four but one died – on inspection a smaller fourth is in position. Susan said that these date palms were 12–15 ft high when they came. Now the crowns have just exploded out into lovely, sculptural herringbone foliage.

The actual garden is only a couple of acres but the impression is one of a bigger scale than that. Because the vistas are all short you can actually see much more by looking up than around – so everything seems huge.

The design is very simple. Steps lead down the steep slope from the front door to the pool, crossing a paved flat patio that is dominated by a large fountain. A path crosses this fountain yard from the car park area to a small lawned space leading to the side of the house. Within this uneven quadrant the slopes are massed with view-blocking planting. But the details and permutations of this are subtle and beautifully done. I notice that every hedge or wall has another lower hedge in front of it. This double-stress of the horizontals balances out all the soaring verticals of the trees and anchors them. It is a simple thing but works incredibly well. Another detail to borrow when I get home.

The hard landscaping is, as you might expect, of the highest order with walls, paths and steps completed with a degree of solidity and permanence that is unusual in anything but the grandest gardens. The more I think about it, this is what extreme wealth buys you in a garden: infrastructure. Plants come and go and can, like the dodgy date palm, be quickly replaced. But to have the infrastructure of your garden built with exactly the same solidity as your house is true luxury. Garden writers and designers talk a lot about the 'bones' of a garden but they are as important as the cheekbones in a starlet's face. The better the bone structure the better the flesh sits.

It costs, of course. Susan told me that she and Roland went 'tree shopping' and spent a cool $500,000 in the process. Everything was placed by a huge crane that only just got up the road. That was just the beginning. The first 'pot shopping' expedition set him back another $100,000. There are over 300 pots in the garden planted beautifully with, in just one corner, strelitzia, cordylines, citrus, cacti, aloes. The effect is amazing. Magnificent even. But the gardener in me pitied the poor sod that has to water them all. The entire hillside had to be stripped of 10 ft of soil and recompacted to stop slippage – remember this is earthquake city. The fountain – which had been in the original garden – ended up on exactly the same spot but 10 ft higher in the air. In all, about $2 million was spent on

*Everything in the garden was brought in and planted by crane. All the enormous verticals, created chiefly by the tall Mexican fan palms (*Washingtonia robusta*), are beautifully balanced by a whole series of horizontal lines, making a surprisingly balanced scene.*

the hardscape and pool. So the total cost was probably $3 million. Susan seemed to think that this was generous but not unexceptional here in southern California. She reckons that 10 per cent of the value of a home should be spent on landscaping for 'small lots of half to two acres'.

Inevitably this extreme instant gardening (although it took two years) means nothing now needs to be done. It has no sense of becoming. It is complete. The ubiquitous maintenance man does just that: he maintains the garden rather than nurturing and growing it in any sense.

This is impressive and very lovely but also has a sense of stasis. It feels like a holiday home or a very luxurious hotel. Compared to the sense of studio that I found in the homes of great garden designers like Jacques Wirtz, Fernando Caruncho or Juan Grimm it lacks energy and life. But Rousham, the most perfect garden in England, is also a performance. All big gardens are. The one thing that this one lacks is a sense of *place*. It could be anywhere. The mega-rich and successful buy beauty, inspiration and luxury but not that one vague, subliminal element of place that no money in the world can buy. It is the wrong currency.

But Susan McEowen has made a garden that is just lovely to be in. There is nothing brash about it. If it is like a hotel then it is a hotel I would be very happy to stay in. The whole place has great restraint despite the exotic luxury. It has a real sense of style. This gives it substance and strength. She has created a green refuge in the middle of the city entirely free from prying eyes. It may not have a sense of place in terms of landscape but it has in terms of culture. Privacy is the great commodity in this vast and open country, opulent privacy in the midst of others.

Mia Lehrer Garden

Brentwood, Los Angeles, California

From the outset the garden and house had equal billing. And when it was finished, the architect said, 'You know this is a garden with a house, not a house with a garden.'

MY FINAL GARDEN VISIT IN CALIFORNIA was to a house that had been wholly reinvented in every detail. The owners, Mr and Mrs Greenberg, had lived on the site in Brentwood, one of the most affluent areas of Los Angeles, for several decades. They had amassed a large collection of 1960s art and wished to have a house suitable to accommodate it. But instead of moving to such a thing, in 1986, having reached retirement age, they decided to pull down the Santa Barbara-revival Spanish home that they had raised their family in and rebuild a new, very modern house, literally in its place. To start all over again and reinvent their house and garden from scratch. They hired the architect Ricardo Legorreta after going to a lecture by him and he in turn suggested they use the landscape architect Mia Lehrer for the garden.

Ricardo Legorreta had been an associate of Luis Barragan and having visited three of Barragan's houses in Mexico I could immediately see the connections. There were the same huge windowless planes painted brilliant colours, the same sense of mass weighted against areas of light and almost delicate colour. It is a very beautiful building. Mia worked on the garden from the outset, before the original building was bulldozed and salvaged many of the trees that were on the site for replanting.

I love this. The scale of it. The ambition. Bulldozing buildings, starting again, moving mature trees. It is outrageous. Hubristic. Completely life-enhancing.

The electronic entrance gates open to reveal a large gravelled yard, surrounded by ochre slabs of stuccoed building and devoid of detail, including any immediate indication of where a door might be – save for a cluster of agaves against the street wall and seven vast Washingtonian palms grouped in one corner. I met Mia Lehrer at the garden. Going round the garden with her I had an insight into how most design issues are practical and logistical. Inspiration affects and changes everything but most of the time is spent making these aesthetic decisions possible.

For example, Mia told me that all seven Washingtonian palms had been dotted around the former garden but not together. She positioned them in the corner of the building like a grove to balance the two towers of the building, 'but then I had the task of convincing everyone that the base of the palm was as interesting as any other part of the plant.' She is right. It is. But it challenges all your preconception of how trees work when you can only see this part of it unless you stand and crane your neck up 65 ft into the bluest of blue skies. The slits in the front of the house play with the lines of the palms, and house and trees really work together in a way that is rarely so deliberate. But there was the problem of where to store all the trees until the building work was finished and they were ready to plant out. In the end they decided to position them in their final planting places before work began and to build around them.

Out of the back of the house the land falls away from a paved seating area, down to the pool – all Californian gardens have a pool – and then, in a ravine below this, a tennis court. Two large jacaranda trees were replanted immediately behind the house, softening the drama of the building. Most gardens are added to houses at some stage but this is inextricably entwined and you have to see it like this – architecture and plants almost dancing together. Mia is married to an architect and for her the relationship between buildings and landscape is always important and wherever possible umbilical. But for that to happen you also need the complicity – and money – of a willing client. In the wealthy suburbs of Los Angeles these are more available than probably anywhere else on earth.

Pale honey-coloured stone steps run down the slope with a raised rill in the retaining wall on one side and a terraced lawn on the other. Stone water and grass stepping down. Looking back up from the pool area the house is magnificent. This is the main view and performance. Swimming pools can be a problem for any gardener, falling somewhere between a trampoline and a canal or formal pond. Mia's pool seems to answer all the questions, partly through the elegance of its lines but especially the wonderful deep Prussian blue used in the tiles.

The only part of the garden I would have changed was the way that the view was not enclosed but seemed fudged with a half-hearted screen of king palms and two *Butia capitata*, the only two trees brought into the garden that were not originally there. I would have kept the screen that backed half the pool right across to the end.

But then it is not my garden. It is not for me to criticise these people's private home. But the very fact that I was thinking like this shows how much I liked it. I wanted every tiny detail to be perfect because it practically is. I also wondered what the future of this garden might be. If the Greenbergs sell it, will new owners pull it all down and rebuild their own version of a house and home? Will there come a time when Californians wish to preserve houses and gardens as having intrinsic artistic value ?

A garden like this resembles a very well-cut suit or frock. The secret of such simplicity is that it be immaculately done with the very best materials and then worn almost carelessly. Now clearly I am biased here. I found the lean, blocky minimalism of these lines incredibly exciting and inspiring. It was the opposite of Roland Emmerich's garden – which I also liked and admired. Both were almost entirely devoid of European influence. Both rely on the sun and optimism – and money on a scale that is rarely spent on European gardens. The added element of Mia's design is the duet with the architecture which I love. It gives a garden immediate context and identity rather than just being the selection and arrangement of plants, however beautifully this may be done.

Following pages *The wild landscape of the Drakensberg and the richness of its flora helped me to understand the plants of South Africa.*
Below *Every garden I have seen in California has a pool but few are as stylish as this one in Brentwood.*

There are new and confident gardens being made, using indigenous plants and drawing on a heritage very foreign to Sissinghurst or Hidcote.

10 Growing Free

South Africa

South Africa

South Africa was always going to be a problem. Growing up in the 1960s and 70s, the country's apartheid regime was considered by many, myself strongly included, as an impassable ideological barrier. Although I met and made friends with liberal white South Africans at university and they often spoke with longing and homesickness of the beauties of their country, to go and visit it seemed to be an act of support for the governing white regime. This view fossilised into an automatic association and by the time that the country had free elections I was almost forty, had no good associations with the place and no desire to go there.

And yet as a gardener I was, of course, aware that many of the plants that I grew in my own garden, some of them long-time favourites, were South African and could be seen growing gloriously in the wild. Not just any wild either but a spectacular wild, with scenery and animals that could match anything else that the world has to offer for range and beauty. I had seen the pictures.

If the experience of travelling round the world looking at gardens had taught me nothing else then it was that gardens are, to an extent, plant zoos and that you cannot really understand a plant until you have seen it growing in its natural habitat. So gladioli, pelargoniums, crocosmia, helichrysum, agapanthus, leonotis, restios, galtonias, lobelias, dieramas, strelitzias, arum lilies, brizas – to name a tiny selection – could be placed in a context that would immeasurably enrich my own understanding of them, as if seeing something lovely in a lovely place needed extra justification.

There were gardens to be seen too. Here was a country that had established its identity through colonisation, war, extreme politics and the most extraordinary bloodless revolution of the last century. That identity was still clearly unravelling and it was tempting to think that this might be revealed in the way that it made and tended its gardens. I could go and explore this forbidden place and try and understand something of it in my own currency.

However, fate did its best to stop me getting there. I came back from Trømso in the Arctic, intending to spend a month at home before heading off to the Cape, hoping especially to catch the spring flowering of Namaqualand. Three days before I was due to leave I got peritonitis and as I was wheeled into an ambulance at 2 am, the morphine blissfully kicking in, I remember saying to Sarah that at least I would not have to go to South Africa.

The trip was rescheduled so that it became the final leg of my adventure. It meant that I missed the autumn bulb flowering but it was a much more desirable time for the gardens, being the equivalent to late spring in England. The weather and the plants would both be better. But I still had reservations right to the point of boarding the aircraft. It was hard to summon up positive thoughts about a place that had represented oppression for so many years. The only real saving grace seemed to be that I would get a few weeks of unbroken sunshine at a time of the year when Britain is at it grimmest, skulking worst.

Kirstenbosch National Botanical Garden

Cape Town, Western Cape

Above *A spotted eagle owl chick sits in the branches of a pine tree in Kirstenbosch.* Previous page *The Dell boasts a collection of more than 400 cycads planted by the first director of the gardens in 1913.*

I ARRIVED IN CAPE TOWN and stayed at Newlands, in the affluent, razor-wired, 'armed-response' protected suburb on the slopes of Table Mountain. This was just five minutes by car to the first garden I was to visit, Kirstenbosch.

Kirstenbosch is not just the most famous garden in South Africa but one of the world's great botanical gardens. The gardens themselves are vast, covering almost 100 acres of carefully tended land but actually only make up a small proportion of a 1,300 acre estate that runs right to the top of Table Mountain. Apart from its size and astonishingly beautiful location, what makes Kirstenbosch exceptional is that it is devoted entirely to indigenous plants of South Africa. So for me to see as wide a range of South African plants as possible in both a garden and naturalistic setting there could be no better place to start.

The original site was partially enclosed by Jan van Riebeeck when he landed with his first hundred settlers in 1652 to establish a replenishing base for ships of the East India Company heading round the Cape of Good Hope to the Far East. His original wild almond hedge still survives in part of the garden. Gradually the native stinkwood and yellowwood trees were largely cut down for timber and European and Australian trees took their place. In 1895 Cecil Rhodes bought a tract of land on the eastern slopes expressly to preserve them as a national heritage. When he died in 1902 this was bequeathed to the South African people and became government land. In 1913 Kirstenbosch, which was by then overgrown and occupied only by ruined buildings and pigs, was set aside specifically as a garden for South African plants.

It is now a hugely influential establishment, visited by 600,000 people every year and perfectly maintained by its sixty gardeners. I met one of the senior horticulturalists, Cherise Viljoen, who showed me as much of the garden as we could see in a leisurely morning stroll. Just two days before, by complete chance, I had bumped into someone I had worked with a few years back, who heard I was off to South Africa. 'If you go to Kirstenbosch, look up my old friend Cherise. She is lovely, completely mad and be careful if you eat with her. She'll have your sandwich in the blink of an eye.' I can vouch that all but the last is true. But then she was at the other end of the table during lunch.

I asked her how many plants there were in the garden. '7,000 species,' she said, 'and still more to be discovered.' We started with some of the fynbos plants (pronounced 'fayn-bos') that come from the 'fine-bush' around the Cape. 'Proteas, ericas and restios are particularly fynbos plants,' Cherise told me. She laughed when I said that restios are being used more and more in the UK. 'They are like weeds to us and there are over 300 different kinds. But they are water-wise plants and can be strikingly beautiful and are used as thatching reeds for our roofs.' 'Water-wise' was an expression I was to hear again and again throughout South Africa, meaning plants well adapted to mak-

KIRSTENBOSCH IS NOT JUST THE MOST FAMOUS GARDEN IN SOUTH AFRICA BUT ONE OF THE WORLD'S GREAT BOTANICAL GARDENS.

ing the most of available moisture. The restios like damp conditions but will grow right at the stony top of Table Mountain, surviving by soaking up water from the tablecloth of shifting cloud that almost always covers it. This cloud falls on the mountain and filters down to springs appearing lower on the slopes, making the area so fertile. Restios are also very fire-resistant, regrowing fast after the fires that sweep across the fynbos every few years. In fact they need the fire because their seeds need smoke to germinate.

There were huge sinuous bushes of regal pelargoniums, another fynbos resident. I was bought up with regal pelargoniums carefully raised and grown in terracotta pots in the musky sexiness of the greenhouse before they were planted out in the warmest spot in the garden in June, after the last risk of frost. Here they grew like sprawling shrubs as big as rhododendrons. It was odd to see something so umbilically connected to my childhood growing in so unBritish a setting and so obviously at home. Nothing reveals the limitations or bonds of home like a handful of childhood plants.

Kirstenbosch smelt good. It was not just the pelargoniums. Cherise told me that the High Veld (pronounced 'felt' – one of the few Afrikaans words that soften in the mouth) smell musky and lemony, not least from *Salvia africana-lutea*, a bushy salvia with tawny flowers.

Pink watsonias with spathe-like leaves were splashed across the garden and out into the slopes of Table Mountain. The mountain is bunched behind the garden like the

I walked through the Kirstenbosch National Botanical Garden with senior horticulturalist Cherise Viljoen. The setting on the slope of Table Mountain makes it one of the most beautiful as well as most interesting botanical gardens in the world. Pink pelargoniums, yellow Anthanasia dentata *and mauve* Scaboisa africana *mix with the grey leaves of* Helichrysum petiolare *in the centre.*

wings of a mantling hawk, a vast fort on the skyline. The eye is irresistibly drawn to it and it is a wonder the way the garden moves easily up its slopes, seamlessly becoming forest. Looking the other direction, you gaze out over the city and to the Atlantic. There can be no garden in the world with a better situation.

The delicate flowers of pale mauve scabious floated on tall stems. Cherise told me that almost all wild scabious are that shade of mauve although recently a white one had been found. I recognised leonotis (*Leonotis leonurus*) but instead of the 12 ft tall annuals that we grow at home, this was a thick woody bush perhaps 5 ft high and covered with a mass of the livid orange ruffles of flower. In fact, as Cherise showed me, the corollas of the flowers are not orange at all but cream. It is the fine hairs that cover them that are orange. I have grown them for perhaps fifteen years and never noticed this before.

Then Cherise brought me to the proteas. I had only ever seen them before as part of spectacularly hideous florists displays. I was convinced that I hated them. How to put this sensitively and politely to Cherise? 'I hate proteas,' I said. She, being lovely and bonkers, roared with laughter and took me to a huge drift of *Leucospermum erubescens*, an explosive thrust of orange, pink and yellow flowers set on upright branches with narrow glaucous leaves. I liked them. 'These are pin cushion proteas,' she said. 'The Afrikaans name is *vuurhoutjies* which literally means fire, wood, little wood or matchsticks.' Looking at them closely you can see how the bundle of unfurled florets look exactly like a bunch of matchsticks. How can you hate a plant with that degree of charm?

But I did not learn to love the King protea. It is an ugly artichoke of pink and grey. As it is the national flower of South Africa that is an entire nation offended at a single pass. However it is only one of many. In fact there are over 350 different types of protea in South Africa. They are all upright, with quite stiff flower heads, mostly oranges and reds to attract pollinating birds. As there are no hovering nectar-eating birds in the Old World, all bird-pollinated plants have flower heads strong enough to take the weight of birds that land on them. In the New World, where there are hummingbirds, bird-pollinated plants evolved to have drooping blooms, like fuchsias.

A tortoise crawled gently through the border and I picked it up and admired it, to which it quickly responded by retracting seamlessly into its shell and then peeing all over my trousers.

Then we went down to the Dell, the first bit of the garden to be planted, back in 1913, where the first director, Professor Pearson, planted his collection of over 400 cycads. These plants with their thick leathery foliage have not changed at all since they evolved to resist dinosaurs 50 million years ago, and create a lush world as different from the fynbos as can be imagined. Sitting in a pine overlooking the Dell was a spotted eagle owl and its chicken-sized chick. I could not have been more excited if it had been a leopard and cub.

Botanic gardens are a bit like reference libraries. You dip in and out of them, look things up, trying to make connections, put things in context. Seeing plants in their natural habitat is always deeply informative, even if you have grown them for years, and provides an emotional and cultural context as well as a botanical one. My day at Kirstenbosch was the ideal way to immerse myself in Cape flora against the most dramatic of settings. The next step was to go back in time and visit a garden that displayed South Africa's links to its European heritage.

Stellenberg
Cape Town, Western Cape

I DID NOT HAVE TO GO FAR. Stellenberg is just round the mountain from Kirstenbosch. Built in 1742, it is the oldest private house in South Africa. It was created by an Englishman called John White who changed his name to Jan de Witt and built his house in a Dutch colonial style, using Dutch craftsmen and German furniture makers.

The day that I visited it rained from morning to night. Stellenberg, like Kirstenbosch, is on the wet side of the mountain and claims to be the wettest place in the Cape, getting 60 inches a year. But not usually in summer. Perhaps the weather was appropriate though, because the 5-acre garden has a strong English influence and appearance, with large oaks and immaculate borders packed with exquisitely tasteful blend of flowers.

When you visit a new garden, especially one that is rather grand and well-established, it is often best to wander round and let it filter in and then go back and talk to people to fill in the information. So this is what I did, unable to write notes because of the rain, so forced just to let the garden emerge around me.

When you walk in and see the White Garden with its impeccably tasteful blend of perennials and annuals you could be in Hampshire on a rainy June day. This is the international language of educated Good Taste. In fact, like all white gardens, the green is accentuated by the white flowers – and in this case the white house too – so the trees, emerald lawns and hedges all combine to glow with an emerald intensity. A single cloud of bright pink came from what I later discovered was *Rosa* 'Russelliana'. A joy.

The lawn gently climbed to a parterre of white roses via very shallow steps, just the thickness of a single brick, almost buried in the grass, almost just horizontal lines on the gentle slope. This may not sound much but it was lovely. I kept slipping back to look at

Part of the former tennis court has been made into a parterre of clipped box. Designed by David Hicks and filled on one side by very English plants and on the other with more santolina and lavender, it is beautifully done.

As we walked through the vegetable garden, it was pouring the kind of rain that leaks through the best waterproofs and the interior of cameras. Being British we soldiered on and made jokes about it while we filmed.

it. The parterres (of a plant I failed to recognise) were precisely clipped, sloping out to a much-widened base, so that they assumed a monolithic quality. Later I learned that this was entirely the whim of the gardeners rather than careful design. Like the rose, I plan to nick the idea for my own garden. The vegetable garden, tucked away up some steps and round a corner, is small and perfectly kept, with four beds in a quadrant around a basin. Leeks are allowed to seed for their flowers, chards and lettuces are banded by colour. I could see that a good eye rather than the desire to grow as much food as possible was the guiding spirit. Beautiful baskets, originally designed for harvesting grapes, lay scattered, ready for weeds, pruning or crops.

Across the unblemished lawns there is some exotic, lusher planting of yellow cannas, melianthus, orange brugmansias and, through a green, dripping jungle, of cordyline in flower – I had to be told that as I had never seen it in flower previously. Tree ferns, bamboo, the leaf straps of *Clivia* formed lapping layers of green shapes and textures modified by the purple leaves of *Canna* 'Durban' with *Prunus cerasifera* 'Pissardii' behind.

Then on into a walled space (it used to be the old tennis court) made up of two halves. One has four beds packed with a sublime mixture of pastel English flowers – *Verbena bonariensis*, foxgloves, delphiniums, verbascums, pale pink roses, penstemons, gaura, knautia. The other half is also made of clipped box but as a parterre infilled with the very blue-green of santolina and lavender and paved with gravel. As a performance it is faultless. Everything here works. They do what they have set out to do without a flaw.

Having dried off, I went and spoke to Sandy Overstone, who made the garden. She is an elegant woman of great charm and modesty who clearly has a wonderful eye. I asked her what her influences were. 'English gardens. Sissinghurst, Hidcote and Laurence Johnson's garden in France,' she said. British horticultural aristocracy at home and abroad. The late David Hicks was a good friend and profound influence and his mark too is everywhere in the garden. It is as though she has distilled all the best taste of British gardens and applied them to the Cape climate. But it did not happen immediately. She came to Stellenberg in 1973 when she was thirty, with three small children and no time for gardening. I asked her what the garden was like then. 'There was no garden at all. It was just lawn and trees.' It was not until 1987 that she felt she had time and confidence enough to transform it. She first made the herb garden and then the white garden. David Hicks 'designed and gave me the walled garden where the tennis court used to be as a birthday present in 1989. When I did that garden I couldn't find enough hedging plants in the whole of South Africa. Now it would be easy. Gardening has changed hugely since then. One of the biggest changes is that we have more indigenous plants available.'

Despite the Englishness of her garden she says that it is water-wise, full of indigenous plants that are exciting and that are changing South African gardens. When she started gardening there were hardly any indigenous plants in South African nurseries. Now there are. Sandy has a nursery where all her plants are raised. 'Everything is grown outside, organically and hard. They are healthy plants.' For the parterre she has used *Rhus crenata* and this is the first time that she has used indigenous hedging. It is clearly an important move away from the instantly defining European *Buxus*.

It is a garden made with care and love; the Dutch house, German furniture and English garden measure out a colonial past with elegance, style and beauty. You would love it. Anyone would. But it was rather like visiting Sissinghurst or Hidcote – a great house and garden celebrating the past of a continent far away in distance and time. It was time to look for the South African present and future.

Henk Scholtz's Garden

Franschhoek, Western Cape

TO HAVE A LOOK AT CONTEMPORARY South Africa I travelled to Franschhoek, a small town a couple of hours east of Cape Town. It is a countryside of orchards and vineyards at the foot of the high mountains that defined the limits of the Cape colonisation for centuries. I went to see the garden of Henk Scholtz, a garden designer and artist and, significantly, an Afrikaaner. His Dutch ancestry was as European as any Englishman's but the lineage veered sharply away from all things English at least two centuries ago.

Henk's house is a small thatched bungalow set on the diagonal of a small square plot with the garden pivoted in a circle around it. You could fit thirty of them in Stellenberg and have space to spare but every inch here is clipped or adorned with artefacts and sculptures, all made by Henk. I don't think I have ever seen a garden of such intense, manicured control and yet, against all odds, it survives and seems balanced and calm. All this is apparent as you walk down the narrow path to the front door between steeply battered parterre hedges of privet. In London privet hedges are invariably threadbare but these are glossy and furnished with leaves right to the ground. The beds contain strelitzia but only one last flare of orange flower remained when I was there. Around the outside, filling the gap between the curved hedges and straight boundary fence were clipped balls of what I later learnt to be plumbago. Plumbago! Until then I had only thought of it as a house plant.

A mannequin clothed in porcelain fragments and wearing a headdress of rusty metal and porcupine quills guards the path to the back of the house where a semi-circular lawn curves like an amphitheatre round a long veranda with a vine-covered wooden canopy. Everywhere there is stone, wood, rusty metal, white shells and wire all balanced against subdued but subtle planting. This is a composition, an arrangement. I blush inwardly when I think of the anarchy of my own garden back home.

I ask Henk about his background. 'I grew up in the Kruger National Park and was a country boy. I went up to Jo'burg and did computer science first, then changed careers and studied horticultural and landscape design. I came to Cape Town and I've been here now for about twenty-three years.

'Coming from the Kruger National Park I saw the thatch and I had to have it. It took me six months to renovate. The garden took another year before I started on it. I wanted to bring aspects of my childhood. I decided that I wanted to have living art, utilising a lot of indigenous art material – in a formal concept. That's what I like. I am originally from Europe and the formal concept is the connection to Europe – but with South African plants.

'Using indigenous plants is absolutely an aspect of being South African. We have

Henk Scholtz's garden is tiny but manages to contain many fascinating elements. The garden is a circle centred on the house and is set against a backdrop of stunning scenery.

Henk sees his garden as much an expression of his sculpture as a garden with sculpture. It is a 'living artwork'.

such richness of plant material. There is a vast misconception about indigenous plant material in South Africa. But you have to be selective about the plant material of the area. I mean I can't bring plant material from Natal to this area. My main criteria is to be water-wise. I did a close study of the plants in Franschhoek itself. When came I saw roses and it was this really English set up and I tried it. But what I have now is really who I am. My garden is a complete expression of myself. I enjoy recycling. It's very important to me. Even a lot of the plant material is recycled. I rescue them wherever I can.'

I pointed out that this was very different from the attitude of lusting after certain plants and scouring the nurseries of the world for it. 'Yeah. I take what I have and explore. Once I have the plant, it will tell me what to do. I don't want to have special plants that need extra protection. That's for the collector. I have really worked with the conditions – particularly of the immediate area. We have extreme cold here and extreme heat. Sometimes it goes up to 45ºC. In winter we have constant rain. You have got to cater for all this. You need really good drainage and tough plants.'

I asked him about the bright and incredibly seductive blue wall along one side of the garden. 'The blue wall began because the next-door neighbour built a house and put up a hedge then a wall. First I thought I would plant against it and then I thought no, blue. And I like that blue because you look through it. It has depth.'

He is right. The sculptures and aloes make deeper blue shadows that intermingle, plant becoming sculpture – an assembly of rusted barbed wire, tools and old tin cans flickering like foliage. Bright red 'flowers' carved out of palm fronds are ranked against the blue and stuck in gravel. Across the garden a shocking pink bougainvillea clashes precisely and perfectly with the blue. Barragan would be proud of it.

In one corner is a tiny horseshoe of an unknown clipped plant enclosing a space just big enough for two chairs. It is like a mini earthwork and is seductively enclosed, almost cosy. I brush the hedging and recoil, more in surprise than disgust. It smells distinctly fishy. Henk laughs (something he does a lot of). 'That's *Rhagodia hastata*. It grows really fast and is very tough but is not pleasant to smell. Best not to touch it. But a very good silver plant to look at and clips well.

There are a lot of clipped plants in the garden. How often does he trim them? 'Every twelve days.' What? Three times a month? Again I think of my own garden's shagginess before its biennial trim. But this is his gardening. It is, as he himself says, small enough to manicure every inch, and that's how he likes it.

The garden is small but holds an enormous amount of images and ideas. It shows that small gardens can be interesting at every level without resorting to the predictability of a plant collection. Henk also showed me that there are new and confident gardens being made, using indigenous plants and drawing on a heritage that is very foreign to Sissinghurst or Hidcote.

I had enjoyed Henk's company and his garden immensely. But so far on my trip, so cosy. How did any of this relate in any way to the life of a township or that of the poor black South African that makes up the vast majority of this country? How do their gardens grow?

'Lil' Eden', Donovan's Garden

Hout Bay, Western Cape

HOUT BAY, ALSO ON THE CAPE PENINSULA, is astonishingly beautiful. Elton John and David Beckham apparently have homes there. So do a mass of poor black South Africans although I suspect the style of accommodation is rather different. We went to visit Donovan van der Heyden, a fisherman, gardener and charity worker who is also a Rastafarian with a prize-winning garden in a township.

We had passed townships on the Cape flats near the airport and on the way to Franschhoek. They were a mixture of shanty shacks assembled from tin and wood and basic brick flats that the government were hastily building, apparently to bring ANC voters into the Cape. The crew and I were told to be watchful, sensible and stick with our minder. South Africa can be a violently lawless place. The small township is on a north-facing hillside over looking Hout Bay with its fishing boats, fishery, yachts and a good beach. In other words, a prime and prestigious location. Yet it is a shanty town, a collection of wooden and tin huts thrown up cheek by jowl on the steep slope. None are much bigger than an allotment shed and there is no sanitation – although electricity has been got to most and the view is blocked at almost every point by a pole and tangle of wires.

I meet Donovan in his garden, which is very small, probably 30 ft by 15, in tiers rather than terraces, held by stonework. There are water pools and pumps. Things work. Skulls, pebbles, stone constructs are placed as artfully as at Henk's garden. It looks healthy, expertly tended and coolly sophisticated and I am ashamed to say I am surprised by this. I think I had expected mostly vegetables and perhaps a few flowers in recycled containers.

How did the garden begin, I ask. What was your inspiration? 'This garden started long, long time ago. Spending a lot of time with my grandparents, with nature, going to Seal

Donovan is dignified, and charismatic. He has an aura. We sit on the steep wooden steps to his two-roomed house and talk.

Donovan's garden
draws upon the natural
landscape of South
Africa for inspiration.
This knowledge in
turn is passed on to
the children in the
community, who also
work in the garden.

Island, spending time fishing and growing in that environment and spending time with elders that used to be into gardening gave me inspiration. But most of all from God's garden, spending a lot of time in his garden, going to the mountains and the water streams, you know just studying the textures and the forms of the plants and how they compliment each other. Their relationship.'

Donovan speaks softly but the words tumble from him, picking up sentences from pauses. 'It is all natural. The local people lived close to nature and that is my inspiration. The koi and the bushmen – they had that respect towards nature.'

Do you think that people are losing that? 'Definitely. I think that we are becoming too Europeanised and Westernised and we are losing that connection that used to be there in Africa – that closeness to nature and the environment. People are so dependent on doctors and prescription drugs as opposed to how we used to live – using indigenous plants for healing. I use predominantly indigenous plants in this garden with healing aspects.'

I know that he works with children and I ask him about this. 'Well, if you want to see anything in the future preserved or sustained then you have to start with the kids because it is the only way that you can secure that future. When I spent a lot of time with elders in their gardens they knew that investing in us was good. The elders knew that if they planted the seeds in us as young people then the fruits would ultimately be reaped when we were grown. So in that tradition I am planting the seeds in young people and seeing those gardens grow and more importantly seeing the seeds inside them grow.

'It is challenging to get the kids involved with making a garden because it is one of the less interesting things to kids I would say. But when you make it fun and you show them the benefits then it works. When they can plant something today and use it tomorrow to heal a sore or something then it becomes interesting. Also I take them out a lot. I take them swimming, hiking. Take them to see nature. For now it is based in Hout Bay. This project started as a garden but other people are now making little gardens and we have taken it to the school and we want to make it a practical part of the school curriculum.'

What do your neighbours think? 'This initiative has been met with mixed feelings. Some people thought I was biting off more than I could chew. Also this is a squatter camp and any available space is used to put up another bungalow, so when you take space to make a garden you get challenged. But by using the children to make the garden then the parents appreciate it. And some people have been inspired and made their own little gardens.

'This is not just a garden but a recreational area where neighbours can have a brai and relax and enjoy the beauty around them. If you show people the true benefits that they can reap, that's when people start realising. In a sense people have lost touch with the closeness with nature and the land. We have to take a step back and see where we have gone wrong and put it right. We have an interest as humans to protect what we have.'

I asked him if he thought that there was a way of taking the good from European influence and constructing a modern, South African way of doing things? 'I am sure we can if we are careful to look at both worlds and how we can manage the two. You can make the best of both worlds. The kids have seen the result of improving this space. They have been an instrument in it. And they are planting in little boxes, making their own space and gardens. This is for the people and it is being done by the people.'

But the practicalities of his work are grinding. The children appreciate what he does but he showed me smashed sculptures – done apparently by four year olds. His biggest problem is maintenance. Apart from anything else he has few tools. Nothing is easy. Nothing straightforward. But his vision is true and in its optimism and expression with-

The Drakensberg
KwaZulu-Natal

I LEFT THE CAPE and flew to Durban where I met Elsa Pooley, an expert on the flora of the Drakensberg and KwaZulu-Natal who was to show myself and the TV team a little of the wild flowers in the Drakensberg mountains. The Drakensberg (Afrikaans for 'Dragon's Mountain') are the highest mountains in South Africa, running about 600 miles south-west to north-east along the southern border of Lesotho. They are also filled with wild flowers that are essentially alpine and which therefore cope well in northern conditions. Winters in the Drakensberg are cold and dry with the temperature dropping well below freezing in the lower slopes and reaching –22°C higher up, and snow falls thickly. In summer it is wetter and warm and until the late 1950s the area was used mainly for summer grazing so was largely unspoilt and uninhabited.

We drove north from Durban for about four hours, passing signposts with names like Ladysmith and Spion Kop that I had learned as a child from the Boer War. As it got dark the sky seemed to expand until it was a vast, glimmering, epic thing. African skies seem bigger than any other.

The landscape is epic too. We passed plains with zebra, ostrich and wildebeest and a series of peaks unfolded on the horizon. It is like a version of cowboy country, the rolling plains punctuated by unglaciated, flat-topped peaks, always with a parapet of high basalt cliffs.

The next morning we set off for a day's botanising. Straight away we passed by a ribbon of arum lilies, *Zantesdechia albomaculata*, in a ditch by the road, their unfurling trumpet of flowers gleaming. We also passed the horror of a manicured golf course, imposed upon this lovely wild landscape. As we passed I saw what seemed at first glance to be a pair of women both driving off from a tee. Then I saw that their golf clubs were in fact mattocks and they were digging the thing. Elsa explained that there is a policy to provide work for women, which is clearly good in many situations but also means that there is a growing number of unemployed young men. Nothing is ever easy.

She took me to a meadow in the foothills that shimmied with flowers. It was an amazing sight. In amongst the thin (but highly nutritious for grazing animals) red grass (*Themeda triandra*) were scillas, asters, vernonias, *Helichrysum* and a few of the great pink inflorescence of the candelabra lily *Brunsvigia*. No, I didn't know it either, but then I had Elsa to guide me. Mark, my plant-obsessed director, irritatingly knew it at once.

We came to a valley a bit higher up and walked along a wooded track by a stream where asparagus, orchids, streptocarpus, begonia and a huge scilla with leaves like an amaryllis all grew. Sitting by the stream eating our sandwiches in warm sunshine (the previous night Sarah had told me over the phone that it was snowing back home), with a spray of phygelius growing out over

THIS IS AS REMOVED FROM THE AVERAGE GARDEN AS COULD BE IMAGINED AND YET BROUGHT ME CLOSER TO THE PLANTS OF SOUTH AFRICA.

the waters, after a morning finding and filming lovely wild flowers in one of the world's great natural wildernesses was not such a bad way to earn one's living.

Then, as if to balance out the hint of smugness, the clouds built up with amazing speed, lightening fizzed through the air and an enormous rainstorm broke. We made the long trek back to our vehicles, without any waterproofs, the path racing with water.

That is the point of mountains. They are essentially unpredictable places. The next morning we set off at 5 am to climb higher, getting up to 8,530 ft. A storm in the lower parts means a noisy soaking. Up near the exposed top of the mountain the risk of being hit by lightening is real and to be avoided if possible. The storms nearly always happen in the afternoon, so the plan was to be off the mountain by midday.

The cloud was like billowing fog and the air noticeably thin. It was cold. The plants had become distinctly alpine, tiny and bunched into the rocks. But there was an extraordinary range of them. There was thyme-like *Helichrysum*, *Eucomis*, *Gerbera* and the occasional gladioli, tiny, an abbreviated version of our garden glad, but the real thing. Then the clouds rolled down the slopes to reveal enormous green valleys stretching endlessly out below and the peak of the Sentinel above us.

This is about as removed from the average garden as could be imagined, but this diversion into the Drakensberg both brought me closer to the plants of South Africa and also to the truth that in all our back gardens, be they ever so urban, humble and small, there grows the ghost and memory of every plant's homeland. When I see *Eucomis* or gladioli growing in my garden next year, they will bring the Drakensberg with them.

I was bowled over by the sheer immensity of the Drakensberg and the enormous range of alpine plants and flowers in the meadows.

Kirklington

Ficksburg, Free State

Kirklington is an amazingly ambitious garden. It took fifteen years to prepare the stonework alone.

FROM THE DRAKENSBERG we went through the Golden Gate National Park, stayed a night in the nearby village of Clarens, and then headed towards Johannesburg. But on the way we stopped to visit a garden in the veldt called Kirklington. The attractions were twofold. Firstly it was a garden made by an English settler after the Boer War, creating a garden where gardens were hardly known, and secondly it was an organic farm – in an area where being organic was regarded as something close to being a commie. This suited us fine. I am organic to my bones and if not a commie certainly a fully paid up member of the awkward squad. Also Elsa had not seen it for years. All in all a visit seemed due.

The farm is at 6,000 ft on land traditionally good for cherries, beef and wheat. It is big, fertile country, probably grindingly hard for farmers but there is a smell of liberation in the air. It is big, open and exhilarating. We turned into the farm track which took us up the hill through trees and fields where organic medicinal herbs are growing and Aberdeen Angus cattle grazing, to a house tucked into a steep, rocky slope. At first glance you could see that the garden was buttressed with solid stone walls, steps and paths and woven with a mass of flowerbeds, languishing slightly in the heat but pretty and packed with flowers.

The Moffett family live here. John and Gill, the parents, ran farm and garden for many years until both were handed to the next generation, son James taking over the farm and his wife Vanessa overseeing the garden. They also home-school their three sons there and the three generations live together with an easy and open familiarity.

Gill Moffett is a splendidly elegant, matriarchal figure, dressed in ruffled collar, improbably gleaming gardening boots and a magnificent straw hat. The garden has clearly been slightly neglected since her heyday but it has history and there is a sense that it will endure more than a slight lack of labour.

The history of the garden is fascinating because it paints such a vivid story of life on a farm in the high veldt. Gill told me that the farm was bought in 1910 by a man magnificently called Tudor Boddham-Whetham. He originally came from Nottingham, which is why the farm is called after a village in Nottinghamshire. 'He saw wonderful visions of creating beauty,' Gill told me. 'That was totally unusual because in those days you farmed to your front door and your back door. This was a totally new concept.'

Tudor laid out the garden by bringing stone down from the hillside directly behind the house, employing a stonemason to cut and dress it and laying out terraces, paths, steps and walls. It was fifteen years of work.

This struck me as an extraordinary thing. Why would an Englishman come to this spot and go to such extraordinary lengths to make a garden, especially when there was absolutely no gardening culture there at the time?

Gill told me that Tudor 'came out in the Boer war, loved the country and married a woman bought up in a similar estate where her father had created a beautiful garden. Ruby was involved in the making of the garden from the outset too. They stripped what was here and made the garden from scratch. There were very few nurseries in South

Africa at that time and those only sold English plants. But it was a battle trying to grow them. It is extreme here. In winter the temperatures will range from 20 degrees down to –10 and in summer it gets very dry and hot. But there is a massive shortage of water. It is a dry farm. There is just about enough water for drinking but not for a garden. At times we have to bring in tankers but the cattle and the crops get it first.'

In fact Tudor made extraordinary and extreme measures to trap rainwater for the garden. Along the back of the house he built a 150-yard long retaining wall with the path between this and the back of the house acting as a gully to channel the water along, under the house and out again to a huge tank, 22 ft deep, holding over 20,000 gallons of water. Later he added another 11,000 gallon tank. So his plans and schemes for the garden were grandiose from the very outset. It was not a garden that expanded organically bit by bit, but a large ambitious plan that was carefully executed. To put that in context, it would be like someone buying a croft in the Scottish highlands and creating an Edwardian garden on the scale of Hestercombe and hewing the stone from the hillside. This is garden-making on the most ambitious of scales in the most improbable of circumstances. As James said, 'the neighbours, all Afrikaans, thought he was nuts.'

I like that. Tudor sounds my kind of man. In fact the Moffett family are all terribly easy to admire and like with their self-sufficiency, home-schooling and organic ideals

Kirklington was designed as essentially an English garden on the high veldt but evolved into something totally unique.

withstanding the market, opprobrium of neighbours and a country evolving into being. There is a Quaker-like simplicity and purity to their lives that makes things tough for them but is enviable.

But there is little that is simple about the garden. As I walked down through the steps into what appeared to be rough fields with a tangle of trees, I realised that they were part of a long flight that led me down through an overgrown avenue of walnuts to a grand double flight retained by a huge wall. Another flat terrace led to more steps that led to the drive. A tennis court stood to one side. Looking back up the steps to the cliff face behind the house, you could see the grandeur – eccentric grandiosity even – of Tudor's scheme. It was fantastic. Later Gill showed me a map, drawn in 1938, that clearly shows the walnuts but also a full orchard, layered into eight terraces and planted with cherry and oranges. The borders are there too, with their thick, solid stone paths and edging weaving through them. It is all still there, albeit sleeping a little.

The truth is that Vanessa cannot possibly maintain the garden, run the household and educate her children with the minimal help that they have. But you can't help feel that the garden, with its bones hewn from the stone of the hillside and its soul born of the dogged eccentricity of a crazy Englishman, will survive.

The Rock Garden

Magaliesberg, Gauteng

There are few flowers – this is a garden made of stone, wood, water and plants and the overall effect is extraordinary.

WE DROPPED ELSA OFF AT A PETROL STATION where she met her lift to take her back home to the coast and then we went on north to Johannesburg, and another widescreen sky with the sun setting on one side and a mauve storm cloud riven with lightening on the other. The next morning we left for a two-hour drive to a garden in Magaliesberg. None of us had seen it but we had heard interesting things about it. It was, we knew, made by a couple of artists and was 'interesting' and 'unusual'. Where I come from this is either a code for something that is either thoroughly unpleasant that has to be politely dealt with or extremely odd. I was prepared to take the risk either way.

It might be odd but the Rock Garden (it has no name – I am calling it that because it is very rocky) is most certainly not unpleasant. The garden is perhaps 2 acres, set in a further 90 acres of hillside. Geoffrey Armstrong is a sculptor and his partner Wendy Vincent a painter and printer. The house and garden seem to be a seamless part of their life and work to an extent that I have never seen before. It is as though through the garden they have become self-sufficient, not on vegetables but aesthetics.

It is common enough to see works of art placed within and as part of a garden and quite frequently artists make excellent gardeners. But it is very rare that the garden itself transcends these distinctions and becomes the artwork itself. This garden is unequivocally a work of art. There is no compromise. I confess that when I see a garden fly free from the constraints of horticulture in this way I am immediately thrilled and long to rush back to my own garden to work in this vein. I just adore it. British horticulture can be so pompous and self-referential that is often just plain dull, but to visit a garden like this rekindles every kind of enthusiasm.

What is there to adore? The garden is entirely constructed from stone, wood, water and plants. In other words it is as artificial and unnatural as any formal Dutch parterre. But rocks in particular are used where trees, hedges or shrubs might be expected in many gardens. They pile on top of each other, lean, poise, balance, peering and posing like courtiers in attendance. I discover that every one of these rocks, every single one of tens, hundreds of thousands, from the smallest pebble to the huge monoliths, have been carefully positioned by Geoffrey.

He describes the process as if it was the obvious thing to do. 'This was a cattle stomping ground. Bare, eroding bush. We could have left it and let nature reclaim it. But we hadn't reached that point. So we bought in rocks to cover the bare earth.'

The natural slope of the hillside has been gauged and hollowed just like one of his sculptures – it is one of his sculptures – so ravines, hillocks and rocky passes leading nowhere map this new, made-up land. Wooden bowls, boulders and bony carcasses jostle the stones until they marry into a kind of composite, organic material. There are no paths – or if there seem to be then they are usurped and invaded by new developments, nipping their progress in the bud. Huge wooden constructs, walkways,

THIS GARDEN IS UNEQUIVOCALLY A WORK OF ART. THERE IS NO COMPROMISE.

viewing platforms, jutting piers of plank all echo the rhythms of the trees. These wooden sculptures are obviously strongly influenced by the work of David Nash but also clearly made without any plan other than to add, extend, create.

And there are plants too. Mainly grasses, agaves, aloes and other succulents with the occasional exclamation of colour. The plants people the garden, giving it a warmth that mitigates the underlying severity of Geoffrey's vision. The plants have also dictated when, where and how the additions have been made.

They both go on rescue collections, gathering plants from the path of roads or buildings in virgin country much as Burle Marx did in Brazil, and then they come back with a mass of plants that have to be planted in order that they might survive. So a new space is cleared and carved out – often literally – for them. The plants and their love for them, have driven the garden.

Geoffrey likes very bright colours in his paintings but prefers to 'not see too many flowers in a garden. I like interesting flowers but rare and small ones. It is texture and form that excites me. I love aloes. Some of them have such personality. You can go up

Every stone is carefully composed and the aloes have become living sculptures in amongst them.

and talk to them.' Wendy is much more of a plants person and you sense that it is her hand and eye that is manipulating and positioning the plants around the rock and woodwork.

We sat and chatted on vast surreal chairs made by Geoffrey. Wendy's paintings and prints were on the walls. There seemed to be no division at all between their life and work. They say they live very simply and earn just enough to get by. The garden is their work.

They came in 1990 and there was nothing except a piece of African hillside that they loved. They had to make the road and lived in a tent and bathed in a shower heated by the sun. They were not young, and as South Africans hating the apartheid regime clearly had a tough time. But they knew that this was where they should be. Wendy says, 'It was fantastic. Something clear and free about it. It was nice as a beginning. And then slowly we started to build this ourselves.' Everything – house, garden, furniture – has been created and manufactured by them.

'What transformed things was water. We had no water and were prepared to even get it tanked in but a neighbour then showed us his spring up on the hillside and said that we could have half of it. It was a wonderful solution. It now comes through the garden, into the house and then back out of the garden into his cattle trough.' Water is a key feature of the garden, running through rock channels, carved wooden pipes and conduits into a series of pools. The dry, orange rock and the succulent plants everywhere increase the surreality of the garden with so much water by them.

Wendy is serene and thoughtful and looks at you with a gently quizzical eye. Both of them have a habit of making eye contact and visually assessing things before they

One of the many striking examples of the precise placement of stone and wood in the Rock Garden.

speak. They literally eye you up. Geoffrey is wiry, intense and effortlessly practical but is also clearly more troubled although it is equal clearly that the garden brings him a kind of peace.

'This is the longest I have looked at the garden for ages. We are too busy for that. Everything here is done by hand. No machines. I have never photographed the garden or drawn it. I am more interested in the doing than recording it. It is pleasant to have people see it but that is not the motivation. It is a form of power, of trying to understand. But realising that I don't have the capacity to understand but at the same time it can intuitively feel right.'

I recognise completely that process of physically working to make sense of things yet knowing that the result, if successful, will be felt rather than articulated. Perhaps all gardens are simply an attempt to make some kind of order out of life's chaos.

Geoffrey deflates the risk of over-intensity. 'It is just playing with sandcastles really. I get joy and pleasure from manipulating forms. That's all.'

I tell them that they have made something completely wonderful and extraordinary. They look a bit bashful. Then Geoffrey looks away at the garden. 'Yes,' he says, 'we are beginning to realise that.'

Brenthurst

Johannesburg, Gauteng

BRENTHURST, IN THE MIDDLE OF JOHANNESBURG, is the grandest and best known of all of South Africa's gardens. It has belonged to the Oppenheimer family since the early 1920s, famous, amongst other things, for their interests in the De Beers mining group. Johannesburg was built on the mining boom of the late nineteenth century and Brenthurst was part of that. It was built in 1904 for the manager of the Goldfield company by the architect Herbert Baker (who worked with Lutyens on New Delhi). Sir Ernest Oppenheimer bought the estate in 1922 and named it Brenthurst.

Since Sir Ernest's son Harry died in 2000, the garden and estate have been run by Strilli, the wife of Harry's son, Nicky Oppenheimer. As soon as she took over Strilli turned the garden organic and began to apply her own principles of gardening which were radically different from what was described to me as the 'petunias and pansies' former style. This is no small change. Brenthurst is a 45-acre garden, employing forty-five gardeners, open to the public by appointment and regarded as an icon within South Africa. All staff, including Strilli, take part in tai chi at 11 am every day. I can imagine that, at the very least, there are raised eyebrows amongst the old guard. So I was as intrigued to meet her and talk about this process as I was to see the garden for myself.

Strilli and Nicky Oppenheimer are warm, charming hosts with none of the patrician easy imperiousness or over-hearty, but rather thin, friendliness that I have come across many times in similar situations in Britain. Strilli has a donnish air, gentle, elegant and thoughtful but slightly reserved.

Walking through the garden the first impressions are of an imposing and traditional garden set below a large Cape Dutch house. But very quickly the details start to reveal themselves as unusual – even unlikely. Grass is trimmed to different lengths and borders are a medley of grasses and bulbs without obvious attempt to tidy where tidiness would be expected. Many banks of shrubs are left unpruned, shrubs are mostly allowed to follow their own pattern of death and regrowth and grass and flowers are free to spread up steps and in the cracks of paths. They do as little tidying as is commensurate with an open garden. This, of course, has created a tension with people's expectations.

Strilli tries to encourage as many insects as possible. 'I say that it is really a reserve for insects! You used to see jacaranda and wisteria in flower all over Johannesburg but not now because there are no pollinators.'

The large mixed 'butterfly' borders have been planted with a general colour and then left to establish themselves. They are only gently weeded (what the head gardener Dawid Klopper calls 'gardening with fingertips not the hand'), never mulched or staked although fallen foliage is allowed to lie and naturally return to the soil. Over-vigorous, bully plants are gently restrained or removed but on the whole the borders have a constantly shifting, evolving life rather than attaining set performances throughout the season. I found this a delightful and wholly inspiring approach. It is as though a gentle anarchy is creeping through the garden spreading by influence rather than revolt. This gives what would otherwise be an impressive but predictable garden that essential dimension of charm.

Yet there is much control too. Grass is still cut in many places and many shrubs and hedges are clipped, creating rhythms and counter-harmonies to the looseness elsewhere.

Looking down from the Japanese garden at Brenthurst it is hard to imagine the scale of these enormous sculptures.

It is an intriguing and sophisticated mix that creates a dynamic of balancing tensions, and ideologies. It gives the place energy.

The fusion is deliberate and in places extreme. Strilli and Nicky have created a huge Japanese garden that involved six of the Emperor's gardeners living there for four years. It is pure in every Japanese aesthetic and yet different in many ways, such as the use of grass instead of moss. All the grass is hand-clipped twice a year – and there must be a good acre of it.

Strilli and I sat by the labyrinth, on the site of the old tennis court and part of the quiet garden area, not only is it a place of contemplation but also an area where no machines are used. To complete the actual and symbolic break with the traditional European past, the pattern of the labyrinth is planted in elephant's food (*Portulacaria afra*), which is native to South Africa.

Strilli is clearly the presiding genius of the garden but has forty-five gardeners at her disposal – did she ever garden herself? 'Yes. You have to have a direct, personal relationship with the garden. Whether it is a garden, a plant or an animal, it is when you actually make a relationship and you are not just viewing it then you are connected to it. I think that what shook me when I started gardening at Waltham Place [in the UK] was that I thought that gardens could be similar every year, but then I found that it wasn't, particularly as I am not a tremendous controller. So then I started going with the flow.' She is intense and passionate about this. The relationship obviously runs deep.

But can you do that in a public garden? 'What I have tried to do is to see that it is still a historic garden and that it is accessible and actually if you look at my patch of garden as opposed to the rest – I say to groups that it could look like this! But I also feel that I could quite easily – and find it exciting – do nothing at all with a garden and just watch it become totally wild again and meet its climax, then find another rhythm.'

I asked her about the background of the family's relationship to the garden. 'This was originally a house on a hill with the rock all around it. But it quickly became an Edwardian garden because they wanted the theatricality of it. I married in 1968 and we came to live here in 1969. So I have been here for almost forty years. But my mother- and father-in-law managed the estate and the garden and they loved it. They employed Joane Pim – who I think really was a genius. She was the first person to use indigenous plants in a professional way. I liked her a lot and I related very closely to the way that she gardened. Then as Harry and Bridget got older and it was open to the public more, I think it took on that typical public persona. And people who visit gardens always say "where's the colour?" So the gardeners would provide colour through annuals and seasonals. And that is the antithesis of the way that I feel comfortable in nature.

'I hope that people will go away having consciously made a choice whether they like it or not. Once they see and understand this then they go away feeling that was an interesting experience, that they have relooked at nature.'

I ask her whether African gardens exist outside the European influence? 'If you look at black African languages there is not a term for a garden. I think it is an alien idea to paint a symbolised picture of paradise or of a landscape. I think that it is because we live in this wonderful Garden of Eden so there was no need. But there is a whole life force that happens when you start relating with nature. And I think that is happening in South Africa.'

I think that she is right. But before I left South Africa I had one last garden to visit, to inspect another mark of this future, and so was going from one of the wealthiest, white households to a school in a poor black township.

Thuthuka School Garden

Tembisa Township, Johannesburg, Gauteng

The older pupils are allowed to grow their own crops for eating and selling.

TEMBISA TOWNSHIP IS AN HOUR or so's drive outside Johannesburg. It is home to a million people, largely living in permanent brick buildings rather than the shanty shacks of Cape Town, athough they are all much closer together than anyone might choose. The dirt streets are busy with people walking to work or selling sweetcorn roasting on charcoal fires. A million people live here which means that it is not classed as a large township. Soweto has 5 million inhabitants.

We were trying to find Thuthuka Primary School, to visit their garden. We were lost. This was rather a scary proposition in a township. Then we saw a man berating a huge earthmover remaking the road for blocking our path. This was Lucas Mbembele, one of the teachers. He jumped into the opened door of the minibus. 'Hello,' he said. 'I am Lucas. Yes!' He had the loudest, biggest voice I had ever heard. 'We are friends,' he said. 'Yes. Because of the little children. That is the thing. Yes!'

Thuthuka has 1,200 pupils aged from seven to fourteen. It was the first day of the holidays but we had asked for a handful of pupils to come in and show us their garden. About a hundred were waiting for us. Lucas bawled them into order and they lined up, singing, dancing and clapping to welcome the BBC. They sang in Zulu, shuffling and rocking with angelic faces and hands that rolled over each other, shoulders twisting, singing their hearts out. The little children were doe-eyed, holding hands, clasping shoulders and waists and the older girls were giggly, clapping and dancing instinctively. They seemed to naturally adopt three- and even four-part harmonies as they sang. Lucas stood before them, bellowing the words and commands surprisingly tunelessly. Although I do not know a word of Zulu the song was familiar. I asked Lucas what it was and he told me that it wwas 'Rivers of Babylon'. 'We are crying,' he said, 'we are *crying*.' (By the rivers of Babylon, there we sat down, yea, we wept...) So was I. So would you.

The children then marched, singing to the garden. We scampered after them with cameras and microphones. This was the eightieth garden I was visiting and for the first time in that number I was just tagging along. The visit seemed to have taken a momentum of its own.

We went through a gap in a pelargonium and cactus hedge to a surprisingly long and fulsome garden. It has three sections. The top part, nearest the school buildings, is an intense allotment with medicinal plants in narrow beds and peach, apple, avocado, lemon and mulberry trees for shade. In one sweep of the eye I jot down the plants I see: fennel, spinach, onions, tomatoes, peppers, sage, pelargoniums, wormwood, cabbages, beetroots, aloes, tagetes, nasturtiums, artichokes. All are used as medicine by the pupils.

It is not just beautiful, it also has an immediately recognisable atmosphere. It is a retreat, an enclosed meditative space. Then there is a classroom area with hay bales for sitting on (and for mulch) and the shade of a large tree. The third area (which is itself divided into three parts) is where the Grade 7 students, thirteen- and fourteen-year olds, can grow crops, mainly spinach, onions and peppers, for eating and selling. They buy the seeds from the school ('Teaching them commerce. Yes!') which uses the cash to buy Christmas presents for the orphaned children ('Every little child must have a present in December. Yes!') and to pay for school prizes such as dictionaries.

The narrow beds are edged with green glass beer bottles from a nearby brewery. The main paths are all covered with carpet. Lucas explained to me that this was more to retain the moisture than to suppress weeds. Although on that bitter, unseasonably cold day it was hard to conceive, Johannesburg is extremely hot in summer and dry in winter. All the temporary bare earth paths between the raised beds in the veg bit are carefully brushed by the children with home-made brooms made from twigs. In fact everything is home-made, recycled or mended. Despite the apparent lack of valuable objects, there is a tall fence of looped razor wire, the symbol of modern South Africa, down one side.

The garden was set up and is helped by 'Food and Trees For Africa' to be sustainable and it is run along permaculture principles, strictly organic and holistic. Lucas told me that when they came to the school in 1978, they made the football pitch and put the spoil from levelling it to one side. For a long while it just remained a hillock. Then, in 1995, he realised that the hillock could be a garden, yes! And so it began.

Lucas showed me round the herb garden which is both visually and ideologically the heart of the garden. 'We need this medicine. People say that 20 or 25 per cent of the

Teacher Lucas Mbembele shows me the herb garden, with its rich crop of plants that are used as medicines by the children and their families.

children have HIV/AIDS. It is not true! It is more like 30 or 33 per cent. Yes! And some are orphans, and many have parents who are very sick. But these medicines can help them. We keep bees so that the honey makes the bitter medicine easier for the children, and lemons to make it taste better. Yes!'

We stopped for lunch, realising that the reason so many children had put on their uniforms and walked, in some cases, for miles to be there, was for the hot dogs that we dished out.

All the children were bright, incredibly polite and yet lively and sharp. On the face of it none of their prospects are very good. I thought of Donovan's Garden in the Cape and the children he encouraged there. Perhaps the seed, that essential life-enhancing seed of hope, was being sown in them through this garden.

And it is not just a piece of educational worthiness. It is truly beautiful. If it belonged to an enthusiastic adult amateur at home I would admire it hugely. Given that it is a garden made by schoolchildren in a township it is simply staggering. It is beautiful, provides essential food and medicines and helps the process of education. Has any garden ever achieved more than this?

Conclusion

We had a small and close-knit team that filmed the journeys with me but we never had exactly the same personnel on any two trips. I was the only constant factor. I suspect that no one has ever visited all these gardens before and no one ever will again. So, what did I learn? I found out, as if I didn't know it before, that I was capable of losing anything, anytime, anywhere, anyhow. During the course of visiting these gardens I lost, in no particular order: my passport, wallet, two cameras, two notebooks, countless pens, a kettle, an ipod and fancy headphones, two pairs of shoes, my suitcase with all my clothes in it, and just occasionally my patience, manners and head, although never, as far as I can recall, my temper.

I gained a mass of new friends all around the world. That surely was the best thing of all. I got most pleasure from gardens made and tended by their owners and the more idiosyncratic and quirky they were, the more I enjoyed them. I had my own perceptions of what a garden might be and do challenged and broadened. It certainly made me realise that the British idea and style of gardening is lovely, sophisticated and admired right round the world, but very limited. It is just one approach and there are many others.

I realised that although British gardens are by no means the best in the world (although I also learnt that such a concept is absurd – no remotely serious gardening could ever be competitive and yet every properly serious garden should always be playful), I came across no other culture that had anything like the same passion or universal skill at actually gardening. Napoleon described the British as a nation of shopkeepers. In truth we are a nation of gardeners.

I am a rotten traveller and have no instinct for it at all. I get sick in most forms of vehicle and I hated going off on each trip, and left my home, family and garden with a deep pang of regret and homesickness. Whilst we were away we worked our socks off, rarely having a day off and constantly travelling as well doing ten to eighteen hours each day filming. All note taking and writing up had to be fitted on top that. The combination of exhaustion and varying foods meant that I was ill at some stage on most of the trips. But other than having more time, I would not have changed a single thing. I loved every minute of every journey.

Nevertheless there is nowhere in that world that I visited that I preferred to my own garden at home. I spent ten minutes on waking and before going to sleep every day looking at digital pictures of it, taking trips around it from season to season via the wonder of digital photography. It was almost a way of reminding myself who I was and where I belonged. This was one of the two big things I learnt. The best gardens are home. All gardens with meaning, without exception, have a human context. They belong to someone. Even the temple gardens in Japan in all their inscrutability were lovingly and cheerfully tended by monks. All gardens are by people and for people. A collection of plants, however rare and wonderful, is only of interest to the collector. Yet a few simple plants in old cans tended with love and shared with friends and neighbours can be paradise.

The final big lesson that popped up again and again is that context is everything. The more a garden is tied into the particular context of its maker, the climate, geology, culture, language, history and even mythology the more interesting and rewarding it will surely be. This is a thoroughly unmodern, unfashionable concept, but increasingly I find themed gardens based upon plants that are not comfortable there and that have to be mollycoddled just to survive an absurdity.

And I will now get outside. I need to get back to earth again having done less gardening in the past eighteen months than I have for the previous thirty years. But as a result of this book my own garden will change. A lot.

Acknowledgments

Inevitably a book like this owes much to a great many people. I was merely the tip of a very big iceberg working, at times frantically, to keep the venture afloat.

At the BBC, the production team of Lynn Rae, Hilary Poole and in particular Avie Littler were fantastic in organising every tiny detail around an impossible schedule. I visited twenty-four countries in twelve separate jaunts, each one of which involved separate travel and visa arrangements and each one went without a hitch. Each trip also began and ended with a journey shared with my driver Mark Thompson. We have covered many miles, Mark and I, and you will not find a nicer man anywhere.

The very best thing about the BBC is the quality of its filming teams out in the field and it is their work that is generally undervalued. It was a privilege to work with them. We all live cheek by jowl whilst filming and it is an intense experience. The fact that it was always an enjoyable one, even in adversity, is a tribute to their decency as people as much as their incredible professionalism. The directors Patty Kraus, Mark Flowers, Andy Francis and Oli Clark were unfailingly encouraging and supportive despite incredible pressures on time and energy. I mentioned the researchers, Almudena Garcia, Katharine Arthy and David Henderson in the introduction but they also took many of the pictures in this book and were key members of the travelling team. The cameramen Gerry Dawson and Keith Schofield and sound recordist Rob Leveritt are simply the best in the world and there is nobody I would rather work with. We saw and did things that will tie us together always. And we laughed an awful lot.

Each trip also had its own team of fixers and drivers that became an indispensable part of the travelling circus, sharing every mile, every garden and every meal. They invariably added much to the quality of the experience at every level.

The more senior layers of the production team were unfailingly supportive. Nick Patten was vitally important in getting the project commissioned and has always been accessible and constructive. Richard Sinclair brought in energy and real enthusiasm and Gill Tierney helped unpick the trees from the wood. But the producer is the rock upon which any progamme is supported or flounders. Sarah Moors got the whole programme going then got promoted to exec and then again to motherhood. It was, as I hope it will be again, a joy to work with her. Kerry Richardson took over for all but the first two programmes and any success of the programme is mostly down to her work. She was fantastic, mothering, guiding, negotiating, making us laugh and popping up all over the world ready for a night out. A true star.

I have worked with a number of publishers but never with one that took a crazy delivery schedule with such aplomb. At Weidenfeld & Nicolson, Michael Dover, Robin Douglas Withers, David Rowley, Clive Hayball, Joanna Cannon, Tony Chung, Justin Hunt and in particular Susan Haynes literally could not have done more to support and encourage me despite receiving copy technically beyond any possible production schedule. They were amazing. The fact that you are holding this book in your hands is their miracle.

My agent Araminta Whitley has nursed (and at times cajoled) me through this, read every word and as ever, a huge thanks to her. Also special thanks to my assistant Marsha Arnold who, despite not seeing me for weeks at a time, has smoothly kept the wheels turning.

There are two final and special acknowledgements to make. The first is to all the gardeners around the world who consented to have myself and a TV crew invade their gardens. I know exactly what that means and the preparatory work that it can involve. Gardens are personal and often private places and without exception we were welcomed and at times entertained with complete generosity. A heartfelt thank you to all of them.

Finally there would be neither a book nor a programme without my wife Sarah. In the past year or so I have spent more time away than at home and when I have been here I have been writing madly. She is a better traveller, a better gardener and a better person than me and yet has stayed behind and held all together with unwavering support and love. Thank you.

MONTY DON, DECEMBER 2007

First published in Great Britain in 2008
by Weidenfeld & Nicolson

10 9 8 7 6 5 4 3 2 1

Text © Monty Don 2008
Design and layout © Weidenfeld & Nicolson 2008

By arrangement with the BBC
The BBC logo is a trademark of the British
Broadcasting Corporation and is used under licence.
BBC logo © BBC 1996

A CIP catalogue record for this book is available
from the British Library.

ISBN: 978-0-297-84450-1

Design director **David Rowley**
Editorial director **Susan Haynes**
Designed by **Clive Hayball**
Edited by **Robin Douglas-Withers**
Proofread by **Joanna Chisholm**

Colour reproduction by D L Interactive UK
Printed and bound in Italy

Weidenfeld & Nicolson
The Orion Publishing Group Ltd
Orion House
5 Upper St Martin's Lane
London WC2H 9EA

An Hachette Livre UK Company

The Orion Publishing Group's policy is to use
papers that are natural, renewable and recyclable
products and made from wood grown in sustainable
forests. The logging and manufacturing processes
are expected to conform to the environmental
regulations of the country of origin.

Picture Credits

Katharine Arthy: 7, 188–9, 191, 193, 195, 196, 197, 202,
204, 205, 207, 208, 209, 210, 212-3, 214, 219, 221, 223,
224, 225, 227, 229, 262–3, 264, 265, 267, 268, 270, 271,
27, 275, 276, 279, 281, 285
Monty Don: 8-9, 14, 18, 19, 20, 21, 24, 27, 39, 40, 46, 48,
53, 55, 57, 62, 64, 65, 66, 67, 68, 73, 74, 78, 80, 81, 89, 90,
96, 102, 103, 104, 105, 107, 108, 109, 112, 119, 121, 122,
125, 130, 131, 133, 135, 136, 139, 141, 147, 151, 152,
154-5, 161, 162, 164, 172, 175, 176, 181, 183, 186, 192,
194, 198, 199, 200, 201, 203, 206, 215, 216, 217, 218, 220,
222, 226, 228, 229, 231, 233 (both), 238, 240, 241, 269,
277, 278, 284
Almudena Garcia: 70–71, 75, 77, 79, 82, 91, 92, 93, 94,
95, 97, 140, 142, 143, 144, 145, 146, 148, 149
David Henderson: 2–3, 4–5, 11, 13, 23, 25, 31, 34, 36,
37, 38, 47, 51, 52, 56, 59, 60, 61, 63, 69, 86, 87, 126 7,
129, 132, 134, 137, 138, 157, 159, 165, 166, 167, 169, 171,
174, 177, 179, 180, 182, 184, 185, 234–5, 237, 239, 242,
243, 244, 245, 247, 248, 251, 253, 254, 255, 256, 257, 259,
260
Patty Kraus: 1, 98–99, 101, 110, 111, 113, 114, 116, 117,
120, 123, endpapers
Rob Leveritt: 280
Kerry Richardson: 12, 15, 16, 17, 28, 29, 32, 33, 35, 42-3,
45, 49, 83, 84, 85

Captions

Page 1 Juan Grimm's garden, Los Villos, Santiago, Chile.
Pages 2–3 Roland Emmerich's garden, Hollywood,
California.
Pages 4–5 The New Summer Palace, Beijing.
Page 287 On the Amazon, Brazil.
Page 288 Atop a Luis Barragan site, Mexico City.